VIKING
CLOTHING

VIKING CLOTHING

THOR EWING

The
History
Press

First published in 2006 by Tempus Publishing
Revised edition 2007

Reprinted in 2009 by
The History Press
The Mill, Brimscombe Port,
Stroud, Gloucestershire, GL5 2QG
www.thehistorypress.co.uk

Reprinted 2012, 2022

British Library Cataloguing in Publication Data.
A catalogue record for this book is available from the British Library.

ISBN 978 0 7524 3587 9

Printed and bound by TJ Books Limited, Padstow, Cornwall

MIX
Paper from
responsible sources
FSC www.fsc.org   FSC® C013056

CONTENTS

ACKNOWLEDGEMENTS

A great many people have given their help and encouragement with this project, too many to mention everyone individually. In particular, I would like to thank Penelope Walton Rogers, whose encouragement fostered my early interest many years ago, and who has provided support and valuable information since the project began; Lise Bender Jørgensen for reading drafts of chapters 3 and 4, and for her very useful comments on these sections; James E. Montgomery, whose help with all things Arabic has always been swift and unstinting (adaptations to translations from Arabic are the result of this correspondence); Andrew Smith ('Old Geoff') for his help with Latin; the staff of Durham University Library, in particular Stephen Atkinson and Jane Roscoe (Jane Roscoe has also written a useful thesis on clothing in Old Icelandic literature, and made her knowledge available to me); Pippa Henry, who first introduced me to the realms of textile archaeology.

As well as the usual picture credits, I should like to thank Lukas Thor Dziubalski for his photographs; Peter Cardwell of Northern Archaeological Associates for providing images of the Adwick-le-Street brooches; Jens Gregers Aagaard at Odense Bys Museer for his photo of the Køstrup dress front; Gill Cannell at the Parker Library; Christine Kyriacou at York Archaeological Trust; Anna Boman and Inga-Britt at Riksantikvarieämbetet.

I am grateful to Antikvarisk-topografiska arkivet, the National Heritage Board, Stockholm, for permission to reproduce line drawings from Agnes Geijer's *Die Textilfunde aus den Gräbern* and Holger Arbman's *Die Gräber*. I am also grateful to The Parker Library and the Master and Fellows of Corpus Christi College, Cambridge, for permission to reproduce the image of King Æthelstan.

Also well worthy of my thanks are many others, including (in no particular order) Eva Andersson, Arne Emil Christensen, John S. McKinnell, Alison Finlay, Signe Fuglsang, Dagfinn Skre, Jesper Hjermind, Margit Petersen, Katrin Kania, Dr Richard Hall, Mytte Fentz, Helga Schütze at the National Museum of Denmark, Bill Schipper, Terrill Heaps, Henk 't Jong, John Dillon of the Memorial Library in Wisconsin, Georg Hansen, Gini Newton of Chimera Costumes, Janet McNaught, Sigrid Wigernes, Are Pedersen, Dagmar Pickles and Catherine Stallybrass of Curious Works, Vanessa Ryall, Andrew Elliot Fabrics of Selkirk, Gerry Embleton, Clive

Fairweather, Kjell Hellesoe, Kerry Fletcher and Tom Sunley, Laura Perehinec and Megan Burns at Tempus Publishing.

I also thank my mother, who guided me in my first attempts at creating historical costumes – and then did most of the work too – without this experience, I doubt I would ever have begun to consider Viking clothing; and my wife Annie, for her patience and encouragement, for helping me to bring some of my ideas into physical reality, and for willingly wearing the results.

Finally, I would like to acknowledge my debt to Hazel Uzzell, through whom I came to write this book in the first place. Hazel began the book with me, but was forced to withdraw due to ill health.

INTRODUCTION

We judge people by the clothes they wear. If we misrepresent the clothes of a historical culture, it will colour our judgements about that whole culture. Our first impression of the Vikings is still founded on a false picture of what they looked like. Indeed, much of the history of Viking studies can be seen as an attempt to reconcile our misguided first impressions with the culture that we actually meet through the primary sources.

Our view of Viking culture, and in particular Viking clothing, is still conditioned by the nineteenth-century image of the horned and hairy warrior. This is the Viking we meet in the operas of Wagner, in cartoons and children's toys and in fancy dress shops, and it is an image which twentieth-century Hollywood has done little to dispel. In trying to get away from this myth, the question for many people will no doubt be whether there can have been anything very interesting or distinctive about the clothes the Vikings really wore. But every culture is expressed in its own unique and distinctive dressmaking traditions, just as through its traditions of poetry and art. Clothing was one of the things which set the Vikings apart from the other nations of Europe.

Whilst popular imagination might dress the Vikings in sackcloth and sheepskins, the truth about Viking clothing was very far from this image. Viking merchants brought luxury silks from the Orient and sold them across Europe, and traded luxuriant furs from Scandinavia in the bazaars of the Middle East. The Vikings could indeed be rather dapper. Not just silks and furs, but fine linens and the finest woollen cloths ever known were worn by the Vikings, decorated with elaborate braids using gold and silver thread. Scandinavian fashions and hairstyles came to be imitated in Anglo-Saxon England, where some people complained that the Vikings washed too often!

In a letter written after the Viking raid on Lindisfarne in AD 793, the scholar Alcuin berates King Ethelred of Northumbria for his adoption of 'pagan' fashions, and it is clear that Alcuin's 'pagans' are Scandinavian Vikings: 'Are you not terrorised by fear of them whose haircut you chose to adopt?' he asks. So, at the dawn of the Viking Age, Scandinavian fashion was distinctively different from that of other European countries.

CHANGING FASHIONS

It is unlikely that fashions remained unchanging throughout the two-and-a-half centuries we call the Viking Age. Similarly, there are demonstrable differences between fashions from different parts of Scandinavia. Foreign fashions appear to have been indicative of status, and may have reflected the wearer's travels and foreign friends; saga characters sometimes return from abroad with fine foreign clothing, which has often been received as gifts. I have sometimes been able to indicate that a particular feature is best seen as earlier or later, or is limited to a particular area, or might have been introduced through contact with a particular culture. However, a general continuity can be demonstrated throughout the Viking era and throughout Scandinavia, while, regrettably, there often is too little evidence to know with certainty how fashions might have differed according to time and place.

The undoubted influence of foreign fashion on Scandinavia does not mean that there was no distinctive Viking style. Thus, the penannular brooch and the ringed pin show the influence of Insular styles on Scandinavian dress, but were used to secure a type of cloak with roots in Roman-era Germania. Frankish strap distributors worn as women's trefoil brooches tell a similar story, while in the Western settlements, a new and unique colonial women's fashion may have emerged. Likewise, oriental belt fittings and caftans show Eastern influence, without necessarily implying that they formed part of a self-consciously oriental outfit; they occur both with and without other indicators of oriental influence. The frequency of these finds suggests that Scandinavian fashion was ready to assimilate foreign elements, and that Eastern- and Western-influenced styles were among the range of options in the Viking wardrobe. These exotic features suggest a dynamic and vital Scandinavian style, which, like Scandinavian art of the period, was open to foreign influence without being dominated by it.

An issue which combines the question of foreign influence with that of changing fashions over time is the question of the use of gores in Viking clothing. Some time in the seventh century, European garments began to be constructed using narrow triangular pieces called 'gores', which were set into the garment to give it shape. These appear first in Mediterranean tailoring, where they had been adopted from oriental fashion. In the Viking Age, they became a commonplace of European clothing, seen for instance in the late ninth- or early tenth-century linen fragments from Llan-gors, Wales. Triangular pieces which could have served as gores have also been found among the textile fragments from Hedeby, which has led to an assumption that gores were as much a feature of Viking dress as they were elsewhere.

However, as more-or-less the most southerly Viking settlement, and as a great international market, one might expect that Hedeby would have been especially open to foreign influence; furthermore, by the close of the Viking Age, Denmark had taken its place alongside other Christian European nations and, under King Cnut and his sons, was actually ruled from England. As it happens, the evidence from the graves at Hedeby is not untypical of Scandinavia, despite a large number of Christian burials. But most of Hedeby's textile remains come from the harbour and foreshore, and might as easily have been discarded by Frisian, Wendish or English merchants as by Scandinavians. Even among the finds from Hedeby, though it would be untenable to suggest that none of the triangular textile fragments were used as gores, individual pieces might have had other functions; the long-tailed hats, for instance, described by the *Hudud al-'Alam* and seen on Gotland picture stones, were probably made up of narrow triangles of cloth.

Putting aside the evidence of Hedeby, there are no Scandinavian garments from the Viking Age or before which use gores in their construction. Although all Scandinavian kirtles or cotes from the later Middle Ages do use gores, they are closely related to mainstream European fashion, whereas Scandinavian fashion during the Viking Age appears to have been distinct from European styles. Only one Viking-age shirt survives in anything like a complete state, and this was made without gores (*50, 51*). It was buried in Viborg, Denmark, in the year 1018 or shortly thereafter, and as such represents Danish fashion towards the end of the period, though before the cultural impact of eleventh-century Anglo-Danish links could have been felt. Similarly, the late Vendel- or early Viking-era shirt from Bernuthsfeld, Germany, is made without gores; it also shares other characteristic features with the Viborg shirt (*56*). These garments appear to represent a distinctive tradition of dressmaking, which survives in Scandinavia throughout the Viking Age. Other aspects of Scandinavian fashion remain similarly independent of European culture throughout the period. On balance then, it seems unlikely that gores were widely used in the construction of Viking shirts before the second quarter of the eleventh century, though they might have made their first appearance somewhat earlier in the baptismal garments given to new converts to Christianity.

The most significant factor for the kind of clothes a Viking wore was not geography, but wealth and status. This is made plain in the Viking poem *Rígsþula*, which portrays three ranks of Scandinavian society according to their typical customs and habits. The clothes of the lowest rank, the slaves, are described only by what parts of the body they leave uncovered, sun-burnt arms and muddy feet. The second rank dresses in good, neat clothing. But the third rank indulges in an abundance of silk and dyed cloth; even their little baby is swaddled in silk.

PERSONAL APPEARANCE AND CLEANLINESS

Not all Scandinavians of the period will have been well dressed, even amongst those who could afford to be; there are slovens in every age and every culture. But personal appearance does seem to have been particularly important in Viking culture. Ibn Rusta describes the Rus as 'fastidious' in their dress. This could be expressed in what Alcuin calls 'immoderate dress', but even for those who could not afford finery, cleanliness was important. Thus, an anonymous verse advises that if one is washed and fed, one need not be ashamed if one's clothes are not the best (*Hávamál*, st.61); another advises that one should be washed, combed and fed every morning (*Reginsmál*, st.25); another stipulates that water and towels should be provided for a guest (*Hávamál*, st.4); another tells how the hands and heads of the dead should be washed, combed and dried before burial (*Sigrdrífumál*, st.34). Even Ibn Fadlan, who deplores the Rus as 'the filthiest of God's creatures', nonetheless confirms that washing and combing formed a daily ritual.

The medieval chronicle attributed to John of Wallingford recalls Viking cleanliness with some distaste, relating that the Danes combed their hair every day, washed every Saturday and changed their clothes regularly. Although he was writing in the thirteenth century, the chronicler was looking back to the beginning of the eleventh century, and was probably drawing on much earlier sources; in particular, the detail about bathing on Saturdays is linked with precise information about the year 1002. This tradition of Saturday bathing is reflected in the word for Saturday in Scandinavian languages, *laugardagr* in Old Icelandic, which translates as 'bath day'.

Washing was a daily ritual which could be performed at home, but taking a bath probably meant a journey to an established bathing spot such as a river or pool, where people would bathe together. Thus, *Völsunga saga* and *Snorra Edda* both relate a traditional story in which Brynhildr and Guðrún bathe together in the river, while in *Laxdæla saga* ch.39, Kjartan and Guðrún meet regularly at the baths in Sælingsdalr. According to John of Wallingford's chronicle, in the St Brice's Day Massacre in 1002, the Danes were attacked on a Saturday so that they could be taken by surprise whilst bathing.

No doubt, their unusual interest in personal appearance was a factor in making Scandinavian fashions a model for others. John of Wallingford's chronicle suggests that the Danish habit of personal grooming led to unparalleled success with English women! Perhaps it was the hope of similar conquests that led a certain Edward to have his hair cut in the Danish style, earning him a rebuke from his brother which survives to this day (Worcester MS Hatton 115 (*olim* Junius 23)).

LINEN

Initially, one of the most surprising aspects of Viking dress is the importance of linen. The Scandinavian climate seems more suited to warmer fabrics, and linen shows the dirt in a way that woollen cloth rarely will; it is also dearer than wool. Indeed, the prevalence of linen in Viking Scandinavia has been portrayed by Lise Bender Jørgensen as 'the triumph of fashion over common sense'. But linen is a hardwearing washable cloth, which can be more economical than cheaper woollen cloth. In a society that lived closer to earth and fire than we do today, this was an important consideration. The laws of the tenth-century Welsh king, Hywel Dda, recognise this when they forbade the use of woollen cloth for the porter, the fuel man and the washerwoman. Perhaps the maidservant washing linens in *Hrafnkels saga* ch.17 is dressed in linen too. It is remarkable that white linen (and later, white cotton) remained a major feature of European fashion until the time that the demise of the home fire and the advent of the washing machine made it easier to keep clothes clean. The Viking emphasis on cleanliness and personal grooming matches their use of linen clothing. The Old Icelandic term *þváttdagr*, 'wash day', as an alternative name for Saturday suggests that linens would have been washed on the same day that people bathed.

Past writers have sometimes emphasised the costliness of linen cloth, but linens need not have been the exclusive domain of the rich. Some notion of the relative values of cloth can be found in an edict of Diocletian, from the late Roman period. This edict, which was issued in AD 301 during a period of intense inflation, allots maximum prices for selected goods. Somewhat strangely from our perspective, cloth is measured by weight rather than by length, but this takes account of the varying width of different cloths, whilst being easier to reckon than surface area. In Diocletian's edict, linen for clothing varies in price from 72*d*. per pound for the poorest sort, up to 1200*d*. per pound for the best with a range of prices in between, while woollen cloth ranges from 25*d*. up to 175*d*. Pound for pound then, linen is indeed dearer than wool, and this is not simply to be explained away by the fact that it can be lighter than wool, allowing more cloth per pound weight. Nevertheless, coarse linen valued at between 72*d*. and 250*d*. per pound is sold for the use of common people and slaves. Linen will have been chosen not just because it was cooler under the Mediterranean sun, but because it was tough and washable.

Only among people from Gotland and western Norway was linen unusual in the Viking Age, leading the eleventh-century writer Adam of Bremen to remark, when discussing the characteristics of the Scandinavian nations, that the Norwegians relied on their flocks for their clothing. But although in these areas wool could be worn next to the skin, this is more a matter of geography than class, and the woollen undergarments proposed by many writers as typical for lower social strata are a modern fiction; fine woollen cloth would have been a greater luxury than coarse linen, and far less practical. In the poem *Rígsþula*, which is at pains to highlight social differences, even the slaves wrap their baby in linen (st.7).

SOURCES OF EVIDENCE

Alcuin's comments, cited above, are a rare insight into Viking fashion through the eyes of a European Christian. Arab sources describe the Vikings under the names of 'the Magi' (*al-Majus*) or 'the Rus' (*al-Rus*); usually, the term 'Magi' is used of the Vikings in Spain, while 'Rus' is used of the Scandinavian or Slavonic merchants and warriors who traded between the Black Sea and the Baltic, but there was some confusion even at the time. Thus, the habits of the Rus cannot be assumed to be identical with those of Viking Scandinavia; however, to insist on a rigid distinction between the Rus and the Vikings is at least as false as it is to insist on their complete identity. I have used the evidence of Arab sources without comment only where it is consistent with evidence from other sources. Extracts from Arabic and Persian sources are quoted, or occasionally adapted, from previous translations.

In the case of the work of Ibn Fadlan, justifiably the most famous Arab commentary on the Rus, we should be aware that, to the extent it describes Scandinavian customs, it describes them in an ex-patriot context. Dr James Montgomery now believes Fadlan's Rus to be the Scandinavian and Slav soldiers employed in the service of the Khazars and billeted in their city of Atil; the same group of warriors was later described by al-Mas'udi.

Such foreign commentaries are just one source of evidence for the nature of Viking dress. Another reliable source of information comes from Viking poetry, which survived in the oral tradition to be written down in later medieval Iceland. Although it is difficult to date poems with absolute certainty, there is often general agreement over their approximate date, based on factors such as traditional attribution, internal evidence and comparison with other sources. The testimony of these poems, coming from within the culture itself, is obviously of prime importance, but it is extremely sparse and often difficult to interpret. Some later poems composed in the same tradition are also relevant, though with the proviso that they might misrepresent the fashions of the Viking Age.

This same proviso applies to medieval Icelandic prose sources including the historical sagas. In citing saga evidence, I have been keenly aware that it dates from long after the period of the Vikings, but nonetheless, approached with caution, it can yield important testimony. Where earlier sources might name a garment, it is often only later saga evidence which allows us to describe it. The saga writers themselves sometimes take an antiquarian interest in past fashions, and although spurious details might occasionally have been added to increase the illusion of historical veracity, even these must have been consistent with whatever historical traditions existed at the time. Of particular importance are some of the underlying assumptions about clothes, and episodes where clothing features in the plot, where there is a fair likelihood that the detail is derived from pre-existent tradition. Of less use are romance-style digressions, where clothes are described in detail; these appear to draw more on fashions contemporary with the sagas' composition than on earlier modes, and are to be seen as a parallel to contemporary medieval art, which portrays biblical figures in the fashion of the day.

A further source of literary evidence describes fashions among related nations. Descriptions of earlier Germanic dress provide useful information about the tradition from which Viking styles were derived, whilst descriptions of the dress of other Germanic peoples, notably the Franks, can provide revealing comparisons.

Glosses, whereby a Latin text is augmented by vernacular translations of individual words, form another sort of literary evidence. Often, these are glosses in Old English, at one remove from Old Norse, the language of Viking Scandinavia, but both languages frequently share the same words for clothing, linked by common etymology.

It is only through literary evidence that we can hope to discover the names by which the Vikings called their clothes, and I have regularly attempted to match names with particular types of garment. Sometimes this can be fairly certain, but not always: descriptions of garments, where they occur in literature, are generally ambiguous and rarely contemporary; glosses can be vague and sometimes inaccurate; etymology, though potentially revealing, can also be misleading – witness the modern English words 'cap' and 'cape', which share the same root. The links which I make here between a name and a garment are thus sometimes more tentative than they might appear, but it is always useful to propose such links, even if some might ultimately break down. To successfully identify a specific kind of garment with a name can greatly enhance our understanding of the meaning of clothing in Old Norse literature.

In the modern study of historical costume, a leading role has been played by archaeology. For Viking dress, this study was begun by Agnes Geijer, who in 1938 published a report on the textiles from the Viking-era cemetery on the Swedish island of Björkö in Lake Mälaren, the site of the city of Birka, which flourished in the ninth and tenth centuries. The Birka textiles, which have been discussed more recently by Inga Hägg, along with the grave plans published in the detailed report on the cemeteries by Erik Holger Arbman in 1944 (3, 49, 72), remain central to our understanding of Viking clothing. Together, they provide a great deal of information as to what was worn and where. Many other excavations have provided further evidence, and similar information has been returned from sites across the Viking world, suggesting that wherever distinctive Scandinavian costume accessories were worn, they accompanied similarly distinctive garments.

However, apart from an almost complete garment discovered during excavations in the Viking town of Viborg, Denmark (50, 51), archaeology has so far revealed only glimpses of Viking clothes. Most of the textile fragments surviving from the Viking Age are preserved through the action of metal salts from dress accessories. In this way, a metal buckle or a brooch might preserve a little of the cloth that lay next to it, and by noting what is found where, we can build up a stratigraphy of the clothes that were worn (7, *colour plates 2* and *3*). In particular, we can look at the cloth which went immediately over or immediately under the accessory. These cloth fragments tell us a lot about the kinds of cloth that were worn, and sometimes we can tell what kind of cloth was used for a particular garment. Occasionally, a sewn seam or a cut edge of cloth reveals clues about the cut of the garment. In York, Penelope Walton Rogers has pioneered the use of chemical analysis to investigate the dyes that were used in Viking cloth.

An amazing collection of Viking-era textiles has been recovered from the harbour mud at the Viking city of Hedeby (Haithabu), in what is now northern Germany, and these finds have yielded vital information about the cut of clothes in the Viking era. Almost uniquely, these are fragments of ordinary clothes, and not the burial garb of wealthy individuals. However, the Hedeby finds are not altogether typical of contemporary Scandinavian textiles, and it is often not possible to establish whether a fragment derives from a man's or a woman's garment. Evidence from Hedeby is consequently treated with some caution in this study.

There has been a tendency to interpret the textile finds from Hedeby and elsewhere in the light of extant later Scandinavian clothing, in particular the wonderfully preserved finds from Herjolfsnes in Greenland. But whilst Hedeby flourished throughout the Viking Age until its destruction in 1066, the Greenland finds date from the fourteenth and fifteenth centuries. This is a gap of about 500 years, and takes us roughly halfway between the Viking Age and modern times; it is as if we were to attempt to understand these same Greenland finds by reference to the clothing of their twentieth-century excavators. Ideally, one should draw only on evidence from the Viking Age itself, but since this is rarely possible, I have preferred to look back to the costumes of the Vendel era, the Migration period and before. Scandinavian fashions of Viking times had their origins in these earlier costumes, whereas the clothing of later medieval Scandinavia appears to have been informed by mainstream European fashion. Thus, the cut of the clothes from Herjolfsnes has more in common with clothing from the fourteenth-century tomb of Cangrande della Scala in Verona than with earlier clothing from Scandinavia.

In the absence of complete surviving outfits, it is only through art that we can see what Viking clothes actually looked like. Of particular interest are the picture stones from the Swedish island of Gotland. This single island had developed a tradition of stone carving, creating tall door-shaped stones covered in pictures. Almost all the stones from Viking times depict people (though they show a great many more men than they do women) and they provide information about a surprising range of garments. From this one source alone, it is obvious that the usual commonplaces of Viking dress do not reflect the diversity of garments available. Gotland's culture during the Viking Age was unique, and the production of picture stones was only one aspect of this. The jewellery and cloth types associated with the island are unlike those found anywhere else in Scandinavia, but despite this, the fashions of Gotland seem to have been essentially similar to the rest of the Viking world. Gotland's idiosyncrasies can be seen as variations within the mainstream of Scandinavian style, rather than as a separate tradition in themselves.

Stone carving was also a tradition in England, which was adopted with alacrity by Scandinavian settlers. Although the English carving style is generally considered more sophisticated, since the designs are deeper cut with a nod in the direction of modelling in the round, they tend to be less precise than the lightly incised lines of Gotland carving. Nonetheless, Anglo-Norse sculpture can be a useful source for the clothes that were worn in the Scandinavian settlements in England. Interesting Danish stone carvings of the Viking Age come from Jelling, Denmark, and Hunnestad in modern Sweden (*20, 73*).

Metal figurines representing men and, more commonly, women, seem to portray a highly stereotypical version of contemporary costume. A similarly conventional picture comes from the gold foil figures known as '*guldgubbar*'. In general, because women are portrayed in fewer contexts and in a more homogenous style of dress than men, particularly given the wide range of male costume on the Gotland stones, it is not safe to assume that women always dressed like the women portrayed in art. More probably, art portrays an idealised image of the woman or lady, and this was probably modelled on the formal wear of women of the highest rank. However, it also seems possible that a number of illustrations of ordinary women have not been identified as such, precisely because they do not show the elaborate formal costumes with which we are familiar.

Textile art, perhaps surprisingly, can also provide valuable information about costume. The rich ninth-century ship burial from Oseberg, dated by dendro-chronology to *c*.834, yielded among its treasures, several fragments of densely pictured tapestry, showing both men and women. Though filled with people, most of the figures conform to a small number of standard types. These standard forms of dress are interesting in themselves, as are the few figures that are dressed differently. Despite its late date and foreign origins, it is impossible to ignore the embroidery universally known as the 'Bayeux Tapestry'. As a work of Anglo-Norman culture at the very end of the Viking Age, the clothes it portrays have close affinities with those of late Viking Scandinavia. Highly stylised glimpses of similar clothes are seen in Scandinavian tapestries from Skog, Överhogdal and Baldishol.

Finally, there are contemporary manuscript illustrations. Some of the most interesting of these come from English manuscripts. Manuscript art is more naturalistic and detailed than any of the other art forms discussed here, which is its great strength. Not only do English manuscript illustrations typically show garments similar to those worn by the Vikings and worn within a related culture, but in a couple of cases it is possible to demonstrate that a given figure represents a Scandinavian, and by looking at these figures in detail, one can see certain differences between Viking and Anglo-Saxon dress. One of the most important illustrations of a Viking comes from the Eadui Psalter (BL MS Arundel 155, *fol.93r*), and has previously gone unrecognised as such (*colour plate 13*); I take it to be a caricature of the Danish leader Thorkell Hávi portrayed as the Biblical antihero Goliath, as I will argue in a future article (in progress); similar illustrations, such as that in the Tiberius Psalter possibly also represent Goliath as a Viking (BL MS Cotton Tiberius C vi, *fol.9r*). The other outstanding illustration is the famous representation of King Cnut the Great from the *Liber Vitae* of Winchester New Minster (*55*, BL MS Stowe 944, *fol.6r*). However, I have not succeeded in identifying any manuscript representations of Scandinavians before the eleventh century and, by this date, centuries of cultural interchange may have minimised earlier distinctions between English and Scandinavian clothing.

THE STUDY OF VIKING DRESS

This is a field which has been somewhat neglected by scholars, partly no doubt, because of a dearth of solid evidence. Archaeology has provided many examples of Viking cloth, but very few of them give any real indication of how this cloth was made into garments; literary evidence is sparse, and the richest sources, the Icelandic sagas, come from a later period; art of the period is highly stylised and often open to various interpretations. Some scholars have indeed made substantial headway, but they have been relatively few. This in turn has led to insufficient debate about the interpretation of such evidence as there is, and, given the uncertain nature of this evidence, that is regrettable. Instead, there has been a tendency to simply accept each new contribution to the subject as a step forwards in our understanding, rather than to rigorously test new ideas through academic debate.

In general, there has been a great deal more interest in women's dress than in men's. This is partly because there is more evidence from archaeology for women's dress than for men's, and partly because it is more obviously different from European clothing. Despite the interest in women's dress, I do not believe that a convincing interpretation has so far been reached. In this study therefore, I have chosen to outline some of the previous and ongoing attempts at understanding this problem, along with the evidence which, as it seems to me, at times supports and at times contradicts these theses. I have also proposed a good many of my own ideas, wherever it seems that current interpretations are inadequate to describe the available evidence. I hope that these ideas will at least serve as a catalyst for further debate and thus, one way or another, they will lead to a better understanding of Viking dress.

The assumption that there is less to know about the clothes of Viking men turns out to be somewhat illusory; the deeper one looks, the more questions arise. The account of men's clothing given here is quite different from the brief summaries to be found in popular books on the Vikings. And the difference is not just in the greater detail possible, but in some of the basics. The Viking man who emerges here is more likely to be found dressed in a neatly ironed and neatly cut white linen shirt than in a loose tunic of coarse wool.

An attempt to pool evidence from all available sources, to arrive at an overall picture of Viking clothing, has not previously been made. As this book has progressed, I have begun to see why. Evidence from many different disciplines must be thoroughly sifted and evaluated, since any one archaeological find, literary reference or artistic detail could change the interpretation of the whole. Inevitably, in attempting this synthesis, I am open to the proper criticism of those who may be more competent in one particular specialism than I am, but I also hope that the cross-disciplinary approach will provide insights which could not be gained from a single field of enquiry.

A great deal of the research and argument behind this book has been original, addressing questions which seldom seem to have been seriously considered before. As a result, this book (with the exception of chapter 3) is not an overview of an established consensus but an enquiry into the nature of Viking clothing. Since Geijer's pioneering work of 1938, the fashion has been for studies to be based solidly in archaeology, looking at the evidence from a single archaeological site (of particular interest are studies by Hägg, Ingstad and Geijer). This study takes a more interdisciplinary approach, drawing on archaeological evidence from various sites and more fully on the evidence of art and literature. Readers wishing to make their own reconstructions are strongly recommended to consult archaeological reports showing extant fragments: detailed drawings and photographs of textile finds from Birka and Hedeby can be found in the works of Inga Hägg (1974, 1985, 1991).

It has seemed important to me not to limit the scope of this book to a description of the garments themselves, but to look at Viking clothing in its wider context, including the cloth it was made from, and its place in the Viking world. In the Viking Age, all cloth was hand-woven and all clothing hand-sewn, and this has major implications for the role of clothing in society. The life of a garment began in the fields, where the sheep were raised or the flax was grown, and its journey from the farmer's field to his back required a massive input of skilled labour at every stage. Thus, sections of this book deal with the making of the cloth and with the place of cloth and clothing in Viking society. The section on clothmaking is a brief overview of a subject which has been considered in great detail elsewhere, and interested readers are advised to read one of the works on textile archaeology listed in the bibliography; of particular relevance to Viking Scandinavia is Lise Bender Jørgensen's monograph of 1986. The final chapter, looking at cloth and clothing within Scandinavian society as a whole, includes an enquiry into contexts for textile production, and considers ideas about best clothes, coloured clothes and clothes as gifts.

Clothing worn for magical purposes is not discussed at length here but, though it might differ to some extent from everyday clothing, it does not amount to a specialised ritual costume. The oft-mentioned skins worn by Thorbjörg in *Eiríks saga Rauða* ch.3, were readily available for sale and trade, and though they may well have held magical significance for her, the same kinds of skins must also have been worn as clothing by ordinary people. Thus, the Varangians presumably just turned their regular clothes fur-side out to perform their Yule ritual called the *gothikon*, which is described in the tenth-century *Book of Ceremonies* by Constantine VII Porphyrogenitus. Two felt masks from Hedeby and a leather mask from Novgorod were probably used in similar ceremonies. Seeresses do dress distinctively, and are often portrayed wearing a hooded cloak or cowl, which would more normally be associated with male dress; this might be simply because wanderers like Thorbjörg spent much of their time outdoors, but magical significance also appears to attach to the garment itself. I hope to return to this subject in another book. Similarly, the horned headdresses which appear occasionally in Viking art are best considered as an aspect of ritual rather than fashion. It need hardly be repeated that the horned helmets traditionally associated with the Vikings have no basis in historical fact.

For simplicity's sake, I have taken all ancient measurements as their closest modern equivalents. Viking Scandinavia will have known various standard systems, but all will have used feet and inches which are roughly equivalent to modern US and Imperial measurements.

Inevitably, in attempting to draw together so many disparate strands of evidence, I have been forced to make omissions and I will probably have made some oversights. In a field as little tilled as this, the more stones one turns, the more one finds to turn, and I am aware of corners which, given unlimited time and resources, I would perhaps have explored further. However, I hope that I have been able at least to clear some ground for future research, and I also hope that many readers will engage with the subject either through public debate in conferences and journals, or by contacting me.

1

WOMEN'S CLOTHING

HISTORICAL

Scandinavian culture of the Viking Age grew out of the heritage of the Germanic Iron Age and before, and the clothing of Viking Scandinavia had its roots in the costume of the wider Germanic world.

The dress of the early Germans is described by the first-century Roman writer Tacitus in *Germania* ch.17:

> *Tegumen omnibus sagum fibula aut, si desit, spina consertum … nec alius feminis quam viris habitus, nisi quod feminae saepius lineis amictibus velantur eosque purpura variant, partemque vestitus superioris in manicas non extendunt, nudae brachia ac lacertos; sed et proxima pars pectoris patet.*

> The clothing for everyone is the cloak, which is fastened by brooch or failing that by thorn … The women's costume is no different to the men's, except that the women often wear a robe of linen patterned with purple, and since the top of the garment does not extend into sleeves, the arms and shoulders and even the near part of the breast is laid bare.

This passage could be understood to describe a linen garment worn with the cloak. But the word translated here as 'robe' (*amictus*) has the sense of a garment thrown around the body like a cloak, suggesting the actual meaning is that women sometimes wore a linen robe instead of a woollen one. Thus, the *amictus* is not a garment worn with the cloak (*sagum*), but is the cloak itself. Pliny notes in his *Historia Naturalis* (xix.i.7) that linen is 'the finest of all clothing known to their women' (*pulchriorem aliam vestem eorum feminae novere*), also suggesting that although linen was distinctive of women's clothing, similar clothes could equally be made from wool. But the women's cloak is worn quite differently to the men's, and Tacitus is stretching his point when he suggests it is the same garment.

Germanic women dressed in the style described by Tacitus are known from Roman art (*1*). Some women wear a single brooch, but many wear two brooches, one on each shoulder. In Germanic women's graves of the Roman Iron Age, identical brooches are usually positioned at the shoulders. Occasionally, as at Juellinge, Denmark, as well as the shoulder brooches, there are one or two other brooches set lower on the breast.

Tacitus's description is brought sharply into focus by finds from Denmark, where two garments of the type he describes have been recovered from peat bogs. These dresses are made from wool, not linen. An unprovenanced dress in the National Museum of Denmark has been woven in a single piece on a tubular loom, and forms a tube without seams, 4ft 6in (137cm) long and 7ft 10in (240cm) round. A similar dress from Huldremose is 5ft 6in (168cm) long and 8ft 8in (264cm) round (*2*). The Huldremose dress would be far too long to wear, unless the top part was worn turned down, or it was hitched up at the waist or hips with a belt. Even the shorter dress was probably hitched up; the average height of a woman in Roman-era Denmark was 5ft 4in (162cm). Dresses of this type are similar to the Ancient Greek *chiton* and *peplos*.

A number of funerary monuments for Germanic women from the Roman era show the same garment worn with a tunic underneath, which covers the areas which Tacitus was surprised to see naked. Perhaps this undergarment was a fashion adopted by well-to-do Germanic women under Roman influence, though the same undergarment is also sometimes shown in scenes depicting Roman captives, and since Tacitus describes shirts worn by high-ranking Germanic men, perhaps he means us to understand that women of the landowning class might also wear these.

This *peplos*-type dress was not the only style available to the woman of Iron Age Denmark. At Huldremose, in the same area of marsh where the long gown was found, a woman's body had already been unearthed in 1879. She was dressed in a pair of skin capes and a woollen scarf and 'skirt'. If she had once worn another garment on her upper body, it must have been of linen which has decayed, but at this date, linen was far from common in Denmark. The Huldremose 'skirt', like the two longer dresses, is woven on a tubular loom. It is 2ft 10in (87cm) long and 8ft 7in (262cm) round, made of checked twill, and it appears to have had a leather drawstring around the top. Another example from Damendorf, Germany, measures 2ft 9in x 6ft 10in (85 x 210cm). If not worn as skirts, these garments could instead have been worn as short dresses, encircling the body below the arms; this use would explain the apparent lack of any undergarment for the upper body of the Huldremose woman.

It is uncertain whether the different costumes may have marked different social status or different age groups, or whether a woman's dress was simply a matter of personal choice. Certainly, although a drawstring skirt might be flattering for a young woman (though the women from Huldremose was a mature adult at the time of her death), it would be less appropriate during pregnancy, while a fifth-century ivory known as the Halberstadt Diptych illustrates the practicality of the *peplos*-type gown for a nursing mother. Perhaps the full dress was the mark of the married woman, like the Roman *stola*, while its length, which makes it impractical for outdoor work, conveys clear messages even today. Worn as dresses, the shorter garments from Huldremose and Damendorf would have made practical working clothes for maidens and mothers alike. Although their interpretation might present problems, without these actual intact specimens, our understanding of Iron Age women's clothing would be a good deal less soundly based. Unfortunately, similarly complete dresses do not survive from the Viking Age.

Above: 1 Roman-era Germanic women portrayed on the Marcus Column, Rome

Right: 2 Tubular-woven woollen dress from Huldremose, Denmark, dating to the Roman Iron Age and similar in design to the Ancient Greek *peplos*

BOSSED OVAL BROOCHES AND THEIR PREDECESSORS

Just before the dawn of the Viking Age, a new brooch style emerged, which is probably the most distinctive feature of Viking Age women's dress within Scandinavia. Worn in pairs on the upper breast, the new brooches were oval and were domed or bossed (*35, 36, colour plates 1–3* and *colour plate 5*). The presence of a pair of these bossed oval brooches (sometimes called 'tortoise brooches') in a grave unambiguously declares it as that of a Scandinavian woman of the Viking Age, and consistently evolving decorative styles allow for more accurate dating within the period.

Paired brooches had been a feature of Germanic women's dress since the early Iron Age. In graves of this period, there are usually two identical brooches, one each side of the throat at the collarbone. Clearly, these paired brooches will have fastened a *peplos*-type dress of the kind described above. Occasionally, another brooch or pair of brooches is found lower down the breast and these presumably fastened a separate garment of some sort.

Iron Age brooches vary considerably in shape and style, and archaeologists have separated them into a variety of categories depending on their form, but most of them can be described by the catch-all term of 'bow brooch'. In essence, they are made of an arc of metal, with a pin hinged at one foot and held by a catch at the other. The arc or bow of the brooch is designed to accommodate the loose cloth of the dress where it is pinned, and it is these bunched folds of cloth that keep the brooch from turning on its side. Sometimes one or more surfaces are set at a right angle to the brooch pin, and these help to hold the brooch upright when in use.

In the Migration era, the bow brooch was joined but not supplanted by the saucer brooch. Unlike the various kinds of bow brooch, the saucer brooch does not have room to accommodate loose cloth from the top of the dress. Where textiles have been found clasped by a saucer brooch, it is always a tablet-woven band edging the top of a plain twill dress. Without the support of the gathered cloth, traditional bow brooches would have turned on their sides, but the flatter saucer brooch is well designed for such a fastening. The appearance of the dress need not have been very different from its predecessors.

The typical position of the brooches changes with the widespread adoption of the bossed oval brooch at the start of the Viking Age (*3*). Unlike earlier Germanic brooches which were worn at the shoulders, the bossed oval brooches were worn on the upper breast, suggesting an altogether different style of dress which went around the body under the arms, with long straps right over the shoulder from the back. Fragments of such straps have often been found, still attached to the pin within the hollow of the brooch.

The new position of the twin brooches is similar to the position of secondary brooches in earlier women's graves such as that from Juellinge, Denmark, and it is possible that the Viking strapped dress is in fact descended from whatever garment these may have secured. Such a garment might not have differed effectively from the Roman-era skirts

Right: 3 Detail of Arbman's grave plan for Birka grave bj.1081, including an iron neck ring with 10 Thórr's hammers (1), twin oval brooches (2), an equal-armed brooch (3), two bronze arm rings (4, 5), a string of 94 beads (6), a bronze needle box (7), iron scissors (8) and fragments of a leather purse with a dirham and two beads (9). *Arbman 1944*

Far right:
4 Earspoon from Birka grave bj.507 decorated with illustration of a woman. She appears to be wearing a suspended dress and a shawl, with her hair probably bound in a head cloth, which is tied to hang down the back

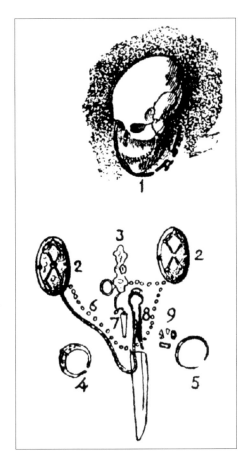

from Huldremose and Damendorf, and is unlikely to have been attached using straps, which would have caused the Iron Age bow brooches to sit awkwardly. Rather, since the lower pair of brooches appears to always occur in conjunction with the commoner shoulder brooches, they probably pinned an outer garment to the dress beneath.

The move from shoulder to upper breast went hand-in-hand with the introduction of the bossed oval brooch, and the new style of brooch swiftly replaced all earlier forms. The fundamentally distinctive feature of the new brooch is its recessed pin, which is tucked away in the hollow of the boss (*colour plates 2, 5*). This makes the new brooch ill-suited to gathering large folds of material in the manner of the old Germanic *peplos*-style dress, or even to pinning through the edge of the cloth like the saucer brooch, but it is an ideal design for fastening the long straps of the new dress. In the new dress, the bulky bunches of cloth are replaced by slender linen straps, but the recessed pin allows the bossed brooch to sit flat on the body, without relying on the bulk of the cloth to hold it in place (*4*). At the same time, the point of the pin is kept away from the skin. Thus, the bossed nature of the oval brooch is its essential feature, which made it an indispensable element of the new style of dress.

On the island of Gotland, Sweden, oval brooches never took hold, but their place was filled by distinctive animal-head brooches, which share the same features of a recessed pin set in a hollow boss. These take over from earlier distinctively local styles at about the same time that oval brooches take over mainland fashions. So, although the archaeology of Viking Gotland is unique, it seems that in this respect, the Gotlanders were expressing their local identity within the framework of mainstream Scandinavian fashion.

Conversely, when small oval brooches appear in eleventh-century Finland, they are flat not bossed, and archaeology confirms that they fastened whole sections of cloth like a saucer brooch, rather than straps like the Scandinavian-style bossed brooches. The unappealingly named 'tombstone brooches' are also flat, and were probably also used like saucer brooches.

EVIDENCE AND INTERPRETERS

Agnes Geijer

The modern study of Viking women's dress begins with Agnes Geijer's 1938 study of the textiles from the excavated cemetery at Björkö in Sweden. This site had been excavated in the late nineteenth century by Hjalmar Stolpe, when it was recognised as the remains of the Viking port of Birka. Geijer's chapter on dress ('Die Tracht' pp134–56) came to be regarded as the standard work of reference on the subject, and it remains invaluable to this day.

It is unusual for textiles to survive well after a thousand years in the soil but in certain conditions, where the soil is waterlogged or where they become saturated with metal salts, they are preserved. At Birka, a large number of braids had used gold or silver thread, which often preserved the braid and sometimes part of the fabric it had been attached to; some textiles were preserved in the rust surrounding knives or scissors; but the largest group of textile remains was preserved in clumps of organic matter surrounding the oval brooches, which were often excavated and stored in their entirety without suffering from the attentions of enthusiastic nineteenth-century conservators. In this way, although Birka had been excavated 50 years earlier, large amounts of organic matter had been preserved. Geijer set about painstakingly cleaning the textiles and opening them out for analysis.

Earlier interpretations had been largely based on pictorial evidence, on the position of brooches in excavated graves, and on comparison with traditional clothing from Eastern Europe. These suggested a dress or skirt with shoulder straps fastened by a pair of oval brooches, and a shawl clasped over the breast with a single brooch. This basic picture has been broadly confirmed by analysis of the textile remains from Birka and from more recent excavations, but it has also been modified and expanded.

Geijer noted textile fragments which confirmed the presence of the dress and shawl as expected, and she also found evidence for a linen shirt, often pleated, which

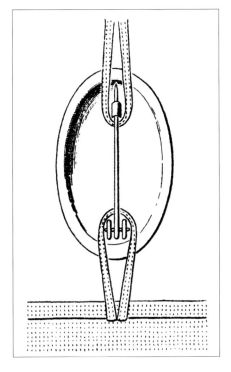 

Above left: 5 Layout of straps inside an oval brooch, based on Birka grave BJ.1084. The actual number of straps varies according to what was worn. *Geijer 1938*

Above right: 6 The Viking suspended dress as reconstructed by Agnes Geijer; two such dresses could be worn together, one around either side of the body. *Geijer 1938*

was worn under the dress itself. Geijer reconstructed the dress worn with the oval brooches by analogy with other dresses worn in the area of the Baltic. She postulated that it was a single rectangle of linen wrapped around one side of the body, with short linen loops to catch the brooch pin at the front and longer straps over the shoulders to the back (*6*). This form of dress would have revealed the shirt at the shoulders and also down one side of the body, where the two sides of the rectangular dress met but were not joined. Geijer suggested, based on multiple strap ends found within the oval brooches and by analogy with Baltic costume, that such dresses were usually worn in overlapping pairs, so that the open side of the overdress revealed not the shirt but the dress beneath.

This understanding of the women's dress has formed the basis for many modern interpretations. Sometimes the side opening is moved round to the back or to the front, sometimes two overlapping dresses are worn, one on each side, and sometimes the back and front sections are separated into two distinct pieces (the so-called 'apron dress'). But the origin for most popular reconstructions is still to be found in Geijer's work.

Inga Hägg

Geijer's main aim was not so much to reconstruct the costume as to understand how the cloth was made. Because of this, she did not attempt a systematic analysis of each find and its relationship to the overall design of the outfit. This work was taken up in the early 1970's by Inga Hägg. She found that organic material which had been excavated almost a century before was still preserved intact. In particular, many of the oval brooches together with their large clumps of surrounding earth were still untouched, and these clumps preserved large amounts of textile remains. Because the textiles had not been separated from the brooches, the whole clump still preserved the layers of textile and other remains in the same order as when they had originally been excavated.

Hägg began the task of piecing together all the information needed to understand how the costume had been put together. Her work has involved examining the various layers of fabric to determine which piece was worn where. Much of the information from the preserved layers of clothing has been presented in the form of schematic section drawings (7).

This analysis represents a hugely important resource for the reconstruction of women's clothing. Working outwards from the body, we typically see the same sequence repeated on either side, representing shirt and dress, followed by the brooch itself which has preserved the collection, and then perhaps out to the shawl, and sometimes to a decoratively woven cloth which wraps the corpse in the manner of a shroud.

Tapestry	Tapestry
Fur and samite	Tweed
Tweed	
Silk	Brooch
Brooch	
	Silk
Twill	Twill
Linen	Linen
Body	**Body**
Tweed	Twill
Fur	Tweed
Tapestry	Wood
Wood	Sand

7 Inga Hägg has used diagrams to represent the layers of textile and other matter surrounding oval brooches from the Birka graves. The tapestry in both these examples probably represents a shroud

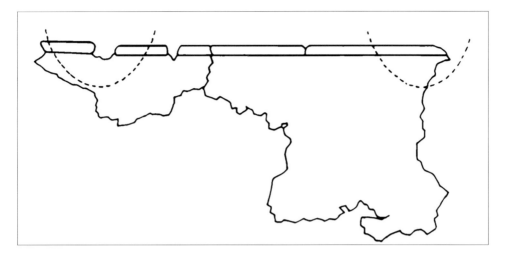

8 Two fragments from Birka grave BJ.597, representing the top section of a dress front. The fabric continues horizontally beyond the point where it was attached to the oval brooches (marked with dotted lines). Scale 1:2

But Hägg found that the picture which emerged from the layers of cloth did not always appear to fit with the conventional image of shawl, dress and shift. She notes that the suspended dress might be made of wool instead of linen, and that the top of the dress is often covered by the lower part of the oval brooch. Two significant fragments from grave BJ.597 preserved the top section of an entire dress front (*8*). Since the top of the dress always appears to have been both straight and horizontal even beyond the strap which attaches it to the brooch, Hägg argues that it cannot have been open at the side and is more likely to have been closed like the earlier Germanic dresses known from Danish bog finds.

She also notes that braided bands were often found in positions that do not appear to fit with any of Geijer's three garments, sometimes running under the brooches themselves, and that occasionally the brooches appear to have sat entirely on top of a woollen garment. Hägg interprets these braids and woollen fragments as evidence for a women's tunic. The most famous of the braided fragments are two sections from grave BJ.735 (*9*). This was a double burial in a chamber grave and, as so often in chamber graves, it seems that the occupants had been buried in a sitting position, which results in a confusing disarray among the grave contents. Geijer thought that the braid constructions came from the clothing of the man, but Hägg convincingly demonstrates that they belonged to the woman's garment. This she interprets as a splendid tunic, decorated with silk and a wealth of costly braiding.

Hägg also observes that the brooches are often overlain with a shaped or tailored garment of silk and fur, which she believes is better described as a 'caftan' than as a 'shawl'. Since grave BJ.967 contains evidence for decorative cuffs, she suggests that this caftan might sometimes have included sleeves.

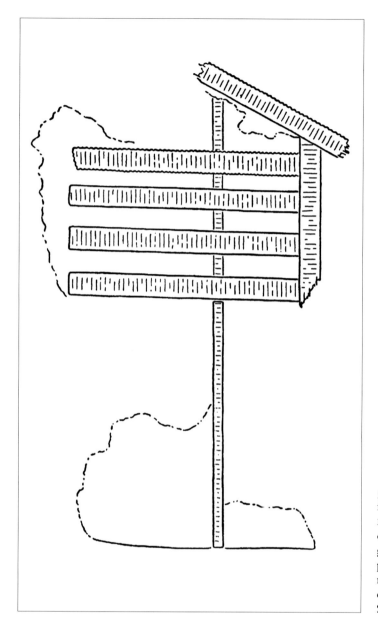

9 Layout of braids from Birka grave BJ.735, showing one of two symmetrical groups of braids probably representing remains of a woman's overdress. *Geijer 1938.* Scale 1:2

The modifications presented by Inga Hägg represent a complete reassessment of Viking women's clothing. Virtually only the brooches remain unchanged from earlier reconstructions. In her reinterpretation of the Birka material, Hägg emphasises that she means to provide a balance to earlier interpretations based largely on iconography, by providing a new viewpoint based in archaeology. Her detailed analyses and observations are presented in an accessible format in her thesis *Kvinnodräkten i Birka* (1974), making the Birka textiles available to others for further study.

Flemming Bau

Hägg's interpretation remains widely accepted today, but in 1986 it was adapted and modified by Flemming Bau. Working from information in Hägg's thesis, Bau noted that her reconstruction appeared to suggest that a richly ornamented tunic was almost entirely covered by a plain woollen dress, and that some metal implements (which had probably hung from the oval brooches) unexpectedly showed textile imprints, which appeared to come from the linen undergarment. Bau therefore argued that the dress could not have been closed as Hägg proposed, but open, as Geijer had originally suggested. But Bau moved the opening by a quarter turn to face forwards, to reveal the splendid tunic fronts described by Hägg (10). Bau also set the shoulder straps slantwise across the back, as they are in almost all strapped garments from Russian *sarafans* to denim dungarees.

Bau pays particular attention to the number of straps preserved in the oval brooches. Because these are right inside the brooch, they very often survive even though they are usually made of linen. Bau notes that there are four combinations of straps found in the brooches. Some have one strap at the top and one at the bottom; some have one at the top and two at the bottom; some have two straps both top and bottom; and some have two straps at the top and one at the bottom. He believes that these variations are to be explained by the occasional presence of two other garments, the apron or forecloth and the train or backcloth. However, his interpretation of strap combinations becomes, in my view, too inflexible.

In cases where the front has clearly been covered, or where there are two sets of straps in the bottom of the brooch, Bau proposes that an apron hung between the brooches. Turning to iconography, Bau notes that some depictions of Viking women include what looks like a pleated train at the back, and suggests that this explains the extra straps at the top of many brooches.

Although Bau is undoubtedly correct in placing the straps diagonally, and probably in his suggestion that some sort of separable train could form a part of the outfit, I find it hard to believe that the dress was typically open-fronted. In some cases, the open dress front does indeed coincide with evidence for either an apron or a tunic, but there are many other cases where an open-fronted dress would expose a woman's underclothing in precisely the areas one should most expect to find covered. Furthermore, for the same reasons that Hägg argued that it was not from an open-sided dress, I am not convinced that the dress front from grave BJ.597 (8) could represent an apron.

In his ethnographical comparative material, Bau fails to present any evidence for an open-fronted garment worn without an apron. Also, except in those cases where they secure the train, there is no real need for brooches in Bau's reconstruction, and the separate straps at back and front could more simply be made as one. Indeed, the whole garment would actually be easier to wear *without* the very brooches which it sets out to explain; without an apron to hold them in place, the heavy brooches become an encumbrance, likely to swing off to one side or another.

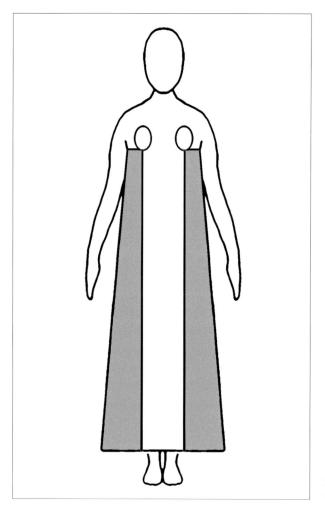

10 Representation of Bau's reconstruction of the suspended dress, with a front opening

REINTERPRETING THE EVIDENCE

In 1980, a small cemetery was excavated at Køstrup in north-west Funen (Fyn) in Denmark. At its centre was a woman's grave probably from the late tenth century, known as Grave ACQ, containing a pair of double-shelled oval brooches from which hung a knife, a key and eight beads, two of them crystal; there was also an iron-mounted maple-wood casket. But more significant than these other finds are the textiles. One group of fragments in particular has, I believe, far-reaching implications for the reconstruction of women's costume. It is clearly the front part of a dress; it cannot be an apron since it continues in a single piece from the front past the brooch and under the arm. The fragment is of wool dyed blue and, quite unexpectedly, much of the surviving fragment, including the area between the brooches is pleated; the construction of the pleating allows the dress to curve down under the arms (*colour plate 4*).

Such a dress clearly contradicts Bau's proposed reconstruction, since it cannot have been open in front. The presence of pleating also makes it unlikely that this dress was open at one side; Geijer's open-sided reconstruction is a simple unstitched rectangle of cloth, but at Køstrup, the dress has been stitched in pleats and there is no reason to imagine that it did not also include sewn seams; the curve of the cloth beneath the arms also suggests a closed garment likely to have included seams, while a pleated front combined with an open side would probably make the dress hang unevenly. Evidence for pleated dresses is not limited to Denmark; a similarly pleated fragment from Vangsnes, Norway, must now be re-identified as belonging to a dress and not a shirt as previously; fragments of wool on an equal-armed brooch from Grave C27997C at Kaupang, and a trefoil brooch from Birka grave BJ.843A also seem to have been pleated.

It seems likely then that the dress from Køstrup Grave ACQ was a closed dress, unlike the reconstructions of Geijer and Bau. Earlier Germanic dresses were certainly closed, and evidence from Viking graves is more consistent with a reconstruction as a closed dress than as an open one. The only evidence suggesting that Viking dresses might have been open at the side or front comes from comparison with traditional Baltic and Eastern European costume. However, this comparative evidence comes from areas where the bossed oval brooch was not known or was not typical; whatever earlier forms modern Baltic dresses may be descended from, they are unlikely to be descended from the Scandinavian brooched dress. Similar dresses are unknown in Scandinavian countries, and their open construction is only necessary because their straps are not fastened with brooches or buttons. Both the distinctive bossed nature of the Viking brooches and the unusual position in which they were worn suggest that the Viking dress was unlike dresses worn by surrounding peoples.

Without evidence to the contrary, we should assume that paired oval brooches were customarily worn with closed dresses. Although for us today, the brooches are our starting point for reconstructing women's dress, it is likely that for the women who wore them, the brooches were secondary to the garment which they supported; that is to say that the brooches were worn with the dress and not *vice versa*. There were clearly possible variations in the style of the dress, just as there were in the style of the brooches; the Birka dress front for instance is unpleated, and the varying numbers of straps attached to brooches suggest various combinations of garments. Inga Hägg has identified a fragment from Hedeby (*11*) as forming part of a suspended dress, and this would clearly have been an elegantly tailored garment made in several pieces; as such, it might represent the shape of the suspended dress towards the end of the Viking period. However, we may assume that the basic garment worn with the bossed oval brooches was a closed dress of one form or another, and that these brooches would not have been not worn without such a dress.

So, it seems we must find a new explanation for Hägg's tunic fronts and for Bau's perplexing textile imprints. I shall turn first to the question of the tunics, for which

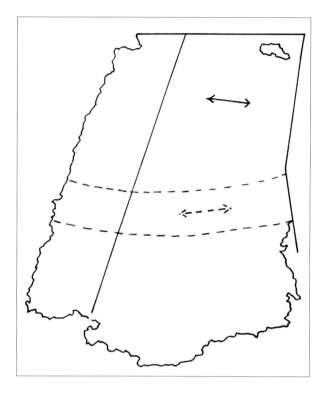

11 Sketch of fragment 14A from Hedeby, identified by Inga Hägg as forming part of a suspended dress. A tear hole in the top right corner might be where a strap was attached. The solid arrow marks the direction of the warp as indicated in Hägg's drawing, the dotted arrow marks the direction as it appears from the photograph. The area between the dotted lines shows signs of wear, as if a girdle had been worn below the bosom. Scale 1:3

Hägg found evidence among the tablet-woven braids from Birka; it simply does not make sense that such beautiful decorative work should have been hidden under a plain woollen dress, no matter how stylishly cut or attractively pleated.

The Birka braids, when found on the body, are usually in one of two distinct areas, that is either in the area of the shoulders or in the area below the arms (*12*). Where the braids are found in both positions (in graves BJ.965 and 950), they differ in type from one area to another. It seems likely then that these braids actually represent evidence for two separate garments, and those from the lower area come from the dress itself, or from a similar garment suspended on top of it.

Some depictions of women in long clothes appear to include a shorter overdress. If these dresses were worn with longer underdresses, this might go some way to explaining the varying numbers of straps found inside the oval brooches. This suggestion is supported by evidence from a rich woman's grave from Kaupang; textile archaeologist Anne Stine Ingstad showed that the costume in Grave C27997C included two dresses of different fabrics, both suspended from the oval brooches. The inner dress seems to have been pleated, and was probably longer than the overdress. A rectangular brooch, between the oval brooches, was pinned through both dresses. Evidence for double dresses also comes from Birka, where Geijer felt that the double dress was the norm. From grave BJ.563 comes a blue-dyed overdress trimmed with a red cord, over a linen underdress.

A short overdress would provide an opportunity for a show of fine fabric and decorative braiding at less expense than in the longer main dress. It is probably such a short overdress that is represented by braid fragments from below the area of the brooches, such as those from grave BJ.735 (9), which have previously been interpreted by Hägg as belonging to a women's tunic. If we return to the braided fragments from grave BJ.735, we can see that the layout of the braids mirrors the line of the Køstrup dress top; there is even a gap between the two sides where there could once perhaps have been pleating. A reconstruction of this garment as a short overdress naturally takes on the swooping hemline shown in illustrations from Hauge (14), Lärbro Stora Hammars (15) and elsewhere.

Similar combinations of short and long dresses are known from Russia where the oft-cited *sarafan* could be worn as a two-piece, and from Norway where the same division between upper and lower garments is typical of some traditional styles of *bunad*. Conceivably, a short, decorative dress might sometimes have been worn with a belted skirt to produce the same effect.

The remaining Birka braids are those from the area of the shoulders. These sometimes run horizontally across the chest, and sometimes pass diagonally under the brooches. Some of these may be fragments of the backcloth or train described by Bau, but more commonly, they appear to define the edges of a garment which covers the shoulders and back, and which hangs down on either side (16). This is not quite the shawl fastened by a single central brooch, nor is it Hägg's caftan, but it is probably the cloak-like garment which is represented on virtually all the female figures of the Oseberg Tapestry (17), and which makes an occasional appearance in other depictions of women, as in figures from Grödinge, Sweden (28), and Hauge, Norway (14). Strikingly, on the Oseberg Tapestry, these cloaks appear to be fastened by the bossed brooches visible on the women's breasts, and it is clear that the garment from the Birka graves was also attached to the bossed oval brooches.

In the few cases where the presence of a tunic has been inferred from fragments of woollen cloth found under one of the brooches, it is sometimes unclear whether this represents cloth which lay beneath the brooch at the point of burial, since the brooches in question have generally become dislodged. However, there is evidence from art and literature which may support the case for Hägg's postulated tunic, to which we shall turn later.

Bau was surprised to find traces of linen on some of the metal objects that hung from women's brooches. But if the women's clothing might have included pleated linen dresses, linen trains and linen aprons, these finds are less surprising. Counting linens and wools from women's graves at Birka, nearly 60 per cent of textiles from clothing are linen, the rest being made up almost exclusively of fine or very fine wools; by contrast the majority of dress textiles from men's graves are coarse wools. These figures may be skewed by the common survival of women's linen undergarments inside the oval brooches, but even allowing for this, they suggest that women's costume was dominated by light fabrics, mainly linens and fine wools.

Right: 12 Diagram showing the position on the body of braids from women's graves with oval brooches at Birka. Most come from the area between the brooches and the hips, where they probably adorned a short suspended overdress. *Based on Hägg 1974*

Far right: 13 Silver figurine from Birka, Sweden, representing a woman. She appears to be wearing a suspended dress and a backcloth, with her hair probably bound in a head cloth, which is tied to hang down the back

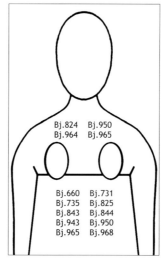

Bj.824 Bj.950
Bj.964 Bj.965

Bj.660 Bj.731
Bj.735 Bj.825
Bj.843 Bj.844
Bj.943 Bj.950
Bj.965 Bj.968

14 Figures from Hauge.

A) *above left*: gold foil showing a man and a woman. Over a pleated suspended dress, the woman appears to be wearing a backcloth, which is fastened to her oval brooches, with her hair probably bound in a head cloth, which is tied to hang down the back. The man wears a cloak of the *feldr* type and a shirt with loose or pleated sleeves fastened at the cuff; his hair is combed back over his head, but is not so long as to cover the neck.

B) *above right*: sketch (after Fleming Bau) of a figure from another gold foil; this woman is also wearing a backcloth fastened to her oval brooches, but over her pleated underdress; she also wears a shorter suspended dress. Short overdresses like this are also seen on other gold foil figures

Tacitus describes a linen overdress worn in his day by Germanic women, while Norse poets of the Viking Age could describe a woman as *lín-Gefn* or *lín-eik*, a 'linen goddess' or a 'linen oak'. Clear evidence for a suspended dress of linen comes from grave BJ.563. Hägg has suggested that linen might have become increasingly common as the fabric of the suspended dress throughout the period. Thus, Bau's linen fragments actually confirm the evidence of other sources. Furthermore, it is by no means clear that suspended objects were always worn outside the dress; they might have hung unseen inside a voluminous dress front.

So, the picture which emerges of the typical garment worn with the bossed oval brooches, is of a closed dress that might include pleated sections and could be made of either linen or fine wool. The dress was worn over a linen undergarment, probably a shirt of some sort, which by the tenth century was generally pleated. This costume is described in the Viking-era poem *Rígsþula* st.16, where it is worn by Amma, the wife of a yeoman farmer:

Sat þar kona … sveigr var á höfði, smokkr var á bringu, dúkr var á halsi, dvergar á öxlum.

There sat a woman … a *sveigr* was on her head, a 'smock' on her chest, a cloth was at her neck, 'dwarf' brooches at her shoulders.

In this verse, the bossed oval brooches are called *dvergar* or 'dwarfs' (a term which can be used of any support), and the dress itself appears to be referred to as a *smokkr* or 'smock'. This term *smokkr* confirms the suggestion that it was a closed garment, as it is related to the verb *smjúga* 'to creep through' – a reference to the way the garment is put on, whereby the wearer almost literally 'creeps through' the dress until head neck arms and shoulders emerge on the other side. The word *smokkr* could not

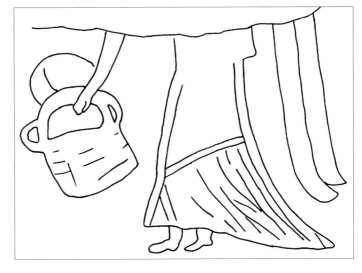

15 Fragmentary figure of a woman on a picture stone from Lärbro Stora Hammars, Gotland. She appears to be wearing a short overdress and a possible pleated underdress. Her underdress resembles garments identified as 'backcloths' on figures from Alskog (*30*), Grödinge (*28*) and Tuna (*31*), raising the possibility that these also represent pleated underdresses

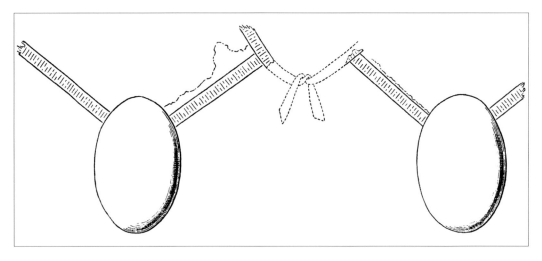

16 Braids and brooches from Birka grave Bj.824. These silver braids were clearly used as trim for a backcloth, suspended from the oval brooches. *Geijer 1938.* Scale 1:3

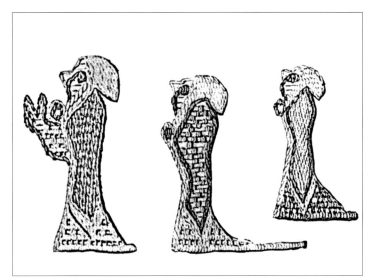

Above: 17 Figures from the procession scene of the Oseberg Tapestry representing women. Most women on the tapestry appear to be wearing an outfit based on the suspended dress with clearly visible oval brooches, often with a forecloth and a backcloth fastened to the oval brooches, and with their hair covered by a head cloth. *After an illustration by M. Storm*

Right: 18 Figure of a woman carved on a stone from Tu, Norway. She appears to be wearing a suspended dress with either a forecloth or a string of objects hanging from her brooch, and with her hair probably bound in a head cloth, which is tied to hang down her back

easily be applied to an open garment which is wrapped around the body, as in the reconstructions envisaged by Geijer and Bau. It is worth noting that the English word 'smock' typically describes a longish garment of cotton or linen, which is put on over the head and often includes a pleated section at the breast.

BROOCHES AS A BADGE OF RANK

Although the brooched dress has dominated ideas of Viking women's fashion, it was not the universal garment that it is sometimes supposed to have been. Only 122 burials from Birka contained oval brooches, out of an estimated 226–252 women's interments. By this reckoning, the brooched dress was worn by only about 50 per cent of women. And there are far fewer such brooches from the cremations or among graves from the surrounding area; other areas of Scandinavia also vary in the density of finds of oval brooches.

In the poem *Rígsþula* quoted above, the brooched dress appears to define the free woman's costume. The brooches or *dvergar*, are specifically mentioned as a part of Amma's dress, and it seems that this distinguishes her clothing from the slave women's costume alluded to earlier in the poem. In the light of this, many have seen oval brooches as the mark of the free woman.

Some caution is necessary. *Rígsþula* presents an extremely simplistic view of Viking society, which does not always fit readily with what we know from other sources. The poet aims to typify the three strata he perceives in society, but his portrayal of these social orders is not definitive. The poem suggests that the brooched dress may have been typical for the free farmer's wife, but not that it was ubiquitous for this class, nor that it was never worn among other social groups. It may also be that Amma is portrayed with twin brooches because of her status as a married woman rather than her status as a free woman.

Clearly, the heavy twin brooches represent an expression of the wearer's wealth, and women's graves at Birka which contained oval brooches were generally richer than those which did not. Even discounting the oval brooches themselves, they are richer on average than those including only women's jewellery of another sort; women buried with twin oval brooches were also likely to wear more beads and more other brooches than those who did not. This could be read as confirmation that the burials including oval brooches represent free women, whilst the others represent slaves, but other evidence suggests that graves from Birka without twin brooches probably represent the unmarried population rather than just the unfree.

This can be demonstrated by a simple if crude comparison of grave lengths (*19*). Whilst a longer grave can sometimes be a mark of status, grave length can often give an indication of the height of the buried person. For simplicity, I have counted only measurable interments having either three or more beads or diagnostically female brooch types; all figures are based on Arbman's *Die Gräber*.

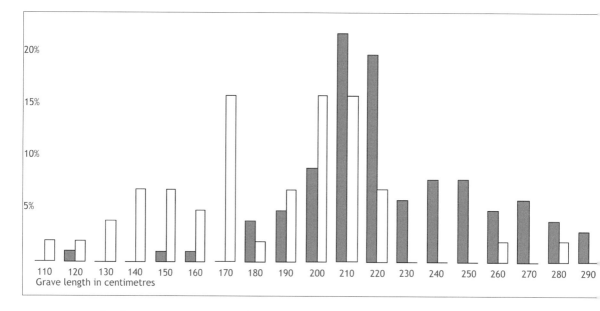

20%

15%

10%

5%

110 120 130 140 150 160 170 180 190 200 210 220 230 240 250 260 270 280 290
Grave length in centimetres

19 Graph comparing percentage figures for lengths of Birka graves with and without oval brooches. Shaded columns represent graves with oval brooches, white columns graves without

The average length of graves with twin brooches is 7ft 6in (230cm), while the average length of those without is just 6ft 3in (190cm). Whilst half (49 per cent) of those graves without twin brooches are 6ft (180cm) or less in length, only 5 per cent of the graves including twin brooches are so short. Some graves are clearly too short to have contained fully grown adults, and the great majority of these do not include oval brooches; perhaps the shorter graves with twin brooches represent child brides. Among graves with twin brooches, half (51 per cent) are 7ft 4in (225cm) or longer; 13 per cent of graves without brooches achieve this length, perhaps indicating that some women might remain unmarried into adulthood.

Significantly, whereas in graves with twin brooches the length of a grave has little bearing on its wealth, the same is not true of those without. In this group, shorter graves (measuring 6ft or less) average roughly twice as many beads and brooches as longer graves. The greater wealth of the shorter graves is consistent with the assumption that graves without brooches represent unmarried women, and suggests a society in which richer girls were less likely to remain unmarried into adulthood and where older unmarried women were less highly valued than their married counterparts.

Thus, the evidence of the Birka graves is consistent with the suggestion that the wearing of oval brooches was symbolic of marriage rather than freedom. However, since it is unlikely that slaves celebrated weddings, it still follows that slaves would have been excluded from wearing twin brooches. However, the twin brooches worn by female companion burials need not be read as evidence that they lived as wives to their co-burials; Ibn Fadlan describes what appears to have been the ritual wedding of a slave girl to her dead master, before she is killed to lie beside him.

In view of the relative scarcity of oval brooches among the Birka cremations and in the surrounding countryside, it is hard to be certain that they enjoyed universal popularity even in their heyday. But there are other explanations for this dearth of brooches, which could be due to a large number of slaves in an unusually wealthy district where slave owners might have been buried in town, or to differing funerary and inheritance customs. The proportion of oval brooches from the Birka cremations relative to inhumations, is similar to corresponding proportions for other types of brooch.

Some writers have drawn attention to a group of high-status graves without oval brooches, suggesting that women of the highest rank did not wear oval brooches. Indeed, the poet of *Rígsþula* does not mention oval brooches among the clothes of the noblewoman Móðir (st.28–9):

… en húskona hugði at örmum, strauk of ripti, sterti ermar.
Keisti fald, kinga var á bringu, síðar slæður, serk bláfáan …

… but the lady of the house was thinking of her arms, smoothing the linen, pleating the sleeves.
A bulging *faldr*, a clasp was on her breast, a full *slæðr*, a blue-dyed sark …

The nature of the garments mentioned in these verses and in the description of Amma's clothing quoted above (st.16) will be considered later in this chapter.

Although there are indeed many high-status women's graves without oval brooches, these date from the late Viking period, especially from late-Viking Denmark, and are probably indicative of changing fashions, rather than representing a long-established social marker. Since the Oseberg mound had been robbed in antiquity, it is not possible to be certain whether its occupant wore oval brooches, but the woman buried in the mound at nearby Borre, Norway, wore an elaborate pair of oval brooches befitting her high status.

Perhaps, *Rígsþula* dates from a period of transition, when oval brooches had been abandoned by the uppermost ranks of society. But it is equally possible that the poet simply omits to mention Móðir's oval brooches because they do not distinguish her rank and dress from Amma's (described in st.16); remarking again on the brooches would involve needless repetition. Thus, Móðir could be wearing a suspended dress or *smokkr* over her blue *serkr*, but the poet is not interested here in a garment which is basically similar to the clothes of the middle rank. It is the dyed linen of her *serkr* with its long pleated sleeves to which the poet draws our attention as a mark of luxury and status, and her long *slæðr*, a style of cloak worn only by men and women of rank.

At the very least, it can be said that twin bossed oval brooches were a popular fashion in Scandinavia amongst women who could afford them, and to the extent that they represent an expression of wealth, they doubtless acted as a status symbol. Besides their monetary value, the twin oval brooches and the dress that went with them, harked back to an ancient Germanic past, and possibly embodied a range of meanings and associations which it is difficult or impossible to understand today. One such level of meaning, according to evidence from the Birka interments, decreed that they should be worn only by married women, and by the same token it is most unlikely that they were worn by slaves.

SLAVES, THE POOR AND WORKING CLOTHES

In *Rígsþula* st.10, the slave woman is barefoot; she wears no jewellery, and her bare arms are tanned by the sun:

> *Þar kom at garði gengilbeina, aurr var á ilium, armr sólbrunninn, niðrbjúgt er nef, nefndiz Þir.*

> She came to the yard, gangly-legged, there was mud on her foot soles, sunburned arms, her nose is hooked, her name is Slavegirl.

Her legs, feet and arms are apparently all exposed for the poet's comment. Similarly, in *Gróttasöngr*, the slave women complain that 'the mud eats our foot soles and the cold above' (*aur etr iljar, en ofan kuldi*, st.16).

From these descriptions, it would seem that the slave was likely to be poorly clad, barefoot and bare-armed. She probably wore a simple knee-length dress of plain wool or coarse linen and nothing more. As well as being more practical for heavy work, a shorter dress would have been simpler to make and more economical in cloth, since the bottom of a longer dress needs fuller skirts if it is not to be too tight for walking.

The image of the barefoot slave girl is also evoked in *Laxdæla saga* ch.13 where the jealous wife Jórunn beats her servant Melkorka with her sock, a symbol of her social superiority. In *Guðrúnarkviða I* st.9, a slave woman dresses her mistress, stressing in particular the shoes:

> *Þá varð ek hafta ok hernuma … skylda ek skreyta ok skúa binda hersiss kván hverjan morgin.*

> Then I was bound and battle-caught … I had to bedeck her and tie the shoes of the warlord's woman every morning.

Tying on her mistress's shoes is a double indignity for the slave, since she must kneel to her mistress and dress her in a garment which is denied to her herself. Confirmation that this is more than simply a literary theme comes from the burial of the Oseberg queen; this mound contained two women and two pairs of shoes, but both pairs had been made to fit the club foot of the older woman.

This image of the ill-clad slave is likely to have been typical, but is a general rather than a universal truth. Some slaves may have been very well cared for and dressed in warm and decent if simple clothes, whilst concubines might well have enjoyed the use of fine clothing and jewellery. When Höskuld buys Melkorka in *Laxdæla saga*, she is described as 'ill dressed' (*illa klædd*, ch.12), and the same phrase is used to describe Queen Ástríðr when she is sold as a slave (*Heimskringla, Ólafs saga Tryggvasonar* ch.52), but, as his concubine, Melkorka is allowed to dress at Höskuld's expense and is then 'well dressed' (*henn semði góð klæði*, ch.13). Although she has been Höskuld's concubine, by the time she is abused by his wife, Melkorka is living as a domestic servant.

Confirmation that short skirts were known in the Viking Age is found in depictions of troll women. A carved stone from Hunnestad, Sweden, appears to show the troll wife Hyrrokin riding her wolf with snakes for reins as she is described in *Snorra Edda*; her dress reaches only to mid-thigh (*20*). *Egils saga Einhenda ok Ásmundar Berserkjabana* is almost certainly drawing on ancient if fantastical traditions, when it describes a troll woman wearing a dress so short that her genitals were plain to see (*mátti þar sjá viðrlita mikil sköp, því at hún var stuttklædd*, ch.11). A similar encounter with a troll woman occurs in *Illuga saga Gríðarfóstra* ch.4. Trolls may be the stuff of fantasy, but it is likely that these sub-human beings were envisaged in clothes appropriate to the lowest orders of people, sometimes perhaps in an exaggerated form of these clothes.

In view of this, some of the Anglo-Norse carvings previously taken to represent men because of their short garments, might in reality be depictions of women. At Kirkbymoorside, a beltless dress with a low-cut neckline, a suggestion of long hair and possible bead neckband contribute to this identification (*21*). Another Anglo-Viking carving from Pickhill in Yorkshire also appears to show a short dress, which in this case seems to be fastened on the breast by twin brooches (*22*). No doubt, scholars have shrunk from identifying this as a suspended dress fastened with oval brooches, because of its shortness, but in the light of other evidence for short dresses, this has to be the most likely explanation of this carving.

The wealth that was worn in the brooches did not necessarily put a woman above hard graft. In *Eyrbyggja saga*, Thorgunna the Hebridean wears fine clothes to attract men, but would no doubt wear something simpler when she works with her rake in the hayfield. A rich burial from Orkney known as the Westness woman, shows that wealthy women were no strangers to work; her grave included paired oval brooches and a very fine Celtic cross amongst other jewellery, yet her spine showed that she had spent her life carrying heavy loads on her back. Likewise, the rich female burial from Kneep, Scotland, included a sickle. Birka grave BJ.739 included what might have been either an iron pitchfork or roasting fork, alongside paired oval brooches, a round brooch, a silver penannular ring brooch and a string of beads. Without any means of hitching up the skirts, a long flowing dress would be inappropriate for the kinds of work these women were carrying out, and there is no evidence that the suspended dress was ever worn with a belt in Viking Scandinavia.

20 Carving from Hunnestad, Sweden, showing a troll wife riding a wolf. She wears a simple short dress or *serkr* with a long slit neck, which comes no lower than her knees. Like the figure from Kirkbymoorside (*21*), this was once thought to represent the Viking god Óðinn

Above left: 21 Carved figure from Kirkbymoorside, England, probably representing a woman wearing a bead necklace and a simple short dress or *serkr*. This figure has also been interpreted as the Viking god Óðinn in a noose

Above right: 22 Figure from an Anglo-Scandinavian carving from Pickhill, England, apparently representing a woman (possibly Eve) in a short suspended dress with paired oval brooches. Oval brooches themselves are seldom found in Britain but perhaps appear in carvings such as this one

Móðir's garments in *Rígsþula* st.28–9, seem to have been long, including as they do a full *slæðr*, but the poem says nothing about the length of Amma's brooched dress, which might have been contrastingly short. Even the many-beaded woman on the Oseberg cart wears a skirt that cannot come very much below mid-calf at the front (*23*).

So, it seems quite possible that some women wore brooched dresses that came no lower than the knee. Short dresses might not have been the sort of formal garment a woman would be buried in or married in (and thus they might feature less in idealised representations of womanhood) but they might yet have had a more important place among her everyday clothes. This shorter style might have been similar to the Roman-era skirts from Huldremose and Damendorf, and might also be reflected in the short decorative overdresses described above in connection with the braids from grave BJ.735.

23 Figure of a woman from the side of the Oseberg cart. She appears to be wearing a skirt, a shirt and a long bead necklace, with hair swept back and tied in a bun; she possibly wears a fillet around her hairline

UNMARRIED WOMEN

So, what fashions could be followed by the free woman (or perhaps the cherished slave) who was not wearing twin brooches? The cart from the Oseberg burial shows a woman restraining a man from attacking a horseman with a large knife (*23*). Around her neck hangs a very long double string of beads, and instead of the brooched dress, she wears a skirt and blouse. The skirt appears to be belted at the waist and hangs in folds around the back; the front of the skirt is either covered by an apron or, more likely, hangs flat like a kilt front, and it appears to be patterned. This waisted, patterned skirt is strongly reminiscent of the shorter garment from Huldremose with its drawstring gathering.

Whilst the image on the cart might conceivably depict an apron tied over a long pleated shirt, the identification of a skirt is supported by a remarkable figure from the Oseberg Tapestry. Almost all the women on this tapestry are dressed alike and are probably wearing the brooched dress, but Anne Stine Ingstad drew attention to two figures which break this pattern. One of these is considerably larger than other women on the tapestry, and, curiously, her face has no features; she may represent a goddess figure or idol (*24*). She is dressed in a long, red skirt apparently belted at the waist with a broad, patterned belt, which emphasises her narrow waist. Her upper body is left white, perhaps indicating a white linen shirt.

Another woman on the tapestry wears a similar arrangement of skirt and blouse, but her top falls over her skirt hiding any belt she might have worn (25). The short blouse worn by this second tapestry figure cannot be the same as the long shirt discussed below for use with the suspended dress, although it could be worn over such a shirt. It is much more like Hägg's 'tunic'. The bride in *Rígsþula* st.23 wears a 'kirtle' when she sets out to be married, which is apparently made of goatskin, and this might have been a short upper-body garment of the sort envisaged by Hägg; its significance here might be that this is her last appearance in her maiden's clothes. However, the goatskin kirtle of *Rígsþula* and the garment worn by the figure on the Oseberg Tapestry, might represent a form of overgarment compatible with the brooched dress (see *Thorax*, ch.2).

Most other depictions of women's costume from the Viking Age are disguised by the shawl, which makes it impossible to say whether the wearer has on a brooched dress or a belted skirt (although the overall shape is usually suggestive of the former).

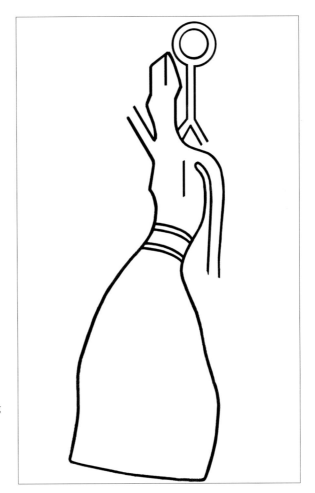

24 Figure of a woman from the Oseberg tapestry. She is much larger than other women on the tapestry, and appears to be wearing a long full skirt of coloured cloth, and a white linen shirt; the representation of her head is also unusual. This figure might portray a goddess or idol

25 Apparently female figure from the Oseberg Tapestry, one of a group of three women close to the hanging scene. She appears to be wearing a skirt and a short kirtle or overshirt, with her hair loose, perhaps representing the fashion for an unmarried woman; only the skirt indicates that this is not in fact a man

One figure, however, from Kinsta, Sweden, wears no shawl, but does clearly wear a belt at the waist from which a series of pleats fall round the back (26). Her hair is curiously similar to the woman on the Oseberg cart and she wears a short-sleeved garment on her upper body, which might be the ancestor of the Scandinavian *oplod*. It seems very likely that this is a third example of the belted skirt, but with such a tiny figure made in cast silver there is inevitably less detail than might be hoped for, and the Kinsta figure has also been interpreted as evidence for a women's caftan.

Intriguingly, this is also the style of dress worn by the hanged women depicted on the stone from Garde Bote, Gotland, suggesting that this image shows seven hanged maidens, which would presumably represent a specific sacrificial offering (27).

If the belted skirt was an option available to women of the Viking Age, perhaps as the fashion for girls and unmarried women, then it is remarkable that Viking women's graves do not seem to yield buckles or other belt fastenings. Presumably, the belt or girdle was made of textile and was tied in place. In Grave 1 at Peel Castle, Isle of Man, the so-called 'Pagan Lady' wore just such a belt of tablet-woven braid. In grave BJ.571, a group of objects was possibly attached to a similar belt. The young female bog burial from Windeby (Schleswig-Holstein, Germany) dates from the Roman Iron Age; the girl was naked, but wore a blindfold of brightly coloured braiding which had previously been used as a belt.

But some of the Birka graves without brooches do not fit this pattern of dress; grave BJ.831 seems to have had objects suspended on the left side of the body above the level of the central brooch, while in grave BJ.649, a chain links a knife to the position which would normally be occupied by the left-hand oval brooch. These

Right: 26 Silver figurine from Kinsta, Sweden representing a woman. She appears to be wearing a belted shirt, a short-sleeved top and arm rings, with her hair swept back and tied in a bun; she possibly wears a fillet around the hairline. The same figure was interpreted by both Hägg and Bau as showing a caftan

Below: 27 Scene on a picture stone from Garde Bote, Gotland, showing seven hanged female figures, all wearing belted skirts

women might have worn a version of the suspended dress without the brooches that commonly accompany it, which would possibly have been similar to the two-piece open-sided Baltic dresses on which previous reconstructions have been based. What social messages might have been implied by this style of dress can only be guessed at.

SHAWLS, BACKCLOTHS AND TRAINS

It was seen above how braids found in the area of the shoulders or running slantwise under the brooches, probably represent the top part of a garment which covered the woman's back. This backcloth could be hung across the back and trailed down at either side, as is worn by women illustrated on the Oseberg Tapestry (*17*) and on the silver figure from Grödinge, Sweden (*28*). In *Rígspula* st.29, Moðir wears a *slæðr*, a garment of the same name was also worn by men (as discussed in the next chapter), which was probably an extremely sumptuous cloak consisting of a massive semicircle of silk. The word *slæðr* probably originally applied to the type of women's backcloth seen in the illustrations from Oseberg and Grödinge, which was fastened to the oval brooches.

Pleated trains have been identified in many contemporary illustrations of women's dress, though in some cases what looks like a pleated train might actually represent a pleated or gathered section of dress, or even a semicircular *slæðr* pushed back over the shoulders and hanging in folds. A picture stone from Lärbro Stora Hammars (*15*) shows a garment that might otherwise be taken for a pleated train, which is worn under a short overdress, and which must therefore be understood as part of the underdress. However, a triangular fragment of fur and pleated cloth was among textiles excavated from the high-status grave from Hvilehøj, and this might have formed part of a fur-lined cloak or train (*29*). The Hvilehøj grave did not contain oval brooches, and if this fragment does represent a train, it could have been fastened by the trefoil clasp found over the breast, in the manner apparently described in *Rígspula*; a similar fragment comes from Grave ACQ at Køstrup, Denmark, where it might have been attached to the oval brooches, and a similar garment might have been worn from her oval brooches by the woman in grave Bj.824 (*16*).

Contemporary illustrations such as those from Alskog, Gotland (*30*), and Tuna, Sweden (*31*), show what looks like a shawl or stole, while fragments from Birka show that a shaped overgarment of wool or silk, sometimes lined with fur, could be fastened by a clasp over the breast; less elaborate woollen versions of this garment might have been worn by ordinary women. A cloth of madder-red mohair from the Oseberg burial was thought by Ingstad to have been from a shawl.

Evidence for the women's caftan has, in my view, been significantly overstated. None of the iconographic evidence which has been cited is convincing, and caftan fragments from Hedeby harbour might equally be from men's garments. Birka textile fragments from a garment fastened by a central brooch have been seen by

Right: 28 Silver figurine from Grödinge, Sweden, representing a woman. She appears to be wearing a forecloth, a suspended dress, a backcloth or shawl (which is probably fastened to her oval brooches), and what looks like a pleated backcloth, with her hair probably bound in a head cloth, which is tied to hang down the back

Below: 29 Sketch of scraps of fur, tablet-woven braid and woollen cloth from a woman's grave from Hvilehøj, Denmark. Scale 1:1

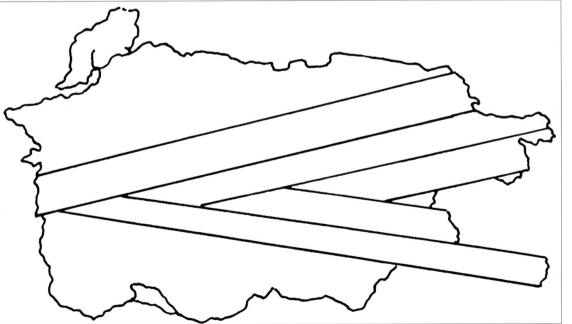

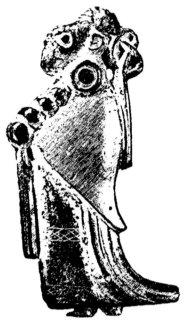

Above left: 30 Figure of a woman on a picture stone from Alskog, Gotland. She appears to be wearing a forecloth, what looks like a pleated backcloth and a shawl, with her hair probably bound in a head cloth, which is tied to hang down the back

Above right: 31 Silver figurine from Tuna, Sweden, representing a woman. She appears to be wearing a bead necklace, a shawl, a short forecloth or string of suspended objects (see *18*), a suspended dress, and what looks like a pleated backcloth, with her hair probably bound in a head cloth, which is tied to hang down the back

Hägg as part of the caftan but probably come from the stole or shawl, while a silver cuffs might have been attached to a long-sleeved shirt. However, it is possible that the 'kirtle' worn by the *Rígsþula* bride (st.23) is an open-fronted garment like a caftan (see *Thorax*, ch.2).

HEADGEAR

Two kinds of headgear are mentioned in *Rígsþula*, the *faldr* and the *sveigr*. These are also the two forms of headdress which commonly occur in the sagas.

The *sveigr* worn by Amma, the free married woman, may well have been the typical headdress of the Viking Age. The word, which is related to the verb *sveigja*, 'to bend, bow', suggests a hoop or twisted loop, and literary evidence seems to point to a simple cloth twisted around the head. In *Þrymskviða*, when Thórr is dressed in women's clothes, he is 'bound' (*bundu*, st.19, 15) in linen, while in *Víglundar saga* ch.14, the hero's father derides a linen bandage which Víglundr wears over his eye as a woman's headcloth. So, the *sveigr* may have been a narrow cloth wrapped around the head and tied off at the back or side. The *sveigr*, or the knot with which it was tied, might perhaps be seen in the circle shown at the back of women's heads in several contemporary depictions.

The word *faldr* means 'fold', and this well describes a form of headgear known from Viking York, Lincoln and Dublin, which may have borne the name (*32*). This consists of a strip of silk or wool about 6½–7in (17–18cm) wide by about 19–24in (48–60cm) long; the cloth is simply folded in half and stitched along one side. Strings run from the corners or from about 6in (15cm) down, and were presumably fastened either under the chin or at the back of the head. Left as it is, this headdress takes the shape of a pointed hood, but the English examples include a dart which cuts out the point; in the Irish examples the point was left in place but a line of stitching separated it from the top of the head. Moðir's *faldr* is described by the participle *keisti*, but the verb *keisa* is otherwise unknown in Old Norse; a comparison with modern Scandinavian languages would suggest protuberance, steepness, swaying or curvature. The Icelandic word *keis* denotes a bulging paunch, and *keisti* should perhaps be understood to suggest that Moðir's *faldr* has a bulging, swollen appearance from being stuffed with her hair; something of this sort might be worn by women on the Oseberg Tapestry (*17*).

As yet, no archaeological evidence for this form of headgear has come from the Scandinavian homelands, which might support the proposition that Moðir's clothing represents a new colonial fashion. However, a turn of phrase in *Njáls saga* ch.129 suggests that a simple piece of unstitched headcloth could also be worn as a *faldr* and, similarly, in *Orkneyinga saga* ch.81, Ragna uses a silk cloth as a *faldr*; in this case the words *faldr* and *sveigr* would not describe different garments as such, but different ways of wearing the headcloth. Edda, who is described in *Rígsþula* as 'old-hooded' (*aldin-falda*, st.2), presumably wears a simpler style of *faldr* than Moðir, which must have been traditional in Scandinavia. Thus, the western settlements might simply have developed a regional variation on an established fashion. Archaeological evidence from the British Isles is for smaller headdresses than those of the sagas: *Gísla saga* ch.12 speaks of 'headcloth' (*höfuð-dúkr*) of 20 ells or 30ft (9m); this may have been split three ways, which gives a more credible 10ft (3m) for each headdress, but this is still a good length; perhaps this would make 'a big *sveigr*' (*en sveigr mikil*) like the one worn by Guðrún in *Laxdæla saga* ch.55.

The headcloth could be either linen or wool; the silk sometimes used in British and Irish finds would be extravagant if used in a longer cloth. In *Laxdæla saga* ch.69, a group of women gathered to attend a women are described as having 'linen on their heads' (*höfðu lín á höfði*), suggesting that at other times they might have worn wool or gone bareheaded. A horsehair headdress features in *Orkneyinga saga* ch.81, but this is a *gaddan*, a Gaelic headdress, and is clearly unusual, perhaps even inappropriate, in a Scandinavian context; interestingly, Ragna puts on a silk *faldr* in its place, another instance of the distinctive silk headgear from the British Isles.

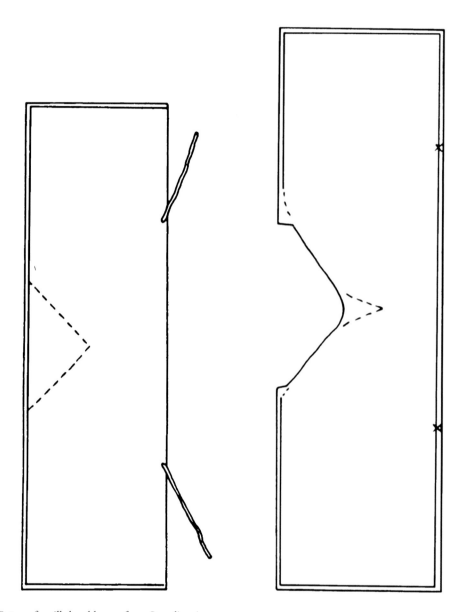

32 Pattern for silk headdresses from Scandinavian
settlements in Britain and Ireland.

A) *above left:* from Dublin (E172:14370), with a selvedge along the front and hemmed at the back and
bottom; a straight line of diagonal stitching forms the crown.

B) *above right:* from York (Coppergate 1332) with rolled hems; a dart has been cut for the crown, and
ties attached at points 'x' on the front edge. Scale 1:4

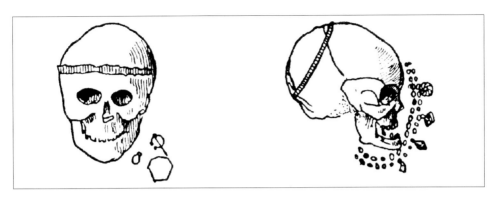

33 Braided bands worn as headgear from Birka graves BJ.707 and 946. *Geijer 1938, Arbman 1944*

As mentioned above, the women depicted on the Oseberg cart (*23*) and on a small figure from Kinsta (*26*) apparently share not only a waist-held skirt, but also a hairstyle. Both women appear to have their hair in a bun, with a band above the forehead. Graves BJ.571 and 707 contained the remains of headbands; both these are graves without oval brooches, and these bands might have been used in hairstyles similar to those of the figures from Kinsta and the Oseberg cart. Similar bands have also been found in eight graves which do contain oval brooches, but not all headgear involving braided bands need have been the same; sometimes the band goes right around the head, sometimes it might simply have edged the top of the headdress, and sometimes it seems to have been worn atop the back of the head (*33*). A tablet-woven band might have been worn, for instance, with either a *faldr* or *sveigr*.

The writer of *Orkneyinga saga* thought it customary for maidens to wear their hair loose (ch.86), but he was writing of a later time and a foreign land. On first glimpsing Steingerðr, the girl he will fall in love with, the tenth-century poet Kormákr recites a verse which suggests that Steingerðr wears her *faldr* before she is married (*Kormáks saga* st.1 ch.3); it would seem she wears it when barefoot and apparently dressed for bed, so perhaps Steingerðr's *faldr* is in fact a nightcap. In *Snorra Edda*, Brynhildr and Guðrún bleach their hair at the riverside; later Svanhildr is ridden down and killed while she sits bleaching her hair. These women are married when these incidents take place, suggesting that the hair even of married women would have been visible, though perhaps only partially visible under a headdress.

UNDERWEAR

Shirts and neckcloths

According to *Laxdæla saga*, wearing clothing appropriate to the opposite sex gave grounds for divorce. Thus, in *Laxdæla saga* ch.34, when Guðrún wants to divorce her husband, she is told to make him a shirt with a neckhole so big that she could divorce him for wearing it, and in the next chapter this is described as having 'a head hole so big, that his bare nipples could be seen' (höfuðsmátt svá mikla, at sjái geirvörtur hans berar). In a woman's shirt, a neckhole such as this would allow easy breastfeeding. Whilst no known Icelandic law actually allows for divorce on grounds of clothing, the law code Grágás orders Lesser Outlawry for a woman who wears her clothes or hair like a man, or for a man who adopts women's fashions. So, although the two sources do not agree in detail, they appear to be independent witness to the rigorous distinction between men's and women's clothing.

In Rígsþula, the slave girl Thir has tanned arms (st.10) contrasting with Moðir's arms covered by pleated sleeves (st.28, though various translations have been offered for the phrase sterti ermar, which I render 'pleating the sleeves'). But Amma's arms are not mentioned (st.16); indeed, though Moðir wears a blue serkr, there is no mention of any shirt worn by Amma, only a neckcloth (dúkr var á halsi). It is dangerous to read too much into the brief epitomes of this poem, but it is certainly possible that Amma is envisaged without an undershirt. Amma's neckcloth might have resembled that worn by the Roman-era Huldremose woman, which measured 4ft 6in x 1ft 7in (137 x 49cm), and which could easily cover the shoulders, back and breast exposed above the smokkr. The possibility that some Viking women might not have worn shirts under their suspended dresses was raised by Geijer among others. If Amma is wearing a shirt, then it probably contrasts with Moðir's in the absence of pleats and sleeves.

At Birka, shirts, or at any rate, undergarments, of smooth linen seem to give way to pleated linen in the tenth century. An indication of the cut of the woman's shirt comes from the direction in which the pleats run, where they are preserved in the back of oval brooches; these pleats invariably radiate outwards over the shoulders from the centre of the breast. This pattern of pleating is at odds with conventional reconstructions, and suggests a very different cut. The pattern is consistent with a neckcloth worn instead of a shirt, but in these high-status contexts, a garment equivalent to Moðir's serkr should be considered, and there is some evidence that a sleeved shirt could be worn with the suspended dress.

A garment which agrees with the various strands of evidence from Rígsþula, Laxdæla saga and from Birka, is illustrated in the ninth-century Italian 'Augsburg Gospel Book' (34). Here in an illumination showing the Massacre of the Innocents, nursing mothers are shown wearing a loose robe which is open in front to below the breast; although it has no sleeves, it is full enough to cover the upper arm. If it were made of pleated cloth (like the similar garment worn by Mary on the eighth-century 'Altar of Duke Ratchis' at San Martino Cividale), these pleats would naturally fall in the pattern found on the back of the brooches from Birka. These depictions are from the early medieval Mediterranean rather than the Baltic Sea, but they are consistent with evidence for the undergarment worn by contemporary Scandinavian women.

The form of shirt shown in the Augsburg Gospel Book is sleeveless, yet would cover Amma's upper arms, so that unlike the slave's they would be protected from the sun. But if Amma's forearms were not as lily-white as she would like, this could

34 Women in a state of undress illustrating the Massacre of the Innocents from the ninth-century Italian Augsburg Gospel Book. Viking women might have worn similar garments under the suspended dress. *Bayerische Staatsbibliothek MS Clm 23631 fol.24v*

still contrast with the description of the slave whose entire arm is probably brown, for since the Norse word *hönd* covers the forearm as well as the hand, the use of the word *armr* in this context suggests the whole arm. A fragmentary garment from Dätgen, Germany, might represent the remains of a similar robe; it has short sleeves of between 4-5½in (10–14cm).

Moðir's blue sleeved *serkr* is consistent with evidence from Birka, where blue-dyed linen is thought to have been found, while pleated linen sleeves might have left their mark on metal objects from Birka graves BJ.980 and 1062; the woman buried in the rich grave C27997C at Kaupang also appears to have worn a long-sleeved linen shirt. Where an arm is shown, women on the Oseberg Tapestry are wearing loose linen sleeves (*17*). Pleating the body of the shirt would take up any excess width of cloth, making sleeves more necessary.

The term commonly used for a woman's shirt is *serkr*. But the *serkr* also appears in *Atlakviða* st.4 among a list of male and martial gifts offered by Attila the Hun to the Niflungar, and is used in kennings to describe the warrior's byrnie or corselet. Despite Moðir's long sleeves, the *serkr* might typically have been envisaged as a sleeveless garment, but it was possibly also distinguished from the men's shirt, or '*skyrta*', by its bagginess. Bagginess was apparently seen as unbecoming in men's garments, though loose clothing was apparently worn by women and thralls. The term *serkr*, then, is possibly equivalent to Latin *tunica*, as *skyrta* is to *camisia* (see below, ch.2); thus, the tenth-century German Liudprand similarly distinguished the clothes of the emperor Otto from the Greek emperor's *tunica*, saying that Otto's clothes were not like a woman's.

Breeches

In *Laxdæla saga* ch.35, after Guðrún has divorced her husband for wearing a low-necked shirt, she suggests that Thórðr divorce his wife on the grounds that she commonly dresses 'in breeches with a gore in the seat, and with bands wound right down to her shoes' (*í brókum, ok setgeiri í, en vafit spjörrum mjök í skua niðr*). Thórðr then divorces Auðr, saying that she wears 'seat-gored breeches like man-women' (*setgeirabrœkr sem karlkonur*). The men's seat gore might have allowed the legs to be spread more widely than was considered seemly. The lack of a gore clearly made women's breeches unsuitable for riding, presumably because the wearer could not spread her legs, and when Auðr mounts a horse later in the same chapter, the saga man comments that 'she was certainly wearing breeches then!' (*ok var hon þá at vísu í brókum*); this phrase and the nickname 'Breeches'-Auðr (*Bróka-Auðr*) might suggest that women's breeches were unusual in themselves, and the troll woman in *Egils saga Einhenda ok Ásmundar Berserkjabana* apparently wears none (ch.11).

We may guess that women's breeches, if worn, were also fairly short (coming perhaps to the knee or to mid-calf), both from the emphasis on the length of Auðr's leggings, and on account of Hallgerðr's nickname 'long breech' (*lang-brók*) in *Njáls saga* ch.9 and in *Landnámabók*.

Stockings and socks

We know nothing of the nature of the stockings which Jórunn used to beat Melkorka in *Laxdæla saga* ch.13, but they are unlikely to have differed greatly from men's hose or from the Roman-era stockings from the woman's grave at Martres de Veyre, France. Short skirts might have been worn with stockings or hose covering the lower leg. If such hose were normally made of linen, this could be why Auðr might have wanted to adopt a warmer alternative. Needle-bound socks, like that from Viking York, might also have been worn (*colour plate 9*).

SHOES

The typical shoe of Viking-era archaeology is the leather turnshoe, which was worn by men and women alike (*colour plate 11*). There are several basic types, but the same general patterns occur right across the Viking world. A turnshoe is made by a similar method to dressmaking. The shoe is sewn up inside out with the help of a wooden last; then it is *turned*, so that the tougher grain or hair side is outermost and the seams are hidden inside the shoe.

Scandinavian shoes typically have straight-sided soles with a triangular heel that rises up in an inverted V-shape at the back. Perhaps the commonest type, and the basic pattern for all the rest, is a two-piece shoe made of a separate sole and upper that comes to just below the ankle. The upper is wrapped around the last and stitched to the sole around the bottom of the foot; another seam joins the edges of the upper either on the inside of the foot, or down the front. Making a shoe from a separate sole and upper allows the use of thinner leather for the upper, and goatskin is common.

In the ninth and tenth centuries, the stitching was often of hide thongs; later thonging is finer than earlier, and it is eventually replaced by thread. At first, thread was only used to sew the seam in the upper where either woollen or linen thread could be used, but linen thread gradually won out, both for the seam in the upper and later for the sole as well. Generally, the stitches pass straight through the upper from side to side (a flesh-grain stitch), but through the topside only of the thicker sole, coming out along the edge rather than on the bottom (a flesh-edge stitch).

Although basically slippers, even low shoes are often tied with a lace, and laces are more important on ankle boots, though at York these were generally fastened with a rolled-leather toggle. Long laces might have marked status. The laces from the Oseberg queen's shoes were 6ft (180cm) long, while in *Heimskringla*, *Óláfs saga Helga* ch.33, King Sigurðr Sýr wears laces long enough to bind around his legs. *De Carolo Magno* describes Frankish gilded leather boots with laces of 3 cubits, which would be 4ft 6in (140cm) or more long. In the medieval Welsh *Mabinogion* story 'Math fab Mathonwy' (written in the twelfth or thirteenth century, but often drawing on older traditions), Gwydion makes shoes of gilded leather for the lady Aranrhod, and gilded shoes with silken seams were worn at the court of Óláfr Kyrr (*Heimskringla*, *Óláfs saga Kyrra* ch.2).

Aranrhod's shoes are made to measure, and likewise the shoes of the Oseberg queen were made to accommodate her club foot. The importance of a good fit was alluded to by the poet of *Hávamál* st.126, who advises against making shoes, pointing out that an ill-fitting shoe is likely to bring a curse on its maker.

JEWELLERY AND ACCESSORIES

Oval brooches

The bossed oval brooch was usually 4–5in (1–12cm) long, and was probably an essential feature of the closed type of suspended dress which seems to have been typical of Viking Scandinavia. The upward-pointing pin did not go through the fabric of the dress or shirt, but was attached to the dress by loops of textile; other loops might sometimes have been attached to a short overdress, a forecloth or apron, or a backcloth or train, or sometimes might have suspended keys and other implements.

There was a surprising degree of conformity in the decoration of oval brooches, so that some commentators have suspected they reflect regional and social origins, rather than the individual choice of the wearer. The different ways in which the ornament is arranged on the brooches has been grouped into more than 50 separate categories, but just nine basic styles account for almost all known examples. The full range of oval brooches was first described in 1928 by Jan Petersen, and the individual styles are now generally identified as P1 to P55 by reference to the numbered illustrations in his book. Petersen's work was expanded and updated in 1985 by Ingmar Jansson. Within each numbered style, there is room for variation in the detail of the ornament.

Vendel-period brooches sometimes decorated with a single crouching beast, which covers the whole surface, and some early Viking brooches show traces of this design. In general, most ninth-century brooches are decorated with animal ornamentation based on Style III, often using gripping beasts. The decorative effect can be enhanced with protruding knobs, which are sometimes cast, but often riveted on to the main body of the brooch.

Whilst in the early period the bowl of the brooch was cast in a single piece, in the tenth century, brooches were typically double-shelled; gaps in the decorative scheme of the outer shell are pierced to reveal the plain inner shell beneath. These double-shelled brooches are also very often gilded. The patterns on the later brooches are still fundamentally conservative however, and are stylistically closer to ninth-century art than to the emerging Jelling style.

The most popular early-period brooch type is P37, accounting for three out of every five brooches from Norway and the western settlements, and half of all those from the east (35, *colour plate 1*). The late-period brooch type P51 is the direct descendant of the popular P37, and was even more ubiquitous than its predecessor, accounting for nine out of ten brooches from the west, and seven out of ten from eastern areas (*36*).

Other important types from the early period are Berdal, which though it makes up one in three from eastern Scandinavia, accounts for just one in eight from the west, where it is challenged by types P25 and especially by P27, which make up one in four between them. P25 does not feature in the east, but P27 accounts for one in five of the total. Brooch type P42 had its heyday at the juncture of the late and early periods, but perhaps only ever made up a tenth of the total. In the late period, brooches of types P52/55 were fairly common in the east where they make up one in four of the finds, but were less popular in the west.

Regional variations in brooch distribution suggest only slight local differences in a pan-Scandinavian fashion. The brooch types and even the relative popularity of types remain largely the same. On the island of Gotland, the usual oval-shape is displaced by an animal-head style, and these appear to have served a similar purpose to the oval brooches, but are sometimes found in threes, where oval brooches are only ever found in pairs; the third brooch was presumably used as a central clasp for a garment other than the suspended dress.

Other brooches and clasps
Turning from oval brooches to other forms, we find the field dominated by round brooches, which account for about half of all brooches other than oval brooches from women's graves at Birka. In Scandinavia, round brooches generally divide

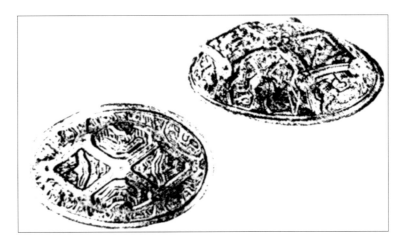

35 Oval brooches of type P37, the commonest type of the early Viking period. These examples are from Nord Fron, Norway, and Meløy, Norway. Scale 1:2. See also *colour plate 1*

36 Oval brooches of type P51, the commonest type of the late Viking period. Unprovenanced. Scale 1:2

into two distinct groups, small and large, but this is not true of round brooches from the British Isles where a good many fall in the middle at around 1½in (4cm) diameter, even though they might be decorated in Scandinavian styles. This suggests that whereas in Scandinavia different roles might be allotted to round brooches according to size, this was not generally the case outside Scandinavia. The distinction between small and large round brooches survives in modern Norwegian *bunad*, where small round brooches are called *knappar* ('buttons') and larger round brooches are *sølvar*. Small round brooches less than 1in (3.5cm) across, become common at Birka in the tenth century; about half of them are positioned above the level of the twin oval brooches, where they probably fastened the neck of the linen shirt (*37*, *colour plate 6*).

Large round brooches from Birka are typically about 2in (5cm) across, while openwork round brooches are larger at around 2¾in (7cm); they were worn either below or between the oval brooches (*37*). Trefoil brooches are generally found in similar positions, and could be worn pointing either upwards or downwards (38). They are usually around 2–2½in (5–6cm) at their widest point, and were particularly popular in the late ninth and early tenth centuries. Early versions were made from the strap distributors of Frankish sword belts, and there must have been a special appeal in turning a piece of Frankish wargear into a woman's trinket. Later versions are made to the same design, but the decoration becomes typically Scandinavian. Curiously, no trefoil brooches have come from cremation burials either at Birka or Kaupang.

The other very common brooch type from Birka was the equal-armed brooch, which has its origins in the seventh century, but maintained its popularity in the Scandinavian world into the Viking period, surviving in Sweden into the eleventh century (39). It is formed of two flat arms on either side of a central boss. Typically, these brooches are about 3in (8cm) long, but they can be as long as 7in (18cm). Of 20 equal-armed brooches shown *in situ* on Stolpe's sketched grave plans, 12 are worn horizontally and eight are vertical. All of the vertical examples are at the height of the twin oval brooches or below, whereas half of the horizontal examples are above this position. The woman buried in BJ.1131 wore an equal-armed brooch instead of one of her oval brooches.

The penannular ring brooch, a standby of men's clothing (86), was not nearly so common in women's graves, and where it does occur, it is worn quite differently. Several of the penannular brooches from women's graves at Birka are very small, approximately 1in across (2.5cm) or even less; these are often made of silver, and were found at the neck, very often to one side, where they perhaps pinned a scarf similar to Amma's *dúkr* (*Rígsþula*, st.16). Larger penannular brooches can be worn on the side of the body and always below the height of the twin brooches. Perhaps the most typical position was at the elbow on the outside of the arm, in such a way that the cloak would have constricted movement in the upper part of both arms; this is most clearly the case in BJ.605A and 860A. It seems that the larger form of penannular brooch might not have been worn without oval brooches; if the brooched dress was worn only by married women, then perhaps the typically male penannular brooch might have a special value in women's costume, either symbolic or sentimental, representing the woman's husband. In BJ.981A a penannular brooch is apparently used in the place of one of the oval brooches.

Typically, these non-oval brooches are worn centrally on the body. In *Rígsþula*, Moðir wears a clasp on her breast, and it is often assumed that the presence of a centrally placed brooch in a woman's grave implies the presence of a shawl or some other form of outer garment worn over the dress. Some brooches have indeed been found with the remains of the silk or linen straps of these garments still attached. But as may be inferred from the different positions of the different brooch types from the neck down to the navel, this is not necessarily a safe assumption.

Many graves appear to show a deliberate relationship between the placement of the central brooch and the twin oval brooches. In some graves, a string of beads

37 Round brooches from Birka.
A) *above left:* large round brooch from Bj.967. Scale 1:1.
B) *above right:* small round brooch from grave Bj.431. Scale 1:1.
c) *left:* large openwork round brooch from Bj.644. Scale 1:1

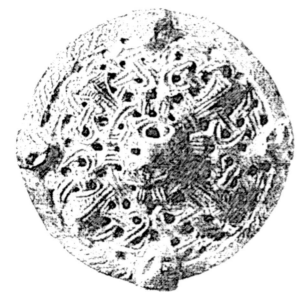

actually links all three (3), while in other cases the central brooch is surrounded by beads in a manner inconsistent with its use as a clasp. Sometimes the brooches were clearly never meant to be central at all, as in Bj.1084 where a string of beads zigzags across the breast from brooch to brooch. In those cases where an equal-armed brooch is worn vertically, it is unlikely that it was worn as a clasp. In Bj.843A fragments of wool on the back of a trefoil brooch suggest it was stuck straight through the fabric of the dress, and the same appears to be true of the vertical equal-armed brooch worn directly below the left-hand oval brooch in Bj.1014. So, it seems that Viking women might wear a brooch simply to look good, just as modern women do, which should scarcely surprise us.

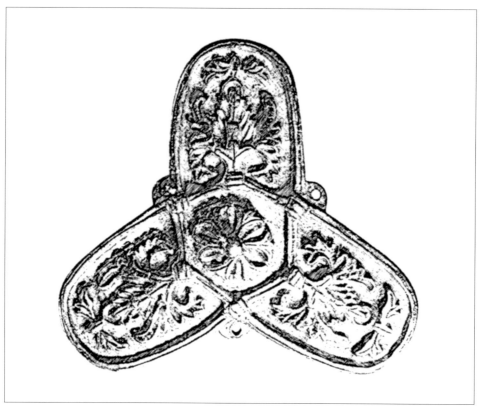

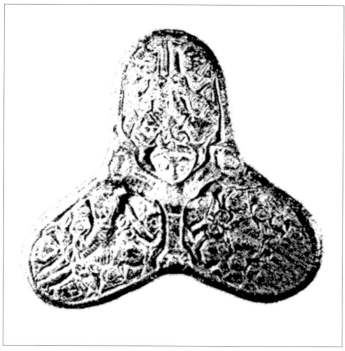

38 A) *above*: Frankish strap distributor for a sword belt, from a Scandinavian hoard. These mounts were reused in Scandinavia as women's brooches. Östra Pådoba, Sweden. B) *left*: Scandinavian trefoil brooch, the design clearly based on that of the Frankish strap distributor. Roskilde, Denmark. Scale 1:1

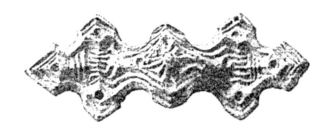

39 Equal-armed brooch from
Birka grave bj.599. Scale 1:1

Beads and pendants

> The jewellery which they prize the most is the dark-green ceramic beads which they have
> aboard their boats and which they value very highly: they purchase beads for a dirham a
> piece and string them together as necklaces for their wives. (Montgomery's translation).

Beads are commonly found in Viking women's graves, but this passage by Ibn Fadlan
reminds us that though relatively plentiful, they were nonetheless prized. They are
usually made of glass rather than ceramic, but often with a matt finish which may
have misled Ibn Fadlan; such beads are found all over the Viking world and beyond.
Glass beads come in all colours (many are multicoloured) and a variety of shapes
and sizes (*40, colour plate 7*). Other beads are made of amber, carnelian, rock crystal,
silver and gold. Although other types of gem and semi-precious stone are rare, a
good number of glass beads are made in patterns which appear at least originally to
have been made in imitation of such stones.

Where beads are worn in a necklace, it can be quite short almost like a choker, but
long strings of beads, like that worn by the woman carved on the Oseberg cart (*23*),
are also known. Very often, in graves containing oval brooches, the beads will hang
in a string between the two brooches, usually suspended from the catch at the top of
the brooch, but sometimes from the hinge at the bottom. Sometimes the beads form
double or triple strings between the oval brooches, and sometimes they also link to
a third brooch (*3, 41*). Or a string of beads might simply hang in a loop from a single
brooch. Some oval brooches and trefoil brooches were pierced by a hole, sometimes
with a small ring, on which strings of beads other objects might be hung.

But not all beads were allowed to hang freely. Some graves from Birka had a perfect
circle of beads on the woman's breast, which must have been stitched in place on one
of her garments (*41*). These bead circlets occur in graves with oval brooches as well
as those without, so they were probably simply sewn onto whatever garment was
most convenient. As well as bead circles, there are also bead squares and bead ovals.
Sometimes, a group of beads has been sewn in a tight group around a central brooch.

As well as beads, many women wore small pendants such as coins, Thórr's hammers,
charms, and loops of wire with a few beads on them. These pendants might form
a part of a string of beads, or might be stitched directly to the costume. They are
particularly popular as a part of the more elaborate arrangements of beads.

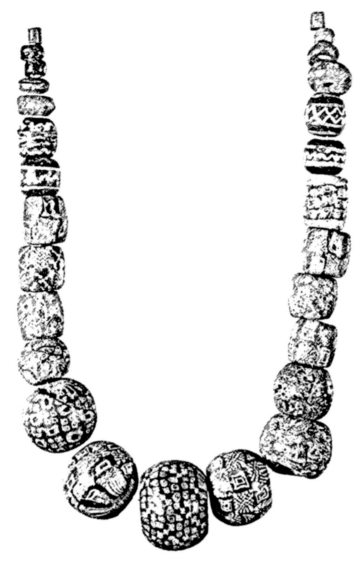

Left: 40 Beads of various sizes and patterns from Eidem, Norway

Below: 41 Some of the many ways of wearing beads and associated pendants from the Birka graves.
A) *left:* as a necklace (BJ.838, 961, 966 and 973).
B) *centre left:* linking the oval brooches (BJ.515, 552, 556, 703 739, 959 and 1012).
C) *centre right:* a triple string linking the brooches (BJ.557, 639 and 660).
D) *right:* sewn onto the dress or shirt (BJ.632, BJ.843A, 791 and 825). Necklaces and sewn beads were also worn by women without oval brooches

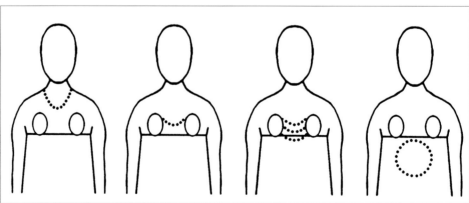

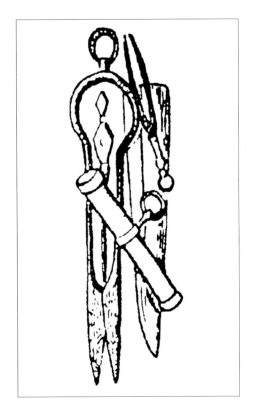

42 Group of objects suspended from oval brooch in Birka grave Bj.1011, including scissors, needle box, tweezers and knife. *Arbman 1944*

Three other classes of object might dangle from a woman's brooches or belt: toilet sets, needlework items and keys (*42*). Toilet sets often included ear spoons, tweezers and toothpick, and dressmaking equipment included a needle box, scissors and a knife. Needle boxes from Birka range from 1½–3in (4–8cm) in length. They were usually made from bone or copper alloy, and over half of those from graves still had needles inside.

Bracelets and Rings

Finger rings, arm rings and neck rings, even occasionally earrings and toe rings, are known from the Viking Age. But although literature describes women decked in gold arm rings, and rings of gold and silver are common in Viking hoards, those found in graves are usually made of bronze and are less common than literary sources would suggest. Perhaps this is a feature of funerary and inheritance customs; if arm rings were given as gifts by the dying woman they would not feature in the burial deposit; in Ibn Fadlan's account of the Rus funeral, the rings are taken from the girl before her death and the same principle might apply to other kinds of jewellery as well. Yet in *Sigurðarkviða inn skamma* (st.46, 49), Brynhildr offers jewellery to entice her slaves to join her in death.

Ibn Fadlan says that the Rus used gold and silver neckbands as an indicator of wealth: 'Whenever a man's wealth reaches ten thousand dirhams, he has a band made for his wife … for every ten thousand more, he gives another band to his wife' (Montgomery's translation). Clearly, neck rings of gold and silver were the jewellery of the very rich, and they are unsurprisingly rare as archaeological finds (*colour plate 8*). Ibn Fadlan's stress on these precious neck rings not only emphasises the extraordinary wealth of the Rus, but also gives an idea of the proportion of wealth that might be displayed in jewellery.

A number of large iron rings, each with several Thórr's hammers, came from among the Birka cremation burials; these were probably neck rings and one was worn round the neck by the woman buried in Bj.1081 (*3*), though in grave Bj.854 one was found at the back of the woman's head. Thórr's hammer rings are not, to my knowledge, ever convincingly associated with men's costume, though one comes from the fill of a man's grave at Birka, and a ring from Gnezdevo, Ukraine, is unreliably attributed to a man's grave.

Finger rings appear to be more-or-less peculiar to women's graves. They are frequently made of precious metal, usually either of twisted wire rings or cast. Earrings, though not unknown, are relatively uncommon in this period.

NEW STYLES OF DRESS

By 1985, archaeologists had already unearthed some 4000 bossed oval brooches. Brooches of this kind have been found in Scandinavian contexts in all the lands that were settled in the Viking expansion, from Britain, Ireland and Normandy in the West to Russia in the East. But wherever the Scandinavians settled into existing Western populations, oval brooches are surprisingly rare; the only colonies where oval brooches have been found in any real numbers are Iceland and Russia.

This scarcity in the West is probably partly due to the swift adoption of local burial customs, which in these Christian communities did not include grave gifts, and partly because many of the Scandinavian settlers will have been men who married local women following local fashions. But if the bossed oval brooch and the strapped dress that went with it were worn as much as badges of rank as practical clothing, perhaps it is also because these culturally-based social messages were simply meaningless for mixed communities on foreign shores, where high-status local women did not wear oval brooches. It might also reflect the opposition of the Church to what might have been perceived as 'pagan' fashions.

Even at home, the oval brooch was losing ground. In the ninth century, the oval brooch had reigned supreme throughout Scandinavia, and indeed in Norway and Sweden the numbers of brooches actually appears to increase. But in tenth-century Denmark, the traditional costume was apparently challenged by

43 Gold figurine of woman from Trøning, Denmark. She appears to be wearing a bead necklace, a long forecloth (or sewn bead decoration) and a backcloth, with her hair uncovered

a new fashion. Charlotte Blindheim first noted in 1947 that some of the richest women's burials of Viking Denmark, such as those from Faarup and Hvilehøj, are without oval brooches. Analysis of Brøndsted's catalogue of Danish grave goods reveals that whereas oval brooches are found in 85 per cent of identifiable women's graves from ninth-century Denmark, this drops to under 33 per cent for the tenth century. Of particular interest is a group of wagon burials, which represent women of indisputably high rank with lavish burials but without bossed oval brooches.

This new fashion appears to go hand-in-hand with increasing contact between tenth-century Denmark and the Christian West. Western artefacts are commonly found in contexts associated with the pattern of high-status graves without oval brooches. When Anglo-Saxon England converted to Christianity, there appears to have been a concomitant change in clothing, and several writers portrayed particular fashions as 'pagan'. Yet in Scandinavia, no easy correlation of broochless Christians and brooch-wearing pagans seems possible. The broochless wagon grave at Fyrkat is undoubtedly pagan, whilst many of the women buried in their brooches at Birka may have been Christian. Nonetheless, the Anglo-Saxons whose 'pagan' dress sense was under scrutiny were supposedly Christian, and it is questionable how deeply Christianised a culture can be where the dead are buried with grave goods as at Birka or in Danish wagon burials.

The richness of these graves has led to the suggestion that they reflect the topmost rank of society. However, tenth-century graves are generally richer than those of the ninth century; thus, whereas only 10 per cent of ninth-century oval brooches from Denmark are gilded and only 4 per cent are found in association with other gilded or silvered jewellery, these figures rise to 64 per cent and 36 per cent respectively for the tenth century. It is also possible that the evidence is distorted by an increase in wealth among a certain group of unmarried women. An attractive possibility is that colonial fashions, which had developed among the Anglo-Danes, Normans and Hiberno-Norse, were becoming established in the Scandinavian homeland through continuing cultural contact. This would help explain the correlation between broochless graves and Western artefacts.

A social distinction, whereby women of the highest rank did not wear oval brooches, has been discerned in *Rígsþula* st.28–9, quoted earlier. If we accept that Moðir is not wearing the suspended dress (and another interpretation of this passage is suggested above), her clothing still differs from the usual dress of the contemporary Christian West. On her head she wears the *faldr*, which is probably to be identified with distinctive archaeological finds from areas of Scandinavian influence, specifically York, Lincoln and Dublin. She also wears a train or *slæðr* (a garment we have mentioned in the context of the suspended dress and which we will return to as an item of men's clothing), which is probably held by the clasp on her breast.

Though the detailed picture may be uncertain, it is clear that the suspended dress and its accompanying brooches went rapidly out of fashion at the end of the Viking Age. The word *smokkr* is unknown from any source other than *Rígsþula*, so, whilst for the poet, the suspended dress typified a social class, by the time of the sagas it had fallen utterly into disuse. The saga writers seem unaware that such a fashion had ever even existed.

2

MEN'S CLOTHING

HISTORICAL

As with women's clothing, men's clothing of the Viking Age was part of a tradition stretching back to ancient times. Tacitus describes Germanic clothing of the Roman Iron Age in *Germania* ch.17:

> *Tegumen omnibus sagum fibula aut, si desit, spina consertum: cetera intecti totos dies iuxta focum atque ignem agunt. Locupletissimi veste distinguuntur, non fluitante, sicut Sarmatae ac Parthi, sed stricta et singulos artus exprimente. Gerunt et ferarum pelles, proximi ripae neglegenter, ulteriores exquisitius, ut quibus nullus per commercia cultus. Eligunt feras et detracta velamina spargunt maculis pellibusque beluarum, quas exterior Oceanus atque ignotum mare gignit.*

> The clothing for everyone is the cloak, which is fastened by brooch or failing that by thorn; they spend whole days at the fire by the hearth in nothing else. The greatest landowners are marked out by clothes, not loose like the Sarmatians' and Parthians', but tight and shaping every limb. And they wear the skins of wild animals – casually near the coasts, more carefully farther off as there is no trading culture. The animals are chosen, and the piebald coats are flayed and the skins of beasts which are born of the Outer Ocean and the unknown seas.

The cloaks described by Tacitus are represented in archaeology by a surprisingly large number of cloak fragments, the best preserved of which have been deposited in bogs. These are large rectangular pieces of woollen twill, measuring in the region of 8ft x 5ft 6in (2.5 x 1.5m), very often decorated with tablet-woven borders and tassels. These cloaks have regularly been represented as masterpieces of weaving, with the implication that they could only have been available to the very rich, but in fact,

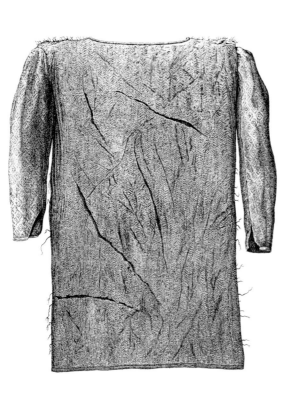
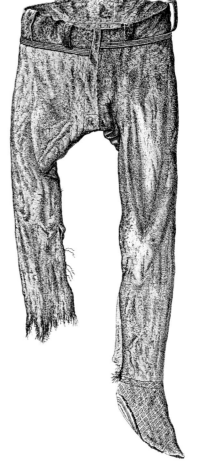

44 Roman-era woollen shirt and footed breeches (F.S.3684) of wool from Thorsbjerg, Germany

the weave of the cloaks is never exceptional. Jørgensen points out that although modern weavers may have struggled to produce accurate replicas, it is only the broad tablet-woven borders of the finest examples that are of outstanding quality, and even these would have been more easily woven by the original weavers than by modern imitators. Many cloaks lack these broad borders, some having narrower borders and others having no borders whatsoever; these simpler types may be underrepresented among the finds, and were perhaps more typical of the common Germanic cloak.

Tacitus suggests that beyond the cloak, other clothing was unusual among the Germans, and Caesar also notes that the Germans wore very little. Some Roman sculpture confirms that they might wear nothing but a cloak, but a large number of Roman sculptures portray Germans dressed in trousers and tunics, which are sometimes just as tight as Tacitus describes them. In later centuries at least, these other garments would become an indispensable part of everyday dress.

The word *camisia* ('shirt') appeared in Latin towards the end of the Roman period, denoting a tight-fitting linen tunic with long, tight sleeves (Jerome, *Epistolae*, Book 64, no.11); this is a form of garment very different from the traditional baggy Roman tunic. The etymology of the Latin word apparently leads through Gallic to a Germanic root, and the garment it describes may likewise derive from Iron Age Germania. The long-sleeved tight-fitting shirt *camisia* in fact tallies perfectly with Gallic costume described by Strabo, and with Tacitus' description of limb-hugging Germanic underwear. An actual garment from a Roman-era votive deposit at Thorsbjerg, Germany, closely resembles these descriptions, though it is made in a fine woollen diamond twill rather than linen; it is just 22½in (57cm) wide, and was laced up either side for a tighter fit (*44, 45*).

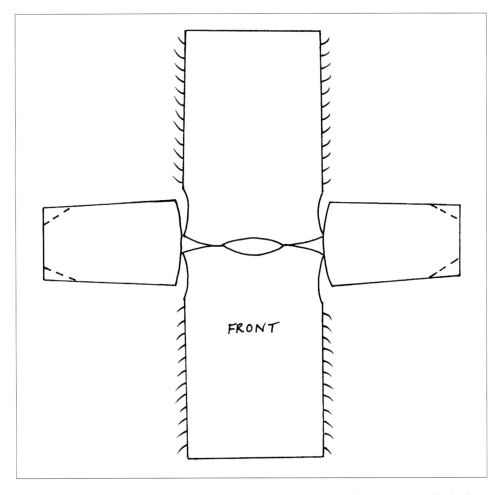

45 Pattern of shirt from Thorsbjerg. The sleeves are arranged so that the seam meets the back about 3in (7cm) below the shoulder seam. The lower part of the sleeve is shaped by sewing diagonally across the cloth. The sides of the garment are fastened with ties. Scale 1:15

Also from the Thorsbjerg deposit, come two pairs of long, tight-fitting trousers (44, 46). These, and a very similar pair from Damendorf, Germany, all show basically the same remarkable method of construction. The trouser leg is made from a single piece of cloth, cut straight up the back and shaped along the front edge. The seam in the leg runs up to meet a separate rectangular or trapezoid seat, and one or two pieces are commonly set in for the crotch. A trouser band round the top has simple belt loops on it. This construction would appear to have developed from separate leggings, which have simply been joined together with extra pieces at the top of the leg. Both pairs from Thorsbjerg have feet; in one pair, these are integral to the design of the trousers, in the other they have been stitched on as if as an afterthought, but these extra foot pieces might replace earlier ones which had worn through. The legs of the Damendorf trousers are torn off at the bottom, so we cannot tell whether they also ended in feet. Similar footed trousers appear on a mural from the grave of a late Roman nobleman at Silistra, Bulgaria. But in Tacitus' day, trousers were the epitome of barbarity, so the pattern must have originated outside the Roman world.

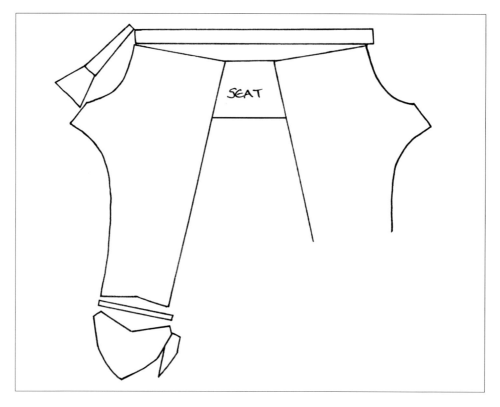

46 Patterns of breeches from Roman-era Germania.
A) *above:* F.S.3684 Thorsbjerg.
B) *opposite above:* F.S.3685 Thorsbjerg
C) *opposite below:* Damendorf. Scale 1:15.

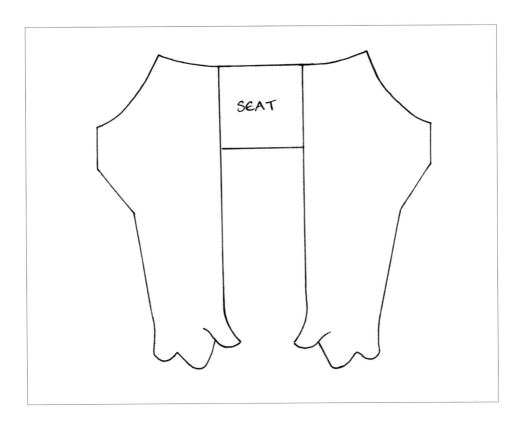

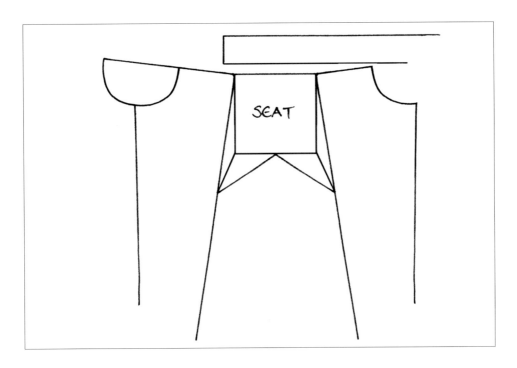

Some four centuries after Tacitus, the Gallo-Roman Sidonius Appolinarus described the retinue of the Germanic prince Sigismer (*Epistolae*, Book 4, no.20):

> *… quorum pedes primi perone saetoso talos adusque vinciebantur; genua crura suraeque sine tegmine; praeter hoc vestis alta stricta versicolor vix appropinquans poplitibus exertis; manicae sola brachiorum principia velantes; viridantia saga limbis marginata puniceis …*

> … their feet up to the ankles were laced in bristly hide shoes; knees, shins, and calves without covering; besides this, a high tight colourful garment scarcely reaching their bare knees, the sleeves covering only the upper arms; green cloaks edged with red borders …

Sidonius goes on to say that they are festooned with reindeer skin, which raises the possibility that Sigismer might in fact be a Scandinavian prince.

Like Tacitus before him, Sidonius notes the typical Germanic cloaks and short close-fitting clothing. These men are either not wearing trousers, or their trousers end above the knee. The short sleeves of this description are matched by a couple of sleeveless tunics from North Germany, from Obenaltendorf (*47*) and Marx-Etzel. At 34in (87cm), the Marx-Etzel tunic is wide enough for the shoulders to give the appearance of short sleeves as described by Sidonius. As well as the tunic, a pair of knee-length woollen breeches was found at Marx-Etzel, of a kind which might also have been worn by Sigismer's retinue (*48*).

Two accounts of Frankish dress come from the Viking Age itself, and I give these here as representations of a parallel sartorial tradition, which shared a common ancestry with Scandinavian costume and which existed alongside it. There was continuous contact between Franks and Scandinavians through trade, settlement and war, and in 826 the Danish king Haraldr Klak returned from the Frankish court with gifts of fine clothing. The first description is by Einhard, a contemporary of Charles the Great. His life of the emperor, *Vita Karoli*, was written *c.*829-36, and describes his typical attire (ch.23):

> *Vestitu patrio, id est Francico, utebatur. Ad corpus camisam lineam, et feminalibus lineis induebatur, deinde tunicam, quae limbo serico ambiebatur, et tibialia; tum fasciolis crura et pedes calciamentis constringebat et ex pellibus lutrinis vel murinis thorace confecto umeros ac pectus hieme muniebat, sago veneto amictus …*

> He wore the clothes of his nation, that is of the Franks: Next to his body he wore a linen shirt and breeches of linen; next a tunic edged round in silk, and hose; then bands enfolded his shins, and shoes his feet; and a jacket made of otter skin or ermine protected his shoulders and chest in winter; he wore a blue cloak …

A monk of St Gall, sometimes identified as Notker, wrote a later account of Charles's reign called *De Carolo Magno*, dated 883-4. This contains a complementary

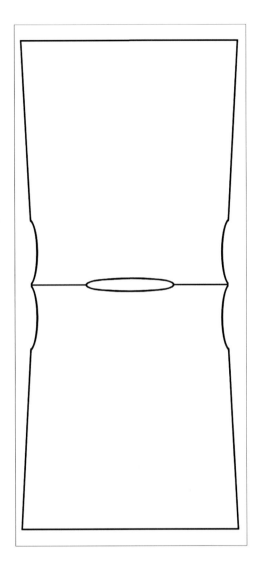

47 Pattern of Roman-era sleeveless woollen tunic from Obenaltendorf, Germany. Scale 1:15

description of traditional Frankish dress, which differs in some respects from Einhard's description of the emperor. The Frankish dress described here is so opulent that it can only have been worn by men of rank and riches:

Erat antiquorum ornatus vel paratura Francorum: calciamenta forinsecus aurata, corrigiis tricubitalibus insignita, fasciole crurales vermiculate, et subtus eas tibialia vel coxalia linea, quamvis ex eodem colore, tamen opere artificiosissimo variata. Super que et fasciolas in crucis modum intrinsecus et extrinsecus, ante et retro, longissime ille corrigie tendebantur. Deinde camisia clizana, post hec balteus spate colligatus …

Ultimum habitus eorum erat pallium canum vel saphirinum quadrangulum duplex sic formatum, ut cum imponeretur humeris, ante et retro pedes tangeret, de lateribus vero vix genua contegeret.

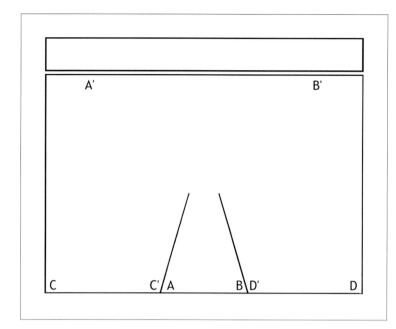

48 Superbly simple pattern for short breeches from Marx–Etzel, Germany. The central flap folds up under the crotch and attaches to the waist band. The same principle could have been used for linen breeches. Scale 1:15

This was the attire or apparel of the Franks of old: shoes gilded outside, adorned with laces of three cubits, kermes-dyed bands on the shins, and under these, hose and breeches of linen, of the same colour but varied with the most intricate work. Above these and the bands, in and out, before and behind, the long laces were arranged in the style of a cross. Next, a shirt of smooth linen, after which a fastened sword belt …

The last of their clothing was the cloak, white or blue, in the form of a double square, so that when worn on the shoulders, in front and behind it reached to the feet, yet down the sides it hardly covered the knees.

Cross-gartered laces of the kind described here were worn by the young nobleman buried in St Severinus Cathedral, Cologne, Germany, in the eighth century. Under his long sheepskin laces, he wore white linen leggings.

Whilst it would be wrong to portray Germanic fashion as unchanging throughout the thousand years that separate Tacitus from Cnut, a surprising number of parallels and similarities exist between what we know of Roman-era Germanic dress and Viking-era Scandinavian fashion.

LINEN CLOTHING

One difference is seen in the prevalence of linen in Viking-era Sweden and Denmark. Archaeological evidence shows that Vikings could be buried in linen shirts, which were worn with a belt and often with a cloak, but without a woollen overshirt or tunic. The silver buckle from the Viking grave at Balladoole, Isle of Man, bore the remains of a very finely woven piece of linen, which must have come from the dead man's shirt. Similar finds from Hedeby indicate that the shirt was invariably woven in medium to fine Z-spun tabby weave, which indicates either linen or possibly a lightweight woollen fabric of similar effect. Fragments of woollen tabby from Hedeby harbour (57), identified as coming from the shirt by Hägg, are not consistent with the fragments recorded on these buckles.

At Birka, in grave BJ.944, were the remains of a linen shirt decorated with silk and with silver braids. This shirt was in fact worn under a caftan, but it cannot have been intended only for use as underwear or nightwear; its rich decoration shows that this shirt was meant for display, and it must often have been worn without the caftan, so it could be seen. Another richly decorated fragment of linen, from Llan-gors, Wales, dating from the late ninth or early tenth century, is probably from a shirt and was embroidered with coloured silken thread. *Orkneyinga saga* ch.55 describes a linen garment, richly decorated with gold, which might also have been a linen shirt.

Linen shirts were also sported by other Germanic nations. As we have seen, Germanic fashion appears to have led to the introduction of the linen *camisia* to the Roman world, while the traditional dress of the Franks, described in *De Carolo Magno*, included a linen shirt worn directly under the cloak without a woollen tunic. Likewise, the Frankish Annals of St Bertin describe the preparation of a linen shirt (*camisia*) for a well-to-do citizen of Thérouanne in the annal for 862. White linen shirts are also to be seen in Carolingian manuscript illustrations, notably the presentation miniature in the First Bible of Charles the Bald (Vivian Bible, Bibliothèque Nationale MS Lat 1). Paul the Deacon, writing in the eighth century, informs us that both the early Lombards and the contemporary English also wore mainly linen clothes (*maxime linea*, *Historia Langobardum* Book 4 ch.22; the colourful trim he also mentions suggests a high-status context), and linen shirts are also mentioned in an Anglo-Saxon context by both Bede and Aldhelm. The Byzantine Leo the Deacon records that the tenth-century Rus prince Svyatoslav and his retinue dressed in plain linen shirts. Scandinavian linen shirts thus form part of a common Germanic tradition.

Linen breeches were worn by the Franks according to the *Vita Karoli* and *De Carolo Magno*. The rich Frankish costume described in *De Carolo Magno* included breeches of kermes-dyed linen which are apparently embroidered, but most would have been plain linen, bleached or unbleached. The Frankish sources *De Carolo Magno* and *Vita Karoli* suggest that linen breeches were worn without woollen overtrousers but with leg windings and hose.

Unique among the Birka finds are two small hooks from grave BJ.905, which were worn just below the knees (49). The hooks held up sturdy woollen leggings, which will have covered the lower leg, but were hooked into iron eyes in what appears to have been a pair of knee-length linen breeches. This rare glimpse of Viking legwear *in situ* corroborates the suspicion that, like the Franks, the Scandinavians may have worn only linen breeches above the knee.

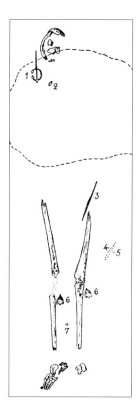

49 Detail of Arbman's grave plan for Birka grave Bj.905, including penannular brooch (1), iron knife (3), bronze garment hooks (6) and bead (7). *Arbman 1944*

In the Icelandic sagas, 'shirt' (*skyrta*) and 'linen breeches' (*lín-brœkr*) are commonly grouped together as 'linen clothing' (*lín-klæði*). Here, the phrase can suggest a state of undress, but this should not be taken to imply that linen clothing was simply underclothes or nightclothes. Linen clothing was worn next to the skin like underwear, and other clothes (such as cloak, hat, shoes and leg windings) would be put on over it, but the shirt and linen breeches remained visible and were indeed the basis of the entire outfit. Far from suggesting anything unusual about wearing linen, the saga phrase 'in linen clothing' (*í linklæðum*) actually suggests that linen clothes were ubiquitous, but that it was unusual to wear only linen outside the house. In *Fljótsdæla saga* ch.18, Gunnar gets up in the night to go to the privy dressed in his linen clothing, and this must have been a common context for this state of half dress, which would have made it familiar to readers and writers alike.

Although linen came late to Scandinavia, it was enthusiastically adopted and had already become widespread before the Viking Age. Thus, despite their discouraging climate, it would seem reasonable to place the Viking-age Scandinavians alongside the other linen-wearing Germanic nations. The Viking attitude to linen was probably similar to that expressed in the eleventh-century Latin debate poem *Conflictus Ovis et Lini*, which notes that whereas woollen clothing would be put on in bad weather, linen was always worn (l.139-56).

Exceptions must be made, however, for the people of Gotland and western Norway, where linen appears to have been little used in Viking times, and the same is probably also true of early Icelanders; thus, in *Fljótsdæla saga* ch.16, Ketill dons a woollen shirt and breeches, and the saga writer notes that equivalent linen clothing was not worn 'at that time', while Adam of Bremen confirms that, even at the end of the Viking Age, the Norwegians were reliant on their flocks for their clothing.

THE SHIRT

In the sagas, 'linen clothing' is sometimes defined by the collocation *skyrta ok línbrœkr*, 'shirt and linen breeches'. Whereas the fabric of the *brœkr* is specifically identified as linen, the fabric of the *skyrta* can apparently be taken for granted. For medieval Icelanders then, the *skyrta* must always, or at least nearly always, have been made of linen, and there is ample evidence for Viking-era shirts made from linen. A group of linen fragments from Viking York has been interpreted as the remains of a child's shirt. Further linen shirt fragments have been found at Birka, and traces of linen garments are not uncommonly found in association with belt buckles in male burials. But the most impressive archaeological survival is the almost complete linen shirt recovered from a posthole at Viborg, Denmark (*50, 51*). The extant shirt from Viborg, which was probably buried in 1018, is of a very similar quality to the

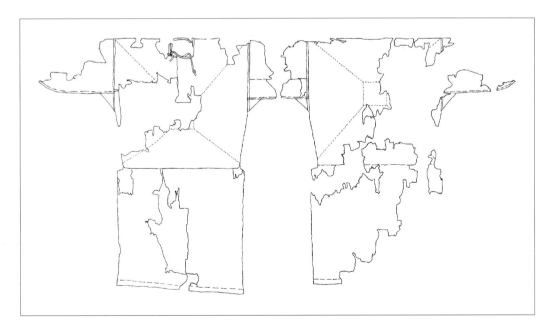

50 Fragments of an early eleventh-century linen shirt from Viborg, Denmark, after conservation. Scale 1:15. *Drawing by Margit Petersen*

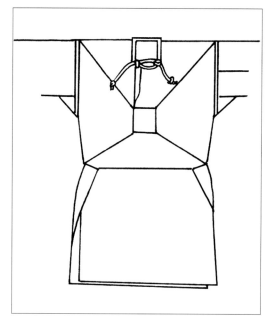

Left: 51 Reconstruction of the Viborg shirt, viewed from the front. The square-cut neckhole is slit on the right side and opens on slip knots to reveal the lining beneath, which is similarly slit on the left. The lining is secured back and front by a series of decorative seams; only the body of the shirt is lined. The shirt tapers slightly towards the waist, where the width of cloth is stepped out and the tail flap overlaps the front. Scale 1:15

Opposite: 52 Pattern of woollen tunic from Reepshold Mose, Netherlands, dated to the first or second century AD. The whole garment is woven as a single shaped piece including arms and neckhole. At 45in (115cm) wide, it is much baggier than its typical Germanic equivalents, represented by the Thorsbjerg shirt. Scale 1:15

fragments from Hedeby graves. The find is truly remarkable because it is extremely unusual for linen to survive in archaeological contexts in Northern Europe.

It would be possible to contrast the linen *skyrta* or 'shirt' of the sagas with the *kyrtill* or 'kirtle', which seems typically to have been made of wool. But the *kyrtill* seems to be unknown from early poetry outside *Rígsþula* st.23; it does occur in a saga verse as *skinn-kyrtill* or 'skin-kirtle', but this, like the 'goat-kirtled' bride of *Rígsþula*, implies a garment of fur or hide rather than wool, as does the account of the Norwegian Ohthere, who told King Alfred that he traded in fur kirtles of bearskin or otterskin (*berenne kyrtel oððe yterenne*), which he seems to have obtained ready-made from the Saami. The Viking 'kirtle' might thus have been a very different garment from the woollen kirtle of the sagas, perhaps denoting the waistcoat or *thorax*, described below. Similarly, the *skyrta* cannot be defined as a linen garment, and a reference to a 'woollen shirt' in *Fljótsdæla saga* ch.16 accurately reflects historical fashions in Iceland and western Norway, where linen was little used in the Viking Age. The word 'shirt' is therefore used here irrespective of whether a garment is made from linen or from wool.

After the introduction of linen, Scandinavian men might have begun to wear a second shirt of wool on top of their linen shirt, and a double layer is occasionally detectable in illustrations from the larger Viking world, as in the Bayeux Tapestry depiction of King Edward on his deathbed. This new distinction between shirt and overshirt could have led to a redefinition of the term *kyrtill* at the close of the Viking Age. However, woollen overshirts were not always worn; they were not used by Notker's Franks or by Paul the Deacon's English, while the author of *Konungs Skuggsjá* felt it necessary to urge against wearing linen outermost even in thirteenth-century Norway.

Etymologically, the word *skyrta*, 'shirt', appears to describe a garment that is cut from cloth, as opposed to a garment like the cloak, which can be woven as a piece. Like the cloak, the Roman-style tunic could also be woven in one piece, as was the extant tunic from Reepsholt Mose, Netherlands, which was woven as a single piece including arms and neckhole (*52*). But a garment which is cut to size is likely to fit better than one straight off the loom, and this was apparently an important characteristic of the *skyrta*.

In the poem *Rígsþula* st.15, the shirt worn by Afi, the free farmer, is described as 'tight-fitting' (*þröngr*). The tightness of the farmer's shirt probably distinguishes it from the clothing of the slaves in earlier verses, which was probably the *kufl*, a relatively shapeless woollen garment. As well as fitting closely around the arms and body, the *skyrta* appears to have been tight-fitting at the neck. Thus, in *Laxdæla saga*

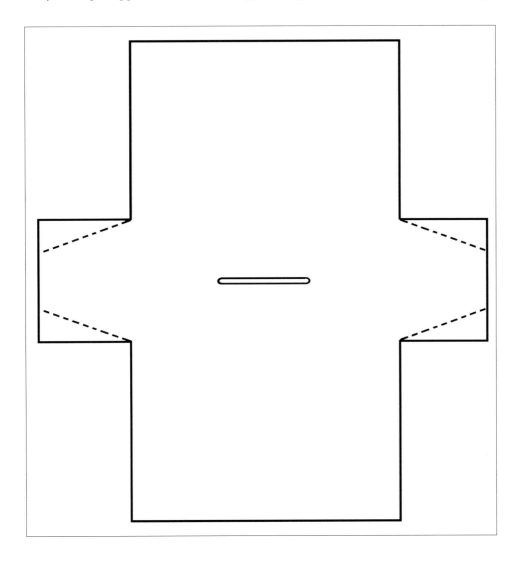

ch.35, Guðrún divorces her husband for wearing the effeminately loose-necked shirt she has made for him (see above, ch.1).

The pattern of the Viborg shirt contrasts markedly with what we know of oriental shirts, such as the shirt from Antinoë with which it has been compared. Amongst other differences, whereas the Antinoë shirt flares out below the junction with the sleeves, the Viborg shirt not only remains close-fitting throughout, but actually tapers slightly at the waist. The contrast is the same as that noted by Tacitus between Germanic clothing and the clothing of the Sarmatians and Parthians.

Length

Like the Thorsbjerg shirt (44, 45), which was only 34in (86cm) long, Migration-era and Vendel-era shirts may often have been fairly short. The fifth-century shirt from Högom, Sweden, was just 28in (70cm) from shoulder to hem, extending only 4-6in (12-15cm) below the belt (53). Similarly short shirts, scarcely reaching the top of the thigh, are seen on the wagon and tapestry from Oseberg (54), as well as on picture stones from Gotland (60), rune stones from Sweden and sculpture from Viking England.

As well as shirts reaching no lower than the top of the thighs, the Oseberg Tapestry also shows men in shirts reaching almost to the knee, and this cut can also

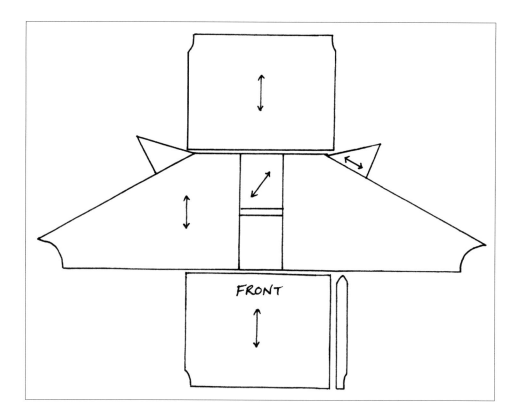

Opposite: 53 Cut of the fifth-century woollen shirt from Högom, Sweden, as reconstructed by Nockert and Lundwall. The extra piece let in on the left side is clearly not part of the original design, but has simply been added to accommodate the wearer's girth. Scale 1:15

Right: 54 Male figure from the procession scene of the Oseberg tapestry. Like most of the men in this scene, he wears a short-skirted shirt and wide-bottomed trousers. Over his shirt he wears a short cloak; the line of the hem and the triangular-shaped opening at the neck suggest a *paenula*-type design with a neck slit (cf. *66b*). *After an illustration by M. Storm*

frequently be seen on Gotland stones and Anglo-Norse carvings; a shirt worn by a hanged man on the Oseberg Tapestry has knee-length skirts with a central slit. These longer-skirted shirts are familiar from manuscript illustrations such as the *Liber Vitae* portrait of King Cnut (*55*) and from the Bayeux Tapestry. The early eleventh-century Viborg shirt was 37in (94cm) from shoulder to hem, and the same measurement in the waist; this was a fairly close-fitting garment but not an especially short one (*50, 51*). A peculiar shirt from Bernuthsfeld, Germany, dated to between AD 660 and 870, was longer still at 41in (105cm), and will have covered the wearer's knees (*56*).

Although the shorter cut of shirt appears to have become less popular in the later Viking Age, perhaps under the influence of mainstream English and European fashion, the longer style does seem to have existed in Scandinavia from the beginning

55 King Cnut from the Winchester *Liber Vitae*. Cnut was king of England from 1016 and lived mostly in his capital at Winchester, but he was Danish and, during his reign, Scandinavian influence is seen in English culture. This illustration affords a rare opportunity to see the clothes of a Viking-age Scandinavian in detail

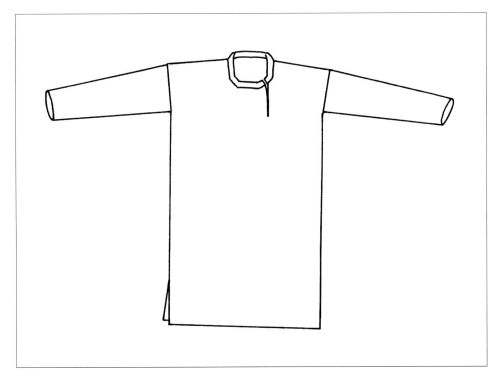

56 Underlying shape of a patchwork woollen shirt from Bernuthsfeld, Germany, dating to around the start of the Viking Age. Scale 1:15

of the era. Shorter garments could evidently be worn by the wealthiest men, since the chieftain from Högom was unambiguously high status; perhaps men who were in the habit of riding favoured shorter tops, which did not overlie the saddle.

The cut of the shirt

The cut of the Thorsbjerg shirt is based on two rectangles of cloth, which are joined with angled seams at the shoulders (45). The shirt from Bernuthsfeld, which dates from the cusp of the Viking Age, seems to represent a closely related tradition to Scandinavian shirts; although it is made from a patchwork of rags, the underlying cut appears to be based on two rectangles with angled shoulder seams, as at Thorsbjerg (56). A particularly interesting cut is seen in the Högom shirt, where the sleeves are integral with the upper body, while the lower body and skirts are cut separately (53); a similar cut was possibly intended by the sculptor at Jelling, who shows sleeves beginning at the neck. But the linen Viborg shirt, despite its late date, elaborate workmanship and sophisticated styling, is essentially simpler, being based on a single length of cloth folded over at the top, with a hole for the head (50, 51); perhaps this is because linen hangs very differently from wool, falling naturally in creases, whereas wool responds well to more careful tailoring.

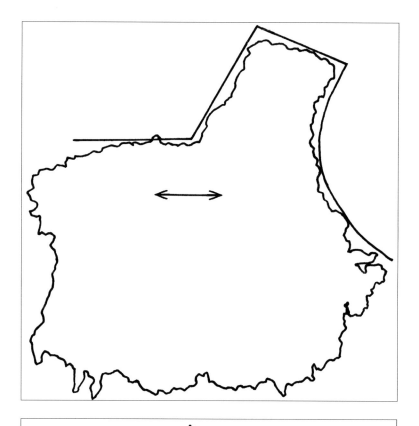

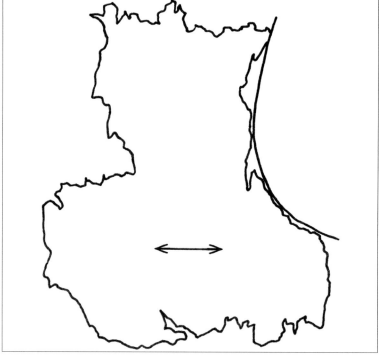

57 Sketch of two woollen fragments from Hedeby, each probably from a shirt shoulder. In each case the warp runs horizontally around the body.
A) *above left:* fragment 72C.
B) *left:* fragment 73. Scale 1:3

Shirt fragments from Hedeby harbour however, are cut with the warp running horizontally around the body (57). This makes it less likely that they were based on the simple lengthwise rectangles of the Thorsbjerg and Viborg shirts, where the length of the cloth gives the length of the shirt. Instead, they were probably cut with a separate body and skirt, a style partly anticipated by the cut of the Högom shirt. Some such pattern must have been used for an eleventh-century style of shirt shown on a runestone at Ledberg, Norway, and on the Bayeux Tapestry, where it is worn by Harold when he disembarks in Normandy. At first sight, the skirts of these shirts look to be made up of a series of gores; indeed, the skirts of Harold's shirt are shown in alternating colours. But the use of colour in the tapestry, where blue horses have yellow legs, is famously impressionistic, and the alternating colours of Harold's skirts might simply indicate folds of cloth falling in pleats. A pleated construction would be consistent with the tradition of Scandinavian tailoring known from archaeology, and could be seen as a Scandinavian response to the new European gore-skirted shirt. If so, perhaps Harold is deliberately shown in a Scandinavian-style shirt on his arrival in Normandy, to reflect the Scandinavian heritage he shared with his Norman hosts. However, the pleated skirt might equally be a common Germanic feature, which is possibly depicted in pre-Viking Anglo-Saxon art on the Franks Casket and the Repton Stone.

The shirts worn by Cnut in the *Liber Vitae* (55) and Thorkell in the Eadui Psalter (*colour plate 13*) probably also used a two-part construction. Unlike the garments from Thorsbjerg and Viborg, they are not at all tight around the waist and have very full skirts. This cut of shirt appears to be more-or-less universal in early eleventh-century England, and an Anglo-Saxon calendar shows harvesters in similar shirts, which appear to have a seam up the back (58). A number of belts on the Bayeux Tapestry are shown doubled, as if the belt wraps around the body twice, which could

58 Harvesters representing the month of August in the Anglo-Saxon Tiberius Calendar. Note the hitched-up skirts, and what appears to be a seam up the back of the shirt. *BL MS Cotton Tiberius B.v. fol. 6v*

possibly indicate that the join between skirt and body is hidden by a woven braid, the ends of which extend into the belt. Unlike the Ledberg-style shirt, the skirts appear to have typically been pleated only at the back and at either hip rather than all round, which would allow for a possible combination of pleating and gores in their construction. Pleated or part-pleated skirts, which must be cut separately from the body, continue to appear in art of the twelfth century.

Laced-sided 'kirtles' are mentioned both in *Egils saga* (ch.78) and in *Heimskringla* (*Óláfs saga Kyrra* ch.2). Side laces or ties were also used in the Roman-era Thorsbjerg garment, and the kirtles described in the sagas might have been made in a tradition which looked back to shirts of Roman times. But the similarity could be merely coincidental; the word used in both sources for these ties, *laz*, is derived from Old French, and laced sides were sometimes used on later medieval European cotes and kirtles. The word 'kirtle' used to describe these garments, and the fustian cloth from which Egill's is made, also look towards later fashions. Indeed, the laced sides of the kirtles worn by King Óláfr's courtiers might have been a novel trend, which would cast doubt on their earlier use by Egill. If there really was a continuous Scandinavian tradition of laced-sided shirts, by the time of the sagas it had become confused with more modern European traditions.

The neckhole

The manuscript illustrations of Cnut in the *Liber Vitae* (55) and of Thorkell in the *Eadui Psalter* (*colour plate 13*) show a square-cut neckhole, with a central slit at the front; in the Eadui Psalter, long decorative ties fasten the slit. This style is unusual in Anglo-Saxon art, and might have been a distinctively Scandinavian feature, which was adopted more widely under Danish rule; later and less perfectly square examples can be seen in the death scene of King Edward on the Bayeux Tapestry, and in the Tiberius Calendar (58). The slit construction allows the neckhole to be closed as tightly as possible around the neck; the importance of a close-fitting neckhole is recognised in *Laxdæla saga* (ch.34, 35), as cited above (ch.1).

Square-cut neckholes are known from archaeology too, most importantly from the Viborg shirt, but here the slit is to one side; the opening was backed by a separate piece of linen cloth and was fastened with linen ties (50, 51). Similar neck openings are found on the Högom garment (53), and on the coat of patches from Bernuthsfeld, Germany (56). All are more-or-less square and fairly small, with a slit at one corner to allow the head to get through. Only at Viborg has the means of fastening the neck been preserved, but it may probably be assumed that the garments from Högom and Bernuthsfeld also relied on linen ties to secure them, and they were probably also lined with linen.

The side slit is in many ways a simpler construction, and the central slit probably evolved later in the period, though the Viborg shirt is itself an eleventh-century garment. The design of the square-cut neckhole suggests the use of separate front and back pieces (at Viborg, the lining is in two pieces), and indeed, the variety with a central slit is dependent on correctly angled shoulder seams; by contrast, the round neckholes often seen in Anglo-Saxon manuscripts would be a more natural design for a simple poncho-cut shirt.

Sleeves

Artistic traditions from England and Europe often show puckering at the bottom of the sleeve, suggesting that very long sleeves may have been sewn tight to the arm above the wrist, a section at the bottom would have been sewn up every time the garment was put on, a daily chore referred to in *Grettis saga* ch.17. However, a similar effect could have been achieved by sewing pleats into the fabric, and it is possible that the saga account reflects later fashions.

A well-preserved fragment from the harbour at Hedeby appears to have been cut down from a two-part woollen sleeve (*59*), and a sketched seam line in the *Liber Vitae* portrait of Cnut suggests that his sleeves might have been made to a similar pattern (*55*). Only the top part of the sleeves of the Viborg shirt is well preserved, but in the lower part they appear to curve inwards towards the wrist, unlike the steadily tapering pattern of the Hedeby sleeves, so whilst the woollen sleeves from Hedeby probably ended in puckering or pleating, the same would not have been true for the linen sleeves from Viborg (*50*). This might suggest a distinction between shirt and undershirt. If linen shirts were worn in bed, or even slung on casually first thing in the morning, elaborate puckered or pleated cuffs would seem unlikely. As well as closed puckered sleeves, Anglo-Saxon manuscripts sometimes show simple loose sleeves, and loose sleeves were clearly worn by Eyjólfr in *Njáls saga* ch.138, when Snorri spots a gold ring worn under his sleeve. Occasional sleeves visible in the procession scene on the Oseberg Tapestry seem to be wide, loose and relatively short (*54*). The sleeves of the Högom and Thorsbjerg shirts were each made from a single steadily tapering piece of cloth (*53*, *45*), and similar sleeve shapes are shown on picture stones from Gotland (*60*).

On the Bayeux Tapestry, armoured men have distinctively drawn sleeves, with a fastening at the wrist; most have their forearms apparently wrapped in cloth bands, similar to those worn as leg windings (see below).

Securing the skirts

One of the harvesters in the Tiberius Calendar has his skirts hitched up to the waist at either side (*58*). This practice appears to develop at the same time that full-skirted shirt is universally adopted. By the time of the Bayeux Tapestry, a whole new style of skirt seems to have developed that could be transformed into two separate leggings, divided by a front flap which buttons under the crotch. The split-leg style appears to be worn on the Tapestry for practical purposes; it is worn by many if not all the riders, and by many men doing physical work. This division of the skirts into leggings could only be possible if the skirts are constructed separately from the body.

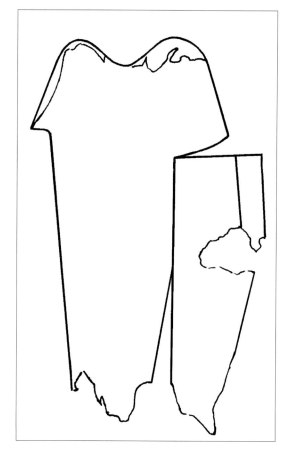

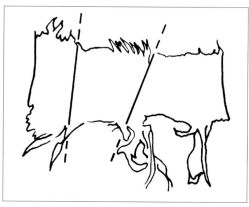

59 Sketch of sleeve fragments from Hedeby.
A) *left:* fragment 57: a tube of woollen cloth which appears to have been cut down from a sleeve. Scale 1:6

B) *above:* fragment 28A: this short length uses the same two-part construction as Fragment 57, and the cloth is cut at a similar angle. Scale 1:6

In *Kjalnesinga saga* ch.7, Kolfinnr, dressed in poor clothes, is wearing a hood (*koll-hetta*), with the flaps fastened between his legs; he also wears ankle breeches and hairy calfskin shoes. In *Eiríks saga Rauða* ch.8, Scottish slaves wear a garment called a *bjafal* or *kjafal*, which also fastens between the legs.

LEGGINGS

We have seen that linen breeches were commonly worn by men in Viking Scandinavia, usually in combination with other legwear. The shape of these linen breeches is probably best seen on an eleventh-century silver crucifix in Statens Historiska Museet, Stockholm (*61*); Christ's breeches here are probably typical of linen breeches of the time, reaching to a little below the knee. Similar, though slightly longer linen breeches appear to be worn by a barefoot haymaker representing the month of July in a Carolingian calendar in the Austrian National Library (*62*). All these examples appear to have been cut with a straight leg, and linen breeches probably eschewed the elaborate patterns of the woollen breeches from Thorsbjerg and Damendorf (46), and more closely resembled later medieval linen braies.

Woollen overbreeches might sometimes have been worn, of similar length to the linen breeches or longer. The very word *línbrœkr*, 'linen breeches', suggests the existence of other forms of *brœkr* made from other kinds of cloth, and the term 'trouser wadmal' (*bróka-vaðmál*) which occurs in *Reykdœla saga* would confirm, if confirmation were needed, that breeches could be made of wool as well as linen. As *Fljótsdœla saga* points out (ch.16), linen breeches were almost unknown in Norway and Iceland in the Viking Age. However, when woollen breeches are mentioned in the sagas, they are typically low-status clothing of coarse cloth.

The poor might sometimes have gone without breeches, as Thórr does in *Hárbarðsljóð* (st.6), and bare-legged figures, presumably slaves, occur in the Anglo-Saxon Tiberius Calendar throughout the year (58). The English placename 'Brocklesby' appears to be derived from a Norse byname *⋆bróklaus*, 'breechless, without breeches', though this presumably refers to someone of higher status.

60 Figures on a picture stone from Lärbro Tängelgårda, Gotland, wearing short shirts, some with very wide sleeves and others with sleeves tapering from the waist upwards as on the Högom shirt. Their high breeches are less baggy than at Stenkyrka Lillbjärs and Halla Broa (*66*). Their hats have long tails hanging down their backs, as described in the *Hudud al-'Alam*

Hose

Under the bands that bound their legs, according to *De Carolo Magno*, the Franks wore dyed linen hose (*tibialia*). Undyed linen worn under leather cross straps by the Frankish burial in St Severinus Cathedral, Cologne, was probably from hose. There is thus some reason to consider hose as another possible item of linen clothing. Such hose will typically have covered the foot and lower leg like the surviving eleventh-century silk hose of Pope Clemens II (*63*).

The tenth-century poet Kormákr refers to 'lichen-red hose' (*hosu mosrauða*, *Kormáks saga* st.38 ch.12), and although linen was normally left unbleached, it is possible that Kormákr is thinking of dyed linen here (his verse suggests that he has never worn them, but that some people might wear lichen-red hose for luck). Where hose are mentioned in sagas about the Viking Age, they are often dyed and associated with other markers of high status. Most notably King Sigurðr Sýr wears blue hose wound round with long laces in *Heimskringla* (*Ólafs saga Helga*, ch.33); again, while we would normally expect dyed clothes to be made of wool, it is possible, especially given his obvious status, that Sigurðr's hose are in fact linen, like the kermes-dyed hose worn by the Franks. Other examples in *Egils saga* (ch.78) and *Njáls saga* (ch.134) are dyed red, possibly with kermes. None of these hose appears to be hidden by woollen bands. Perhaps in these cases, it is not so much the hose as use of high-status dyed linen that prompts the saga writer's comment. Ibn Fadlan's account of the Rus funeral also mentions hose (*ran*) as well as breeches (*sarawil*).

On the picture stone from Etelhem Railway, Gotland, at least two of the three figures in the top section of the stone have double lines drawn below the knee, apparently representing a garter for hose (*hosna-reim*, *64*), and King Cnut wears similar, though more elaborate, garters in the Winchester *Liber Vitae* portrait (*55*). Hose from Gotland will have been woollen, and there is archaeological evidence for woollen hose, in the shape of an undyed woollen fragment from the Hedeby mud, which appears to have been the top section of a tubular hose leg, complete with tie. Among the many wares made by the shoemaker in Ælfric's *Colloquy* are 'leather hose' (Old English *leþerhose*, Latin *caliga*) and something similar appears to be illustrated in the presentation miniature from the First Bible of Charles the Bald and in illustrations of Louis the Pious from *De Laudibus Sanctae* (*78*), where they look rather like high boots. Leather or fur hose can be denoted in Old Icelandic by the terms *leðr-hosa* and *skinn-hosa*.

The fourteenth-century man from Bocksten, Sweden, wore ragged footcloths inside his long hose, and similar combinations could have been used in Viking times. A single needle-bound sock from York, England, testifies to what might have been a fairly common garment which could have been worn with or without hose (*colour plate 9*). The illustration of Thorkell Hávi in the Eadui Psalter shows his feet covered in red footcloths, which might be the 'lichen-red hose' which Kormákr mentions, while his calves are wrapped in blue-green bands (*colour plate 13*). Gale Owen-Crocker has drawn attention to an apparent distinction in Anglo-Saxon sources between *hosan* ('hose') and *meon* or *soccas* ('socks'), suggesting that they could be worn together.

Left: 61 Swedish silver crucifix probably showing linen breeches

Above: 62 A haymaker illustrates the month of July in a Carolingian manuscript; he is barefoot, and his white linen breeches flap around his shins. Figures representing other months wear hose which reach to just below the knee. *Östereich Nationalbibliothek Vienna MS Salz. 9Jh Cod.387 fol.90v*

Leg windings

The lower part of the leg would typically have been covered by woollen bands, as worn by the Franks according to *De Carolo Magno* and *Vita Karoli*. The Franks seem to have wound bands over their hose, but bands could have been worn without hose just as hose could be worn without windings. According to *Laxdæla saga* ch.35, men (and only men) wore windings (*spjarrar* or *vindingar*) on their legs. Suitable bands woven in 3-4in (7.5-10cm) breadths have been found at sites across the Viking world; these are typically in fairly fine zigzag twill, either dyed or undyed. Such windings seem to have been the standard covering for the lower leg. The Vendel- or early Viking-era bog body from Bernuthsfeld, Germany, wore woollen bands around his lower legs, and no doubt was originally dressed in linen breeches above the knees. Likewise, the occupant of Birka grave Bj.905 wore linen breeches on his upper legs, with woollen leg windings, or possibly woollen hose, below (*49*). Similar bands appear to be wound around the forearms of armoured men on the Bayeux Tapestry.

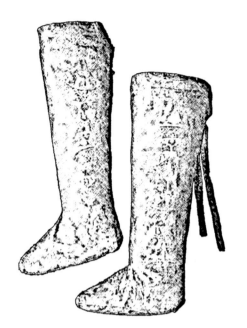

Above left: 63 Eleventh-century hose of patterned silk worn by Pope Clemens II

Above right: 64 Figure from a picture stone from Etelhem Railway, Gotland, showing garters securing hose

High breeches

Inga Hägg has drawn attention to textile finds from Hedeby (*65*), which show elements of construction similar to the Roman-era footed breeches from Thorsbjerg (F.S.3684, *46*). It seems very likely that these do indeed come from Viking-era trousers, which were constructed on the same basic principle as Germanic trousers of late Antiquity. *Laxdæla saga* ch.35 refers to 'seat-gored breeches' (*setgeira-brœkr*) as indicative of men's clothing, which again suggests that a construction similar to the earlier examples remained in use in the Viking Age.

But despite their similar construction, Hägg believes that these fragments do not come from the same style of tight-fitting trousers as the Roman-era examples. Wrinkles still visible today could be the result of deliberate immersion of the light woollen cloth in hot water, and such wrinkled cloth would only have been used for a baggy garment. The *Hudud al-'Alam*, a tenth-century Persian source dedicated to an Afghan prince, describes the wide trousers of the Rus: 'Out of a hundred cubits of fine linen (*karbas*), more-or-less, they sew trousers, which they put on tucking them up above the knee' (adapted from Minorsky's translation). Ibn Rusta's contemporary account gives a similar description, though even more incredibly allots a hundred cubits of cloth to each leg.

These baggy knee breeches were not confined to Russian Vikings. They are clearly illustrated on picture stones from Gotland, as at Stenkyrka Lillbjärs and at

1 An unmatched pair of bossed oval brooches from the grave of a Norwegian woman found at Adwick-le-Street, near Doncaster, England. Though not identical, both brooches are versions of type P37, the commonest brooch form in the ninth century. *Photograph: Bill Marsden. Courtesy of Northern Archaeological Associates*

2cm

Above: 2 A back view of brooch AC from Adwick-le-Street, showing the recessed pin. Attached to the pin are the remains of the woman's linen shirt or neckcloth, which have been preserved by salts from the corroding metal (thread count 14 x 9 per cm). *Photograph: Erica Paterson, YAT. Courtesy of Northern Archaeological Associates*

Opposite above: 3 A closer view of the back of brooch AB from Adwick-le-Street reveals the textile remains in more detail (thread count 12 x 9 per cm). *Photograph: YAT. Courtesy of Northern Archaeological Associates*

Opposite below: 4 Fragmentary top section of a suspended dress from Grave ACQ, Køstrup, Denmark, showing pleating. *Photograph: Jens Gregers Aagaard. Courtesy of Odense Bys Museer*

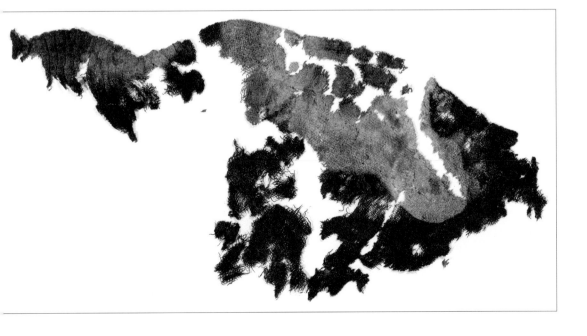

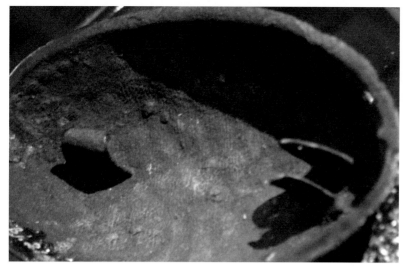

5 Back view of a bossed oval brooch from Sweden, clearly showing attachments for the iron pin, now lost. The inside of the brooch has the texture of the cloth (in this case a diamond twill) used in making the mould. National Museum of Sweden. *Photograph: Lukas Thor Dziubalski*

6 Small round brooch (enlarged; diameter 1in, 2.6cm) from a hoard found at Vester Vedsted near Ribe, Denmark. In excavated graves, such brooches are often found above the level of the twin oval brooches, where they might have fastened the neck of a woman's shirt. National Museum of Denmark. *Photograph: Lukas Thor Dziubalski*

7 Glass beads from a hoard found at Lerchenborg, Denmark. Beads were sometimes worn as necklaces, but more commonly, strings of beads were suspended from brooches or sewn onto garments. National Museum of Denmark. *Photograph: Lukas Thor Dziubalski*

8 Silver neck ring from a hoard found at Vaalse, Denmark. The Arab writer Ibn Fadlan remarked that among the Rus, a man's wealth was displayed on his wife's neck. National Museum of Denmark. *Photograph: Lukas Thor Dziubalski*

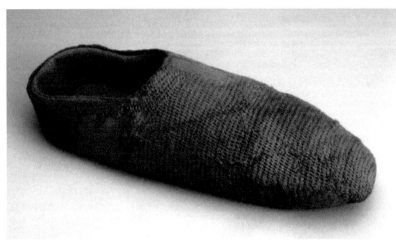

9 A needle-bound sock from Anglo-Scandinavian York. Wool used for the top of the sock was dyed red with madder. Needle binding is not known from the British Isles outside Scandinavian contexts, and this sock was associated with other textiles of possible Scandinavian origin. *By permission of York Archaeological Trust*

10 Penannular brooch from Høm, Denmark, decorated with stylised masks. Penannular brooches were typically used to fasten men's cloaks. National Museum of Denmark. *Photograph: Lukas Thor Dziubalski*

11 Bone skates are well known from Viking archaeology, but this example from York was found with the shoe still attached. Crude wooden pattens could have been worn in a similar manner. *By permission of York Archaeological Trust*

12 A collection of dress pins of bone and metal from Anglo-Scandinavian York, laid on a woollen textile fragment. These pins would probably have been used to fasten cloaks and similar garments. *By permission of York Archaeological Trust*

Ñ EEXAVDI

ORATIONEM MEAM·

13 This illustration of Goliath from the Eadui Psalter appears to represent a Viking. The Psalter was made at Christ Church Canterbury in the early eleventh century, not long after the community had been held to ransom by the army of Thorkell Hávi, who is very probably the subject of this cartoon. Distinctively Scandinavian features are his blue and green clothes, his swept back red hair and moustache, and his square-cut neckhole apparently faced with silk; on his feet he wears either red socks like the example from York (*colour plate 9*) or hose. *BL MS Arundel 155 fol.93r. By permission of the British Library*

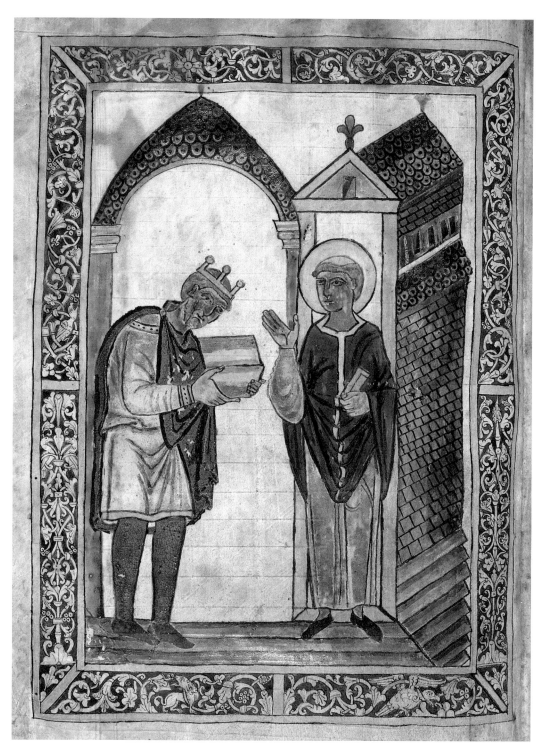

14 This manuscript illustration shows King Æthelstan and St Cuthbert. King Æthelstan's clothing is typical of high-status dress of the period. His shirt is decorated with a braid across the chest, (as is Goliath's in the Eadui Psalter, *colour plate 13*), which probably covers a seam attaching the main fabric to the lining as part of the structure of the neck opening. Athelstan's cuffs are very similar to Cnut's in the Winchester *Liber Vitae* (*55*), while the bottom of his shirt appears to be edged with silk. *CCC MS 183 fol. 1v. By permission of the Master and Fellows of Corpus Christi College, Cambridge*

Halla Broa (*66* on p100); the style was known in Viking England too, where it is shown on a cross shaft from Sockburn (*67* on p101). A pair of wide knee breeches might be worn on a stone from on Hunnestad, Sweden, though these are not tied in at the knee (*73*); the same style might also be seen on a picture stone from När Smiss, Gotland (*66*), on a sculpture from Weston, England (*67*), and by male figures in the procession scene on the tapestry from Oseberg (*54*).

Bagginess was generally avoided in fashionable men's clothing, but an exception appears to have been made for these exaggeratedly baggy breeches. Today, baggy trousers are associated with oriental fashions, and are known from Rajastan, Afghanistan, Turkey and North Africa, but the Arab and Afghan-Persian sources which describe these breeches are clearly amazed at the sheer quantity of cloth used by the Rus. If it did not originate among the Rus and Scandinavians of the Viking Age (perhaps from naturally baggy linen breeches), the fashion for enormously baggy trousers must have been taken to new extremes by them.

From Birka grave BJ.905 comes a hook-and-eye fastening, which might come from baggy linen breeches of this type (*49*). The presence of an iron eye might imply a different construction from the ordinary linen breeches discussed above, which were presumably simply wrapped inside the hose or leg windings. It would be foolhardy to reconstruct an entire garment on the basis of such tiny scraps of cloth, but it is at least credible that the occupant of this grave wore baggy breeches of linen, which ended just below the knee. By contrast, the textile fragments from Hedeby, identified by Hägg as from baggy breeches, are woollen, and if this identification is correct, there is evidence that baggy trousers could have been made in either wool or linen.

The right-hand man of King Haraldr Hárfagri was Hauk Hábrók, whose nickname translates as 'high breeches'. Hauk lived around the middle of the Viking Age; he is supposed to have visited Russia, and so could have adopted his distinctive breeches from the Rus. This same term, *hábrók*, is used in poetry as an epithet for the hawk, a bird whose feathered upper legs are reminiscent of the knee-length baggy breeches illustrated in Viking Age art. So, it may be that *hábrækr* or 'high breeches' was the name by which these breeches were known. The accounts of the *Hudud al-'Alam* and Ibn Rusta suggest that baggy breeches were a deliberately flamboyant fashion, a conspicuous show of excess. As such, they may have been a sign of social status, and indeed, in *Hauks þáttr*, the term *hábrókast* appears to be used as a byword for pride or pre-eminence.

For high breeches to be seen to full effect, a short shirt is a pre-requisite, and this combination is seen on Gotland picture stones. Like the shortness of the shirt, the bagginess of the breeches might have proved particularly suitable for riding. Images of riders are relatively uncommon, but at least in some instances, as at Sockburn, England, and at Stenkyrka Lillbjärs and Halla Broa, Gotland, they wear baggy high breeches. Longer, tighter leggings are worn by a rider illustrated on the Oseberg wagon and by a silver rider figurine from Birka (BJ.825), as well as by two carved

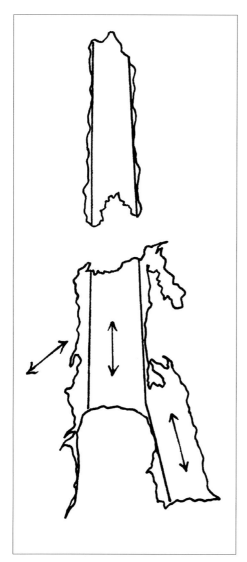

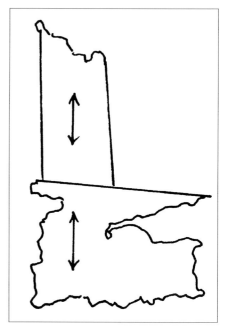

65 Possible high breeches from Hedeby.
A) *left:* sketch of fragment 91A (above) and
72A (below).
B) *above:* another view of Fragment 72A,
showing how the narrow strip attaches to
a fourth piece of cloth at one end. These
fragments are identified as from men's
breeches by comparison with Thorsbjerg
F.S.3684 *(46).* Scale 1:3

riders on another fragment from Sockburn, England. But the suggestion that high
breeches are a mark of status might be supported by a comparison of the Sockburn
riders; those in tight-fitting legwear are carrying spears, while the man in high
breeches is holding a hawk.

Ökulbrœkr

The term *ökulbrœkr, hökulbrœkr* or *höklabrœkr* is used of the leggings worn by ill-
dressed figures such as Refr in *Gautreks saga* ch.9, Kolfinnr in his hairy shoes and
hood in *Kjalnesinga saga* ch.7, or Hreiðar in *Hreiðars þáttr.* However, there has been
some uncertainty over the meaning of the word.

According to one suggestion, it is derived from *hökull*, which can be defined as a *paenula*-like cloak. Some have thought the word refers to breeches made in the form of a *hökull*, citing for comparison the Scottish kilt. However, the word *hökull* refers to the ecclesiastical chasuble, and not to the related laymen's garment, the *hekla* (see below); thus, *hökull* might in fact be a loan word from another Germanic language, introduced at the time of the Conversion, and a new word for a priest's vestments would be unlikely to give its name to poor man's leggings. Furthermore, both Refr in *Gautreks saga* (ch.9) and Hreiðar in *Hreiðars þáttr*, wear a cloak (*feldr*) as well as *ökulbrœkr*, which makes it improbable that *ökulbrœkr* doubled as cloak and breeches in the manner of an early kilt. In any case, the shape of the kilt bears no relation to the shape of the chasuble.

An alternative explanation links *ökulbrœkr* with *okkla*, *ökkla*, 'ankle'; thus, *ökulbrœkr* are simply 'ankle breeches' – the existence of the parallel term (*h*)*ökul-skúaðr* (presumably 'ankle-shoed, in ankle-high shoes') seems to clinch the argument. Ankle-length trousers are worn by seamen on a picture stones from Ardre and Alskog Tjängvide, Gotland (*68* on p103), and by the dwarf Turold on the Bayeux Tapestry; Turold's trousers have been left white by the embroiderers, possibly indicating that they are made of linen; there was probably little significant difference between the cut of ankle breeches in linen or wool. On Gotland however, where linen was not used, there can be no doubt that ankle breeches were made of wool. Ankle breeches in the sagas will probably have been cut to a simple pattern from coarse woollen cloth.

It is sometimes assumed that, though trousers were a mark of low status in later medieval fashion, they were commonly worn by Scandinavians in the Viking period. If so, the use of *ökulbrœkr* as shorthand for an ill-dressed bumpkin would be a saga anachronism, but, on the whole, it seems more probable that long trousers were indeed shunned by men of status even in Viking times.

Footed breeches

In *Njáls saga*, ch.134, Flósi chooses to wear footed breeches (*leistabrœkr*) because he will be walking, and Thóroddr also wears footed breeches in *Eyrbyggja saga* ch.45; a related style, with bands under the foot occurs in *Fljótsdæla saga* ch.16. Flósi has chosen to walk so that he will be on the same footing as his men, who have no alternative. Footed breeches are clearly considered more suitable for walking than riding, and might consequently have been seen as an unusual garment for men of rank. It might also be inferred that whatever leggings Flósi would have worn on horseback would probably have been unsuitable for sustained walking.

Such footed breeches were perhaps quite common; both pairs of Roman-era trousers from Thorsbjerg are footed, while the lower part of the trousers from Damendorf is missing (*46*). Whilst Hägg interprets the Hedeby fragments (*65*) as coming from baggy high breeches, it is possible that the wrinkled appearance of the cloth is the result of treatment after it had been cut up for rags (much of the material

66 High breeches from Gotland.
A) *above:* Stenkyrka Lillbjärs.
B) *centre:* Halla Broa; this horseman also wears a *paenula*-like cloak.
C) *left:* När Smiss, with wide sleeves and open-bottomed breeches

67 High breeches from
England.
A) *above:* Sockburn.
B) *right:* Weston

from Hedeby had been reused for washing and tarring ships in the harbour), and that it was originally part of a pair of tight-fitting footed breeches similar to the Roman-era example from Thorsbjerg (F.S.3684), which it resembles. As long trousers with feet sewn to the bottom, *leistabrækr* are a combination of ankle-length trousers and footed hose, and perhaps represent the rich man's answer to ankle breeches, since they combine the advantages of long trousers with the look of footed hose.

The trouser belt

Breeches of whatever kind must have been supported by a belt, while another belt would have been worn around the shirt. The Thorsbjerg and Damendorf trousers are fitted with wide belt loops (46), while *Landnámabók* contains the account of Lon-Einarr whose belt broke in a fight, so that his trousers started to fall down. However, it is rare to find more than a single buckle in a grave, and where two or more are found, the extra buckles are seldom in the waist area. Where buckles have been found with associated textile remains, it appears that they have been used to secure the shirt, and it makes sense that such comparatively expensive and decorative items should have been openly displayed rather than hidden under the shirt. The trouser belt, then, cannot have been buckled, but must instead have been tied in place.

Since tablet-woven bands from the Viking Age are apparently always decorative and high-status, we can assume that this belt was usually made of leather or rope. A simple tied belt of leather has a slit at one end, through which the other end passes before it is tied off, while in a common medieval variant a pair of slits are cut and the other end is split in two halves which are tied together; the early Iron Age bog body from Tollund, Denmark, wore a leather belt of this kind. However the word used for Lon-Einarr's belt, *lindi*, suggests a rope of bast, the fibre found under the bark of the lime or linden tree; Grettir wears a belt of bast in *Grettis saga* ch.38, and in *Króka-Refs saga* ch.16, Refr wears a belt made of a rope of walrus hide. Belts of this kind were probably the only kind available to thralls and the poor. It is worth noting here that very many graves of the Viking Age contain no surviving grave goods whatsoever, and many people probably had no metal dress accessories of any kind.

THE CLOAK

Tacitus tells us that historically the cloak was the mainstay of Germanic clothing, and several early examples have been recovered by archaeologists. At the time of the Vikings, it was still the commonest pattern of overgarment, and among the Rus visited by Ibn Fadlan it may even have been worn without other garments, just as it had been in Roman times. The saga habit of wearing only a cloak and linen clothing is a testimony to its continued importance.

68 Sailors in ankle breeches on a picture stone from Ardre, Gotland. Wide-bottomed trousers might have proved more practical on board ship

Feldr

The cloak described by Ibn Fadlan, which 'covers one half of his body, leaving one of the arms uncovered' is the same cloak that was worn by the Germans in Tacitus' day; a large rectangle of cloth wrapped round the body and pinned at the right shoulder, leaving the right arm completely free (*69* on p103). This cloak, the *feldr*, is the classic male cloak of the early medieval period, and is the equivalent of the Roman *sagum*.

Like their Roman predecessors, Viking-era cloaks could be fairly sizable. In *Kormáks saga* ch.10, the size of cloak for a *hólmganga*, a kind of duel fought on a *feldr*, is specified as 'five ells in the sheet' (*fimm álna í skaut*); the early medieval Icelandic ell was reckoned at 18in (45cm), so this cloak works out at 7ft 6in (230cm). This would be comparable in size to the Roman-era and Migration-period cloaks, which range from roughly 6ft 6in (200cm) to over 9ft (275cm) in width; they are usually somewhat shorter than their width, so that if the long side is taken to be five ells, the shorter side would be roughly three and a half. This would give proportions of 7ft 6in x 5ft 3in (230 x 160cm) for the cloak described in *Kormáks saga*, but we should perhaps not be too insistent on exact measurements. According to *De Carolo Magno*, the great cloaks of the Franks had been in the shape of a double square, which would be appropriate here too; this would force the duellists to fight along a fairly narrow strip 45in (115cm) wide. A smaller cloak is probably envisaged by the writer of *Svarfdæla saga*, where each man stands on his own cloak. Though the phrase *í skaut* has generally been taken to imply a square cloak, this is unlikely given its great size; a cloak of five ells square would be almost unwearable.

Another standard size for the cloak comes from the Icelandic law code known as *Grágás*, where the size of a 'trade *feldr*' (*varar-feldr*) is set as 'four thumb-ells long and two broad', giving the same relative proportions as specified by *De Carolo Magno*. A thumb-ell is shorter than a standard ell, and these cloaks would have measured just 5ft 4in x 2ft 8in (160 x 80cm). These trade cloaks were made of ruggy, piled cloth, and may have been smaller than other cloaks because of the weight of the cloth. It was an undyed cloak of this kind that was worn by Haraldr 'Greycloak' (*Heimskringla, Haralds saga Gráfeldar* ch.7), but dyed varieties were also available (see ch.3). The remains of a ruggy cloak were found on the cloak pin from Birka grave BJ.736, and similar fragments come from Russia, Iceland and Britain. These legal definitions of cloak size for duelling and trade probably simply give precise formulation to a generally agreed standard.

Coarse fabrics not dissimilar to the thick but loose twills of earlier cloaks, were found in association with some of the cloak pins from the graves of Birka. Such coarse fabrics from high-status graves clearly indicate that the cloak was worn for warmth, but *feldir* and similar cloaks might also have been symbols of rank. In the Bayeux Tapestry, of the 400 or so clothed figures, only about one in eight wear cloaks, and all are men of rank, whether nobles, courtiers or skippers; half the cloaks are worn by major nobles such as Harold Godwinson and Duke William. Although the fastening on the right shoulder leaves the right hand free, no one wearing a cloak on the Tapestry is engaged in fighting or physical work of any kind. In other pictorial sources, the *feldr*-type cloak is also commonly worn as a badge of rank, which is how it was seen by the author of the thirteenth-century Norwegian *Konungs Skuggsjá*.

Perhaps similar to the *feldr*, were the *skikkja* and the *möttull*. The *möttull* is first mentioned by the tenth-century poet Kormákr (*Kormáks saga* st.71 ch.22). As a probable loanword, *möttull* might have described a new Western style of cloak, perhaps the semicircular cloak, which was probably introduced to Scandinavia during the Viking Age. At this period, the semicircular cloak would have been pinned at the shoulder, like the *feldr*; occasional finds of penannular brooches worn at the hip will be considered below. The *skikkja* appears to have been a luxury garment, worthy to be given and received by kings, and worn only by men of rank; as such, the word might have implied more about the cloak's material than its cut, and it can sometimes be used interchangeably with *möttull* and *feldr*. In *Laxdæla saga* ch.75, in an antiquarian detail, Halldórr's cloak pin rips his *skikkja* when he stands up suddenly with his foot on the hem, which suggests the cloak is made from a delicate fabric. A particularly fine example is described in *Ljósvetninga saga* ch.13, and the splendid cloak which Hauk Hábrók obtained for King Haraldr was also a *skikkja* (*Hauks þáttr Hábróks, Flateyjarbók*).

The richness of Scandinavian cloaks was noted by the Spanish geographer al-'Udhri in about 1058 in his description of a Viking city in Ireland, as quoted by al-Qazwini in the thirteenth century: 'Its people have the customs and dress of the Norsemen. They wear rich mantles, one of which is worth a hundred dinars'

(Dunlop's translation). Al-'Udhri also comments that the nobles' cloaks are decorated with pearls, which is reminiscent of the *möttull* set with stones worn by the seeress Thorbjörg in *Eiríks saga Rauða* (ch.3).

Kápa

A type of cloak called a *kápa* or 'cape' is described in *Landnámabók*, where it is worn by Ljótr, and in *Bandamanna saga* ch.5. In each case, the garment is distinguished by a hood and a single sleeve. For a sleeve to be necessary, the *kápa* must have been long enough to be impractical without one, and unlike the *feldr*, it must have been closed at both sides. The most likely reconstruction appears to be based on a rectangular or semicircular cloak worn like the *feldr*, and sewn up the right side where the sleeve is added.

In the sagas, the *kápa* seems to have been a high-status garment, very often made of blue-dyed cloth and worn by men of rank. Thorgils in *Laxdæla saga* ch.62, and Gísli in *Gísla saga* ch.20, swap their *kápur* for common clothes as a subterfuge, and Gísli is said to be 'well dressed' (*vel búinn*) in his *kápa*. Men in *kápur* also appear on horseback, as Vésteinn does in *Gísla saga* ch.12, when the single sleeve would allow the rider to hold the reins.

However, the word *kápa* does not appear to be used in early poetry, and, despite its mention in *Landnámabók*, it probably represents a post-Viking fashion.

Slæðr

In a late tenth-century poem, Egill Skallagrímsson honours his friend Arinbjörn in return for the gift of a silk *slæðr* (*Egils saga* st.43 ch.67). According to the saga, it had been made especially to fit Egill, since he was taller than most other men. It was so long, that when Egill's adult son Thorsteinn secretly borrowed it, it trailed in the mud, to Egill's fury (ch.79). Similarly, in *Vatnsdæla saga* ch.31, the bottom of Bergr's *slæðr* 'of good cloth' (*af góðu klæði*) gets dirty and, in an extravagant gesture, he cuts it off and throws it away. The name *slæðr* itself suggests a long, trailing garment, since it is related to the words *slæða* 'to trail on the ground' and *slóð* 'a spoor or trail'. Clearly, so long a garment made of silk was inherently extravagant. This must be why, although the saga suggests that it was only a part of an entire outfit given to Egill, it is only the *slæðr* which he mentions in his verse. The extravagance of the *slæðr* is also apparent in *Njáls saga* ch.123, where it is offered on top of a previously agreed compensation settlement, in what is characterised by Roscoe as 'an attempt to overwhelm another with generosity'; both the agreed compensation and the *slæðr* are instantly refused.

The *slæðr* appears to have been the garment known in English as a 'cope' or 'pluvial', which is made as a large semicircle of silk cloth reaching from shoulder to floor, and sometimes fastened by two small brooches, one at each shoulder. A twelfth-century Norman cope, originally belonging to Roger II of Sicily, consists of a half circle of scarlet samite, 11ft 4in wide and 4ft 9½in (345 x 146cm) long; it is heavily embroidered in silk and gold, and encrusted with enamels, pearls and gems.

In his verse, Egill says that his *slæðr* is made of silk with gold *knappar*, which can mean 'buttons' but might be translated here as 'small round brooches'.

The saga writer possibly understood Egill's *slæðr* differently, describing it as 'made of silk and heavily stitched in gold, set all down the front with gold *knappar*' (*gerðar af silki ok gullsaumaðar mjök, settar fyrir allt gullknöppum í gegnum niðr*, ch.67), a description which has generally led to its interpretation as a form of long, buttoned coat. However, there is no evidence for such long, buttoned coats from the Viking Age, and Viking caftans were not buttoned below the waist. If the saga writer had in mind a genuinely historical type of garment, perhaps he envisaged Egill in a cope with button-like ornaments along the leading edge, such as is seen on the twelfth-

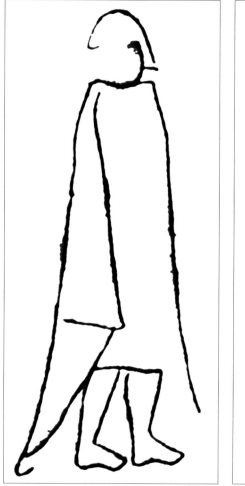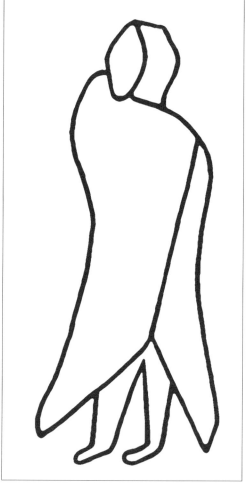

69 Cloaked men from A) *above left:* a carved stone at Tu, Norway, and B) *above right:* the Oseberg tapestry. The figure from the Oseberg tapestry appears to be wearing a hood. These figures, and the man on the gold foil from Hauge (*14*) are wearing the ancient Germanic *feldr*

century west front of the cathedral of St Gilles du Gard, France. Decorative bobbles wrought from silver wire are known from Birka, while a find from Dunmore Cave, Ireland, deposited during Egill's lifetime, included silk patterned with gold, and 16 button-like objects in various sizes woven from silver wire, which could be interpreted as the remains of a silk cope with decorative *knappar* (*70*).

The men's *slæðr* probably took its name from an already existing garment worn by Viking women, which might in turn have been influenced by the men's cope. The long, trailing semicircular cope hangs in folds down the back, like those seen in contemporary illustrations of women's dress, and a garment of the same name is worn in *Rígspula* by the lady Moðir (st.29). This has led to the suggestion that the silk *slæðr* might have been seen as effeminate, and that this might be the reason it is refused in *Njáls saga*. But though the *slæðr* might have been worn by men and women alike, it cannot have been perceived as effeminate, since Viking society was extremely alert to charges of effeminacy, and such a garment would hardly have been well received by the touchy Egill.

Bergr's *slæðr* is apparently also referred to by the word *vesl* (*vesl hafði einn yfir sér ok slæðr af góðu klæði*, *Vatnsdæla saga* ch.31), a word which appears to be a general term for a cloak, and may be translated loosely as 'robe'.

Ólpa

The *ólpa* may have been a short cape, perhaps a shorter version of the *kápa*, with which it is linked in *Jónsbók* and in *Egils saga*. In *Egils saga* ch.75, Egill gives Álfr an *ólpa*, and Álfr remarks that it will make a *kápa* for him; the joke seems to be that a short garment for Egill will make a long one for Álfr, and the shape of the two kinds of cloak is thus presumably similar.

An early reference in a verse preserved in *Hervarar saga ok Heiðreks* (st.16 ch.4), suggests that it might have been an archetypically male garment, and perhaps one better suited to fighting than the larger *kápa*. It seems often to have been made of skin.

Hekla

Óðinn's famous cloak is the *hekla* or 'hackle'. In the sagas, he wears this cloak when he appears in his guise as a mysterious walker, but despite its close association with Óðinn in prose, the *hekla* is apparently unknown in poetry, and in *Grímnismál* he wears a *feldr*. It was probably something like the Classical *paenula*; the related word *hökull* is used of the priest's chasuble or *paenula*, and the word is used similarly in other early Germanic languages. Óðinn wears the *hekla* with a hood, thus his nickname 'deep hood' (*síð-höttr*), but the *hekla* did not necessarily always have a hood, and as with the *kápa* and *feldr*, the hood might have been detachable or even a separate garment.

An illustration on a late Viking picture stone from Sanda, Gotland, shows a figure which might represent Óðinn as walker, who is wearing such a garment, apparently with a hood (*71* on p110). Cloaks of similar cut, but without the hood, appear on the men in the procession scene of the Oseberg Tapestry (*54*), and on a picture stone from Halla Broa where the *hekla* is worn by a mounted rider (*66*). The eighth-century

Northumbrian Franks Casket shows a scene (which might represent the Apprehension of Christ) where three figures wear hooded cloaks, apparently of this cut, and two figures on a carving from St Mary Bishophill Junior, York, appear to be wearing hooded cloaks similar to those of the Franks Casket. From these contemporary representations, it seems that the cut of the *hekla* could be either triangular or semicircular, with a neck slit, to which a hood might sometimes have been attached, cut halfway along the selvedge.

OTHER OVERGARMENTS

Caftans

In several graves at Birka, a row of buttons indicates that the occupant has worn a buttoned coat or caftan (*72*). The number of buttons varies considerably, but they always form a row down the middle of the chest, reaching no lower than the waist. They are usually cast in bronze, but in one case were made of lead; similar buttons could also be used to fasten a pouch. A belt of leather or textile appears to have secured the caftan's waist.

Similar garments can occasionally be glimpsed in art of Viking-age Scandinavia. Most importantly, a caftan-like coat is worn by the axeman on a runestone from Hunnestad, Sweden. This stone is now seriously damaged, but the general lines of the figure can be reconstructed by reference to early sketches (*73*). A carving from Weston, England, appears to show a very similar garment. Interestingly, both figures also seem to wear the same wide knee-length breeches (*67*).

Early caftans are known from excavations at Antinoë, Egypt, and Fayum, Iran. These were buttonless woollen garments fastened with ties, and cut to an ingenious pattern which uses a single piece of cloth for both sides including the upper part of the sleeves. Caftans worn in Viking Scandinavia will have doubtless been derived from similar eastern exemplars.

A splendid fur-lined caftan of patterned Persian silk comes from the Alan burial site known as Moschevaya Balka in the Northern Caucasus (Grave 2; *74, 75* – both on p112); it is 4ft 6in (1.4m) long and dates from the ninth century. Such a fine garment must have belonged to a man of enormous wealth, perhaps a king. The gold-buttoned silk caftan made for the Rus chieftain's funeral witnessed by Ibn Fadlan might also have been similar.

A pair of silver-embroidered cuffs and a collar from tenth-century silk caftans come from the royal cemetery of Valsgärde, Sweden (Graves 12 and 15 respectively; *76* on p114). The ground weave in both cases is red silk tabby. Twelve bronze buttons, much like those from Birka, were found in Grave 12, but no buttons were recovered from Grave 15, and it is possible that, despite its similarity to the cuffs, the collar was originally a cloak trimming. However, the fastenings at Moschevaya Balka were made of fabric, which under normal conditions would leave no archaeological trace.

70 Button-
like ornament
from Dunmore
Cave, Ireland.
Perhaps Egill's
slæðr was
decorated with
objects like this

Hägg believes that some of the trimmings from apparently buttonless male graves at Birka indicate that the occupants were dressed in caftans, and these might have been fastened either with cloth buttons or with ties. An alternative reconstruction for the Valsgärde 'cuffs' suggests that they might have formed decorative ends for a stole or sash, or perhaps for cloak ties similar to those worn by Cnut in the *Liber Vitae* portrait (*55*).

Whilst the caftan was certainly worn in Viking Scandinavia, it is possible that it was never completely naturalised there, and that finds of caftans represent links of gift, trade and travel with the eastern Rus; in two of the Birka graves (BJ.716 and 1074) it was worn with a belt decorated with oriental-style fittings which were probably made in Kiev. Aside from the Weston sculpture, most evidence for caftans comes from the Viking east, but fragments of patterned silk and 16 button-like objects of silver wire from Dunmore Cave, Ireland, have been claimed as a caftan. However, the identification as a caftan relies on the interpretation of these silver objects (which come in three different sizes) as buttons, and they might in fact have been purely ornamental (*70*; see above, *Slæðr*).

A more humble caftan seems to be represented by a find from Hedeby of ordinary woollen cloth, with the remains of somewhat unevenly spaced buttonholes down one edge (*77* on p114). This plain fragment might once have borne rich trimmings, but nonetheless, it suggests that not all such garments were necessarily luxury imports. The caftan in grave BJ.944 at Birka was made of linen trimmed with silk.

71 Scene on a picture stone from Sanda, Gotland. The central figure with the spear is thought to be Óðinn. He wears a distinctive cloak, similar in style to the Classical *paenula*, which is probably to be identified as a *hekla*. Similar cloaks are seen on figures from Halla Broa (*66*) and Oseberg (*53*)

Thorax

A further overgarment is mentioned by Einhard, which, plucking a name from his Classical model Suetonius (*De Vita Caesarum* Book 2 ch.82), he calls a *thorax*. The literary influence of Suetonius on this passage does not seem to me in any way to invalidate it as a source, though it must be taken into consideration in our interpretation.

As the name implies, Einhard tells us that this garment covered just the chest and shoulders; the king's *thorax* is of otterskin or ermine and he wears it for warmth; it appears to be worn with the cloak rather than in place of it. The *thorax* then, is a warm fur-lined garment enclosing the upper torso. Just such a garment is worn in images of Charles the Great's successor, Louis the Pious, where he is portrayed in Hrabanus Maurus's figure poem *De Laudibus Sanctae* as defender of the Cross (*78* on p115). Here the *thorax* is edged in blue, which might represent a dark fur lining such as sable or beaver, but more probably represents a trim of silk or silk brocade. This short-sleeved jacket is worn under the cloak, and wraps around the front of the king, ending just below the waist. Similar but longer wrap-around jackets are worn by figures depicted on Vendel-period helmet plaques from Vendel and Valsgärde, Sweden, and Sutton Hoo, England, and also on the fifth-century Halberstadt Diptych (*79* on p116).

Fragments of the type are among some of the most interesting discoveries from Hedeby (*80* on p117). These are cut to wrap around the front of the body and would probably have reached to just below the waist, just as is shown in the illustration of Louis the Pious. They are lined with pile-woven cloth for warmth, and in one case this fleecy lining is dyed. The method of fastening is not visible in the illustrations of Louis the Pious, but in one of the Hedeby fragments, traces of bronze have been identified near the bottom corner, indicating that it has been fastened with a bronze pin. If the jacket was worn as it is in the illustration of Louis the Pious, this pin would have been located at the right hip. Penannular brooches and ringed pins were regularly found in this position among the Birka graves, and it is most likely that they were used to fasten a garment similar to that known from Hedeby and from Frankish sources. In some cases at Birka, these brooches seem to have been positioned somewhat lower, suggesting the longer style known from Vendel-era art.

This garment might well have been called *kyrtill* or 'kirtle' in Viking times, a word which was later applied to the woollen shirt, but which appears in

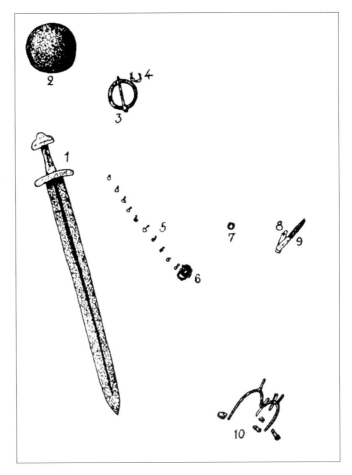

72 Detail of Arbman's grave plan for Bj.752B. This man was accompanied by a sword (1) and shield (2); his cloak was decorated with twisted silver (4) and pinned by a penannular brooch (3). A row of buttons (5) running upwards from the buckle (6) at his waist indicates a caftan. His knife (9) and hone (8) were probably suspended from a belt at his waist, possibly using the iron ring (7). His spurs (10) show that he was dressed to ride the horse which was buried in another part of the chamber. *Arbman 1944*

Above left: 73 Reconstruction (based on surviving fragments and earlier drawings) of a carved figure from Hunnestad, Sweden. He appears to wear a caftan, open-bottomed high breeches and an elaborate hat

Above right: 74 Ninth-century caftan of patterned silk from Moschevaya Balka, Caucasus

early references to be made of skin or fur. Thus, the bride of *Rígsþula* is 'goat-kirtled', while the Norwegian Ohthere took kirtles of otter or bearskin to England. A figure probably representing a 'kirtled' woman on the Oseberg Tapestry has a diagonal line across her body, which might reflect the wrap-around front of the *thorax* (*25*).

Kufl

The *kufl*, *kofl* or 'cowl' regularly appears in the sagas as a disguise. In *Króka-Refs saga* ch.16, Refr appears disguised as an old man sporting a blue *kufl* tied with a rope of walrus hide. A white *kufl* is worn by Earl Thorfinnr as disguise on board ship, and also by Earl Rögnvaldr when disguised as an old fisherman (*Orkneyinga saga* ch.30, 85). In *Bósa saga ok Herrauðs* ch.8, Bósi disguises himself in a slave's grey *kufl*, and in *Hrólfs saga Kraka* ch.3, the princes Hróarr and Helgi wear *kuflar* in hiding.

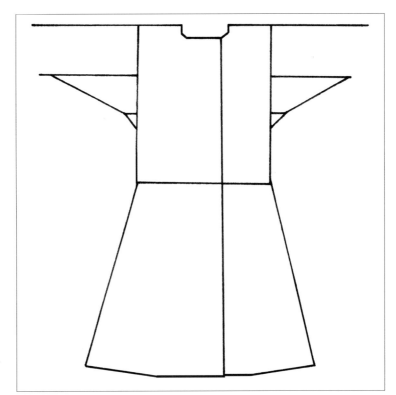

75 Simplified layout of caftan from Moschevaya Balka, Caucasus. Scale 1:15

The *kufl* has a hood, which helps hide the wearer's identity, but another factor must be that it was generally worn by the common people, whilst the men who disguise themselves in it are invariably men of rank. A man in a *kufl* could pass unremarked, without attracting a second glance. As such, it is adopted by Gísli as an outlaw (*Gísla saga* ch.34), and by Thorgils when he poses as an outlaw (*Laxdæla saga* ch.62). The *kufl* then, was probably one of the most common garments of Viking Scandinavia, worn by the slave and the working freeman.

The *kufl* commonly appears in the sagas as sea gear. It is worn in nautical contexts in both instances where it appears in *Orkneyinga saga*, and in *Króka-Refs saga*, Refr has probably adopted the habit of an old and prosperous sailor; he styles himself a 'merchant' (*kaupmaðr*). In *Reykdæla saga* ch.21, Skúta chooses a *kufl* to hide his armour when he goes to the fishing nets, and the term is used in poetry in kennings for armour.

Though large and loose enough to conceal Skúta's armour, and long enough for Refr to fasten with a belt, the *kufl* was also short enough for Grettir, admittedly a giant of a man, to tuck into his trousers when he goes swimming (*Grettis saga* ch.75). It was probably similar to the *cuculla* worn by late-Roman slaves, from which it may be descended (related words appear in all Germanic languages, which might reflect an early linguistic borrowing from Latin). It seems to have normally been girt at the

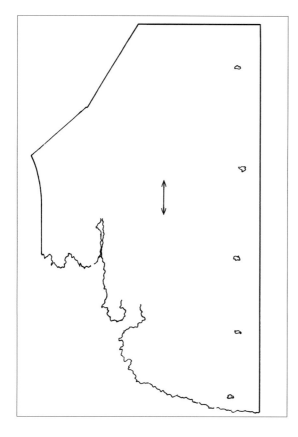

Above: 76 Tenth-century silver-embroidered collar from Valsgärde, Sweden, probably from a caftan

Left: 77 Sketch of fragment of a woollen caftan from Hedeby, Fragment s28. Hägg groups this with fragments 11 and 76 (*80*), but the parallel sides and probable buttonholes suggest that this actually formed part of a caftan. Scale 1:6

waist with a simple belt of rope or leather; this is how Refr wears his, and Grettir belts his *kufl* with a bast rope in *Grettis saga* ch.38; otherwise a belt on a *kufl* attracts no more comment than it would on a belted shirt. A possible illustration of a *kufl* appears on one of the gold-foil figures found at Helgö, Sweden.

Refr wears a blue-dyed *kufl* which, like his walrus-hide belt, might indicate a degree of status within a working community, but usually when the colour is stated, *kuflar* are almost always undyed in natural wool colours, generally black or grey. White *kuflar* are mentioned twice in *Orkneyinga saga*, and are also worn by two lads sold as slaves in *Færeyinga saga* ch.8; these white *kuflar* might have been distinctive of the Faeroes and Orkneys and may indicate that white sheep already dominated the Northern Isles breeds.

Gowns

Some illustrations show what looks at first sight to be a full-length shirt. At Lärbro Tangelgårda, Gotland, near ankle-length garments are shown with full skirts and wide sleeves (*81* on p119). A garment shown on a carving from Kirklevington, England, also has wide sleeves, and falls to at least below the knee, though it does not appear to be belted like the Gotland examples (*82* on p120). The Kirklevington carving might possibly represent a caftan, but its neckhole is strongly reminiscent of a fragment from Hedeby harbour which appears not to have opened at the front (Fragment 18), and the carved vertical band at the front appears to end just above the bottom hem, making it unlikely that it represents a front opening. These and similar illustrations depict a long, loose overgarment, which is quite different from the shirts described above.

78 Louis the Pious as defender of the Cross. His outfit is strikingly similar to Einhard's description of Charles the Great in *Vita Karoli* ch.23; note in particular the waistcoat or *thorax* worn under the cloak

79 Figures on a helmet plaque from Grave I, Vendel, Sweden. The man on the left wears a
garment similar to Louis's waistcoat (78), but longer like a coat, corresponding with the position
of penannular brooches in some Birka graves

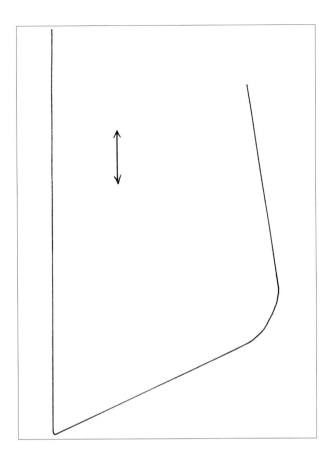

80 Pattern derived from Hedeby Fragments 11 and 76. Fragment 76 showed traces of bronze roughly 12in (30cm) above the corner. Scale 1:6

Generally, long, loose tunics were associated with women's clothing; thus, it would seem Haraldr Harðráði's mail shirt gained the nickname Emma because of its great length (*Heimskringla, Haralds saga Harðráða*, ch.91). But by the end of the Viking Age, long gowns could be worn by European kings and nobles, and are seen on the Bayeux Tapestry where they are worn only by magnates holding court. Long gowns such as these might be compared with the Byzantine dalmatic. Some nations habitually wore similar full-length garments, which might also have influenced Scandinavian fashion. The tenth-century Arab writer al-Istakhri noted that the Rus wore a short *qurtaq*, distinguishing it from the full-length *qurtaq* worn by the Khazars, Bulghars and Petchenegs.

HEADGEAR

Hats seem typically to have been conical in shape. This type of hat can be seen in Scandinavian art on Gotland picture stones, most notably those from Lärbro Tängelgårda (60) and Sanda, and on bronze figurines usually identified as representing the gods Thórr (from Akureyri, Iceland) and Freyr (from Rällinge, Sweden). They also feature in Anglo-Scandinavian carvings from Middleton (*89*) and Kirklevington (*82*). It is not generally possible to absolutely distinguish hats from helmets in these depictions, but in many cases a hat seems more plausible.

The hat worn by the figure of Thórr appears to extend beyond his head into a brim, and might have been made of a relatively stiff material such as straw, birch bark or leather. Other conical hats have their edge relatively flat to the skull, though some of those on the Gotland stones combine a floppy point with a brim at the front, and might have been made from heavy woollen cloth or needle binding. The skin hat worn by the early Iron Age man from Tollund, Denmark, was more-or-less of a type with the simpler hats seen on the Gotland stones; a two-piece skin hat from Søgårds Mose, Denmark (*84*), might have more closely resembled the hat worn by the bronze Thórr. Skin and fur hats are mentioned in the sagas, and such hats might sometimes have been covered in linen, wool or silk.

At Birka, gold or silver trim was found at the forehead in more than a dozen male graves, sometimes with the fragmentary edge of a piece of silk cloth still attached; these fragments are compatible with a reconstruction either as pointed caps or skullcaps (*83*). Where there are no other textile remains, the band might have been used as a simple fillet tied around the head, a fashion which occurs in the sagas; one of the silk bands from Dublin is tied so that it could have been worn in such a way. In grave BJ.944, a section of passementerie concealed a seam which joined two rounded edges of cloth, while the remarkable silver ornaments from graves BJ.581 and BJ.644 must have come from pointed caps, which appear to have been made of silk (*83*) and decorated with trailing ribbons or braids; the granulated decoration on these mounts suggests an origin in the Kiev area.

Gotland picture stones usually seem to show the point of men's hats dangling down their necks. Confirmation of this fashion is found in the tenth-century *Hudud al-'Alam*, which states that the Rus 'wear woollen bonnets with tails let down behind their necks' (Minorsky's translation). It seems most likely that the trailing tails were the floppy tips of tall conical hats, perhaps extending into narrow cloth tubes. Hägg interprets a fragment from Hedeby as a liripipe hood (Fragment s3), which would provide an alternative explanation for the long-tailed headdresses of the Gotland stones, but other evidence suggests that the liripipe hood does not make its appearance before the thirteenth century at the earliest. A hood would, in any case, be unlikely to reveal the line of the neck and shoulder as it is sometimes visible on the Gotland carvings.

The word *húfa* might have been used for this pointed cap or bonnet. A tasselled variety (*skott-húfa*) can be seen on the stone from Sanda, Gotland, and the style is probably related to the silver-bedangled silk hats from Birka graves BJ.581 and BJ.644. Though the *Hudud al-'Alam* specifies wool, a linen *húfa* (*lín-húfa*) is mentioned in *Njáls saga* ch.124, and linen is also suggested by the traditional use of 'Húfa' as a name for a white-headed cow. A close-fitting variety was known as a *koll-húfa* or 'skullcap', and a close-fitting hat appears on each of the front head posts of the Oseberg wagon. This carving is reminiscent of the skin cap found with the Vendel- or Viking-era bog body from Bernuthsfeld, Germany (*84* on p122). A *koll-hetta* is worn by Kolfinnr in *Kjalnesinga saga* ch.7, where his dress is clearly supposed to seem unsophisticated. Similar hats are sometimes seen on picture stones from Gotland. The different terms *hattr* and *húfa* perhaps reflect a difference in cutting patterns, and the *hattr* might have been cut in the manner of a simple hood (see below, 'Hoods') or a woman's *faldr*; unlike the term *húfa*, the words *hattr* and *faldr* are used identically in kennings denoting helmets.

The finest of hats seems to have been the *gerzkr hattr* or 'Russian hat'. When mentioned in the sagas, it is invariably worn by a showily dressed character, and Russian hats are given as kings' gifts in *Njáls saga* ch.31 and *Ljósvetninga saga* ch.2.

81 Figures on a picture stone from Lärbro Tangelgårda, Gotland, wearing long, wide-sleeved gowns

82 Figure of a man from Kirklevington, England, apparently wearing a long, wide-sleeved gown and a pointed hat

Probably, they were something like the hat made from silk and sable which caught the eye of Ibn Fadlan, and which he calls a '*qalansuwwah*', a type of conical hat. These might also have resembled the silk hats with silver ornaments from Birka.

A remarkably elaborate hat is worn by the caftaned figure from Hunnestad (*73*), while a hat made of roots in the manner of a rush hat and shaped like a straw boater was among finds from Viking Novgorod.

The hood

The words *hattr* or 'hat', and *höttr* or 'hood', often appear to be used more-or-less interchangeably, and probably describe the same style of headgear. Thus, for instance, the hood attached to the *kufl* can be called either *kufls-höttr* or *kufls-hattr*. Our distinction between a hat and a hood might be found by distinguishing the *hattr* from the *síðr hattr* ('wide hat' or 'deep hat') or *hetta*. The collocations *síðr hattr* and *síðr höttr* occur so frequently that they probably denote a distinct garment from the simple forms *hattr* and *höttr*. *Síðir hettir*, or 'hoods' are regularly worn in the sagas by men trying to hide their identity.

Hoods are often mentioned in conjunction with another overgarment such as a cloak, but except in the case of the *kufl*, they do not appear to have been integral to the other garment. The hood of Ljótr's *kápa* in *Landnámabók* is 'tied round the neck' (*var hottrinn lerkaðr um halsinn*), while in *Bandamanna saga* ch.5, Ófeigr wears a *kápa* with the sleeve trailing down the back yet the hood does not appear to be on sideways. Similar detachable hoods could have been worn with the *feldr*; in *Fóstbrœðra saga* ch.23, Thormóðr wears a hood with his *feldr*, and so it seems does a group of figures on the Oseberg Tapestry (*69*).

A peculiar skin hood from Krogens Mølle Mose, Denmark, has been dated by pollen analysis to the late Iron Age or Middle Ages, though this dating has been questioned (*85* on p125). It bears some resemblance to the child's hood from St Andrew's Parish, Orkney, held in the National Museum of Scotland, which is also of uncertain date, but which probably comes from the late Iron Age; though recently identified as a 'Viking hood', it might equally be of Pictish origin (*85*). These closed garments cover the head and neck of the wearer, reaching down to the shoulders.

Neither of these hoods has a point or tail, and indeed the Orkney hood is deliberately cut to avoid this feature, in the same way that the peak is cut off the silk and woollen headdresses from the British Isles, which are considered above as examples of the woman's hood or *faldr*. This feature strengthens the assumption that when the *Hudud al-'Alam* describes Rus merchants dressed in hats with points trailing down their backs, it refers to a conical hat or *húfa* and not to a form of hood.

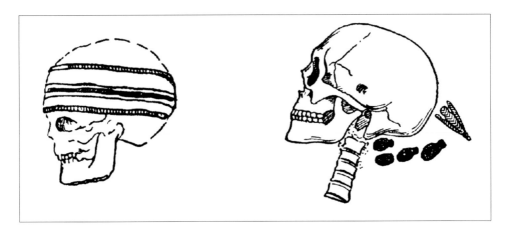

83 Headgear from Birka graves bj.798 and 581. *Geijer 1938, Arbman 1944*

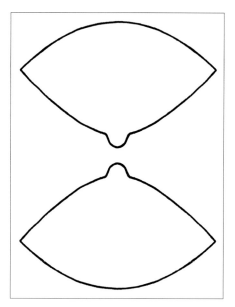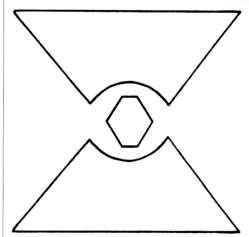

84 Hats from the bogs.
A) *left:* Søgårds Mose, Denmark (pattern partially reconstructed).
B) *right:* Bernuthsfeld, Germany

GLOVES

Snorri Sturluson recounts the myth of Thórr's journey to visit Útgarða-Loki, in which the god and his companions take shelter for the night in a giant's glove, and the same myth is referred to in the poems *Hárbarðsljóð* and *Lokasenna*, where, as in *Snorra Edda*, the glove is called a *hanzki* (st.26). Another word, *vöttr*, which is used in the sagas for 'glove', has a more curious early history; it is referred to by Thorbjörn Hornklofi in a verse preserved in *Heimskringla* (*Haralds saga Hárfagra* st.7 ch.16), where it appears to mean cushion; similarly, the term for a sponge, 'Njörðr's *vöttr*' (*Njarðar-vöttr*) which clearly dates from pagan times, would seem more appropriate to a meaning of 'cushion' than 'glove'. Thus, the word *vöttr* and its diminutive *vetlingr* refer to mittens worn for warmth, while the *hanzki* (originally derived from 'hand shoe') denotes a protective gauntlet. A well-preserved pair of Viking-era woollen mittens with neatly inset thumbs is displayed in the National Museum of Iceland.

The term *glófi* is probably a late borrowing from Old English, and is used for a new style of costly decorated glove, similar to a medieval bishop's glove. In *Gull-Þóris saga* ch.3, *glófar* enhance the description of a richly dressed man, while gold–adorned *glófar* occur in *Njáls saga* ch.31, as well as in the saga romances *Bósa saga ok Herrauðs* (ch.12) and *Örvar-Odds saga* (ch.19). Archaeological evidence suggests that most ordinary gloves will have had just two finger compartments, each for two fingers, but the *glófi* clearly had four separate fingers, and in *Bósa saga ok Herrauðs*, Bósi even plays harp wearing *glófar*.

SHOES AND RIVELINS

Turnshoes worn by men do not appear to have differed significantly from those worn by women, described briefly above (ch.1). But tanned leather turnshoes were probably rarely found on the feet of the poor and the unfree. It has already been noted that female slaves went barefoot, which may sometimes have been the case with male slaves too; the Anglo-Saxon Tiberius Calendar shows barefoot men at work throughout the year (58), while the Julius Calendar shows a barefooted, bare-legged ploughman tilling his master's fields in January. But unprotected feet are easily injured and the Scandinavian winter is too cold for outdoor work to have been done barefoot. Sometimes at least, slaves and the poor must have needed footwear.

In *Parcevals saga*, the Old Icelandic version of the tale of Sir Perceval, the young hero, whose rustic beginnings are well known, wears *hriflingar*. This word *hriflingr* is clearly cognate with the Old English *rifeling*, and survives in Scotland, Shetland and Orkney as 'rivelin', where it denotes a rawhide shoe. Almost all the rural communities of Northern Europe have a tradition of making such simple hide shoes.

Rivelins are made of fresh cattle skin or other hide, the fresher the better. The pattern is based on an oval or rectangle, which measures a little more than the length of the foot by double its width. The edges are laced together with thongs which gather up the hide around the foot, the final shoe having a puckered or 'rivelled' appearance. The hair side may be worn outside or inside according to local tradition; mostly it is worn inside. They can be stuffed with a layer of moss or hay to pad them out and keep the foot warm, and would probably have been worn with footcloths similar to those worn by the Bocksten man.

Such homely footwear may well have attracted ridicule in sophisticated circles, but there is no doubt that it was effective, and that it was in use among the poor. No examples can be looked for from archaeology, since the untreated hide is extremely unlikely to survive except in truly exceptional circumstances, although simple shoes from Dorestad, Elisenhof and York all show rivelin-like features. But in the fictional romance *Halfdanar saga Eysteinssonar* (ch.14), the poverty-stricken wise-man-of-the-woods is given the apt name 'Hriflingr', and to lead a 'rivelin life' (*hriflinga-björg*) is used as a byword for a hand-to-mouth existence. The twelfth-century writer Giraldus Cambrensis describes the Welsh as going barefoot or being shod in rawhide boots 'roughly sewn' (*Descriptio Kambriae* Book 1 ch.8), and Sidonius Appolinarus describes the fifth-century Franks as wearing 'boots of bristly hide' which entirely covered their feet (*Epistolae* Bk.4 no.20); both Giraldus's Welsh and Sidonius's Franks are bare-legged.

Not all rivelins were worn by the poor. The Gaelic for 'rivelin' is either *bróg* or *cúarán* depending on design, and Anlaf 'Cúarán' of Dublin and York was perhaps the longest reigning king of the Viking Age; whether he habitually wore rivelins or just on one notable occasion we may only guess, but like other rivelin wearers he probably went bare-legged, following the Irish fashion. The hairy calfskin shoes worn by Thorbjörg in *Eiríks saga Rauða* ch.3, are probably also rivelins, their thick lacing taking the place of stitching in normal shoes. Hairy calfskin shoes are also worn by Kolfinn in *Kjalnesinga saga* ch.7; he wears them with rustic ankle breeches and a hood with his skirts hitched up between his legs.

Rivelins might not have kept the feet especially dry: the *cúarán* was traditionally pierced to allow water to run out when walking through bogs; Arran fishermen would wear their sealskin pampooties as they walked to and from their boats in the sea (sealskin is said to last better in salt water); and in all lands rivelins have been kept supple by soaking overnight in water before use. But if the feet are damp, at least they are well protected by the tough rawhide, and the lining of animal hair helps keep them warm.

Another form of simple homemade footwear was the rush shoe. A pair of rush shoes was worn by the English ascetic Godric of Finchale on pilgrimage at the close of the eleventh century. In nineteenth-century Denmark, rush-shoe making had become a cottage industry; the women plaited the rushes which the men sewed in the evenings, turning out 70 to 80 shoes a week. Rush shoes were still traditionally worn in Denmark into the early twentieth century.

Clogs and wooden shoes, though not known from the Viking Age, have a long tradition in Scandinavia. Something similar might well have been worn to protect leather turnshoes from the wet and the mud, even if it was simply a matter of fastening short axe-hewn lengths of wood to the feet. The find of a bone skate from York, still tied to a shoe, shows how such simple clogs might have been fastened (*colour plate 11*).

JEWELLERY AND DRESS ACCESSORIES

Penannular brooches and ringed pins are probably the most important form of accessory worn by Viking men. These were worn at the right shoulder to fasten the *feldr*, as described above, and when worn at the right hip, they probably fastened a short jacket or waistcoat (Latin *thorax*). Types of cloak pin were probably not as precisely distinguished in the Viking Age as they are by modern archaeologists, and have a tendency to influence one another.

The penannular brooch (*86* (on p128), *colour plate 10*) originated in Roman Britain, and elaborately decorated versions had already developed in the British Isles before it was adopted by the Scandinavians. The size of such brooches could vary greatly, but the smallest are more often found in women's graves and cannot have been used as cloak fastenings. The penannular rings are often slightly ovoid and most have a greatest diameter of 1½–3in (4–7.5cm); the pin is generally only a little longer than the ring is wide, though there are exceptions, notably the Hiberno-Norse thistle-headed brooches. There was a wide range of styles, some drawing on British and Irish influence, and some on Baltic fashion.

Ringed pins of bronze or iron developed in Ireland long before the Viking Age, and were apparently adopted into mainstream Scandinavian fashion in the second half

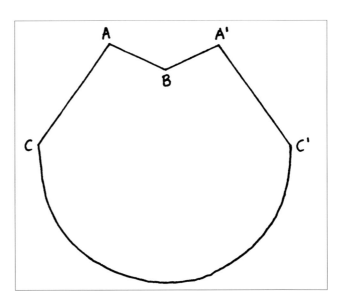

85 Hoods from the bogs.
a) *right:* pattern of a child's hood from St Andrew's Parish, Orkney. A wide braid around the bottom joins points c and c'.
b) *below:* simplified pattern of a hooded skin cape from Krogens Mølle Mose, Denmark. Despite an apparently different pattern, the underlying shape is comparable with that of the Orkney hood

of the ninth century, where distinctive styles quickly developed (*87* (on p129), *colour plate 12*). Most were fairly plain, but some could be elaborately decorated. The ring is typically 1–2in (2.5–5cm) across and the pin between 5–7in (13–18cm) long. The ringed pin would have been stuck through the two layers of the cloak and tied in place with a cord or lace, running through the ring; fragments of this textile tie have been found at Tjørnuvík in the Faeroes, at Dublin, Ireland, and at Kaupang, Norway. The pin is sometimes bent, to help with fastening. A ringed pin was one of the characteristically Scandinavian artefacts found at L'Anse aux Meadows in Newfoundland, Canada. Bone dress pins will have been similarly fastened (*87, colour plate 12*).

Arm rings or bracelets of gold and silver were worn by Viking men. This fashion is mentioned in Ibn Rusta's account of the Rus, and in William of Malmesbury's description of the English before the Norman Conquest. Sometimes these were simple bent strips of metal, which were probably as much a means of carrying silver as of decorating the body, but other arm rings were more elaborately worked. Rings were worn to be seen not hidden, and in *Njáls saga* ch.138-9, Eyjólfr seems to be acting suspiciously by wearing his new ring hidden under his sleeve.

Every man wore a belt of some sort, and belts made of leather or bands of textile could be fastened with buckles (*88* on p130). These were fairly narrow; some were simple undecorated loops of iron, but many were cast in bronze and covered with decorative designs. Carved bone buckles come from Viking York, where one example had been dyed green. Other decorative belt fittings were also sometimes used. Strap ends were generally similar to Anglo-Saxon examples, often terminating in an animal-head design; occasionally they were made to match the buckle. Some belts were adorned with oriental-style decorative fittings along their whole length; moulds for making these belt fittings (one bearing an Arabic inscription) have been found in Kiev, and similar belt fittings found in Birka were probably produced here. In graves BJ.716 and 1074, where ornamental belts were worn with caftans, we can see that they were worn decoratively across the belly in the Hungarian manner.

Purses were also worn by men, and sometimes by women, and seem usually to have hung from a belt. A form of purse with a horseshoe-shaped bronze frame is known from several graves at Birka, and was worn under the left shoulder, where it would have been concealed by the cloak. At Birka, purses of both types were often closed with a bronze button. Whilst purses, knives and other items were certainly worn suspended from a belt at the waist, they might often have been worn inside the shirt on the trouser belt, where they would not have been visible. An Anglo-Saxon riddle describes a key worn in this manner beneath the shirt.

This was not the case with the large decorative fighting knives which were found at Birka, and which might have been worn after the style of the carving from Middleton, England, slung horizontally across the front of the body (*89* on p130). Like other weapons, these large knives were not worn in the grave but were deposited alongside the body, probably indicating that they were not a part of everyday dress. Similarly, when a character puts on his sword in the sagas, it is often remarked on as significant. Travellers and warriors would, however, have carried weapons as a matter of course, while small decoratively inlaid axes, such as the Mammen axe, were probably badges of rank or favour rather than actual weapons; this seems to be the case with Síðu-Hallr's 'little axe' in *Njáls saga* ch.147, and a surviving haft indicates that the wood could be chosen more for its look than its strength; the axe sent by Eiríkr to Skalla-Grímr (*Egils saga* ch.38) may possibly have been larger, but was meant to serve a similar purpose.

The only forms of pendant worn round the neck by men appear to have been the Thórr's hammer and, later, the crucifix. Thórr's hammers seem to have been worn from at least the ninth century onwards, when one was buried with a fallen warrior at Repton, England. The Repton warrior wore his hammer between two unmatched beads, but strings of beads were not worn by men. Mostly, these amulets were probably hung on a lace of leather or textile, but sometimes they were suspended on elaborately plaited silver chains; the structure of these chains might reflect the nature of the textile laces which were used.

TATTOOING

Ibn Fadlan describes the Rus as decorated all over their bodies with dark lines, which he dismisses as un-Islamic representational art. In the warmer climate of southern Russia, the Rus might have had more chance to display their body art than would the Scandinavians, but tattooing was also used in eighth-century England, where it was deplored as a pagan custom by the legates of Pope Hadrian. Thus, although there is no direct literary evidence for tattooing within Scandinavia, since it was practiced by associated cultures to the east and west, and was regarded by the Christian Church as a pagan practice, it seems more likely than not that tattooing was also practised in Viking Scandinavia.

It has been plausibly suggested that the traditional sailors' tattoo representing a wreathed anchor is descended from an original representation of Thórr's Hammer.

HAIR AND BEARDS

One of the most enduring images of the Viking is of his unkempt long hair and bushy beard. But most of the evidence actually points towards shorn hair and neatly trimmed or even shaven beards. True, the Norwegian king Haraldr Hárfagr is reputed to have neither cut nor combed his hair until he had united the whole of Norway, but this was only noteworthy because it was at odds with usual customs. This behaviour appears to represent a traditional accessory to a vow, witness Tacitus' account of the warlike Chatti (*Germania*, ch31), whose young men, in accordance with a vow, would let their hair and beards grow unchecked until they had killed their first man; the same custom, according to Tacitus, was also practised by individuals of other Germanic nations. In *Jómsvikinga saga*, the captured Jómsvikingar apparently have hair long enough to cover their necks, but though the reason for this is not explicitly stated, they are collectively bound by a vow at the time of their defeat (ch.36–38). Similarly, according to *Völuspá*, the mythological figure Vali neither combed his hair nor washed his hands until he had avenged the death of Baldr (st.33).

The normal attitude of the Vikings to their hair is probably exemplified by the bone combs which are common finds in Viking archaeology, and were carried by both women and men. Ibn Fadlan describes how combing the hair was a daily ritual among the Rus, and combing is mentioned in both *Reginsmál* (st.25) and *Sigrdrífumál* (st.34).

86 Penannular brooch from Birka grave
BJ.1059. Scale 1:1

In a letter copied into Worcester MS Hatton 115 (*olim* Junius 23), an anonymous English writer rebuked his brother Edward for following Danish modes 'with bared necks and blinded eyes'; a very similar haircut is seen in carvings on the Oseberg wagon from the early ninth century, and is also worn by Normans on the Bayeux Tapestry. Afi too in *Rígsþula* st.15, wears his hair over his brows and his beard trimmed (*var skegg skapat, skör var fyr enni*). But this is a young man's haircut, and the *Liber Vitae* portrait of King Cnut shows him with his hair cut in a fashion compatible with a receding hairline (55). Longer hair is shown on a helmeted head carved in elk horn from Sigtuna, Sweden, whose straight hair is swept back over the ears towards the nape of the neck (*90*); Thorkell Hávi sports a similar hairstyle in the Eadui Psalter (*colour plate 13*), while both Thórr in *Þrymskviða* (st.1) and Jörmunrekk in *Hamðismál* (st.20) have hair long enough to shake. However, the very long, black hair worn by Brodir in *Njáls saga*, augments the picture of a dangerous and aberrant individual (ch.155).

Not all men wore beards. The back head posts of the Oseberg wagon wear a moustache but no beard, while the men on the body of the wagon, if they are bearded, wear beards so short as to be barely discernable. Nonetheless, most contemporary illustrations of Viking men do show beards, and the taunt directed towards the sons of Njáll, insinuating that they rub dung on their chins to grow beards, hints that the beard might have been seen by some as the mark of a man (*Njáls saga* ch.90).

Beards vary in style and length, but seem generally to have been neatly trimmed and shaped like Afi's in *Rígsþula*; one of Afi's grandsons is called 'Bound-beard' and another 'Jutting-beard' (*Bundinskeggi* and *Brattskegg*, *Rígsþula* st.24). Pointed beards

87 Dress pins.
A) *left:* ringed pin from Dublin, of a type commonly used in Scandinavia.
B) *centre:* an elaborate variation classified as a 'pseudo-penannular ring brooch' from Birka grave BJ.561.
C) *right:* bone pin from Trondheim, Norway. Scale 1:1

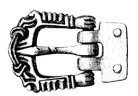

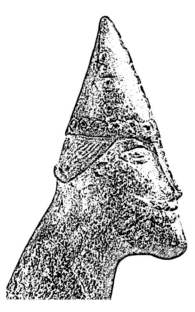

Above: 88 Buckle and strap end; belt fittings from the Gokstad burial. Scale 1:1

Far Left: 89 Carved figure from Middleton, England, wearing a long knife across his body and a pointed hat

Left: 90 Bearded head from Sigtuna, Sweden. His beard is neatly shaped and his hair combed back; Vikings probably rarely grew their hair longer than this

are particularly common in art, usually accompanied by a full moustache; one of the head posts from the Oseberg cart shows a more rounded style that might have been denoted by the term 'spade beard'. Sveinn 'Forkbeard' (*Tjugu-skegg*), of course, took his nickname from his forked beard, but it is hard to know if this was a common fashion. Al-Istakhri says that among the Rus, some beards are plaited like curried horse tails, perhaps like *Rígsþula*'s 'Bound-beard', but he also notes that some men are clean-shaven. Some men of course will have worn longer bushier beards, and *Egils saga* has a character known as Ármóðr 'Beard' (*Skegg*), whose beard is long enough for Egill to grab and cut off with his sword (ch.72). No doubt, the beard worn by Thórólfr 'Beard of Mostr' (*Mostrar-skeggi*), the patriarch of *Eyrbyggja saga*, was at least as impressive.

3

CLOTH AND CLOTHMAKING

In the Viking Age, ordinary people made not only their own clothes, but also their own cloth. Even away from the fields which supplied the wool and the flax, city dwellers were spinning and weaving cloth for themselves. Not all homespun cloth was meant for clothing of course, and professionally woven cloth was available for finer clothes, but most Viking-age Scandinavians dressed in cloth that was woven in Scandinavia from locally grown raw materials, either linen or wool. The same general types of fabric are found throughout Scandinavia, and these are often different from those of the rest of Europe.

TEXTILE FIBRES

Linen

Pliny believed that linen first came to the Germanic peoples in Roman times (*Historia Naturalis*, Book 19 Part 1 ch.2) and this appears to hold true for Scandinavia at least. Although they had been known in Europe from the Neolithic onwards, linen textiles are unknown in the Scandinavian archaeological record before the Roman Iron Age, and appear only rarely until the Vendel period (AD 600-800). But by Viking times, linen cloth had become common. Linen is made from the fibres of the flax plant (*Linum usitatissimum*); other plant fibres can also be used in clothmaking, notably nettle and hemp, but where tests have been possible, plant fibres from Viking-era textiles have proved to be from flax.

Flax fibres come from the stem of the plant, between the pith and the skin. To turn these fibres into linen yarn involves a series of processes with its own distinctive terminology. The plants must first be harvested before the seeds ripen and are 'rippled' to remove the seedpods. The flax is then 'retted', either in shallow water or by exposure to rain and dewfall; during retting, the plant begins to decompose, loosening the fibres but not rotting them. Bunches of flax stems were found in some of the many wells at Næs, Denmark, a site of large-scale linen production, suggesting that these wells were used for retting; the wells were positioned well away from the settlement because of the stench of retting flax.

The retted flax must be dried and then beaten or 'beetled'. At Næs, several rectangular ditches and pits with large amounts of charcoal and fired stones were probably used for drying flax; wooden 'beetles' used for pounding the flax are not uncommon in the archaeological record and they show distinctive wear patterns (*91*). After beetling, the stems are 'scutched' against a vertical board with a wooden scutching blade; the blade strikes the stems to remove unwanted matter or 'shives' from the fibres. Scutching knives have been identified among finds from Viking York and Hedeby, and shives have been found at York. The fibres are now free of the stems, and are ready for 'heckling', when they are drawn through successively finer 'heckles', rows of iron teeth set into wooden blocks. Drawing them through these heckles separates the individual fibres and aligns them together ready for spinning; it also removes any last fragments of the woody core.

Wool

A sheep's fleece has a longer hairy layer and a softer under layer, and different breeds produce different proportions and qualities of these two basic wool types. The type of fleece used is of utmost importance for the nature and quality of the finished cloth. Wool from Viking textiles is normally classified according to Ryder's fleece types as 'hairy' or 'hairy medium'. Wool was presumably sorted before it was used, but surviving textiles can give a general impression of the sort of fleeces available in Viking Scandinavia; similar hairy fleeces are still produced by Icelandic sheep today and by British mountain breeds. 'Medium', and 'generalised medium' wool was also used, and 'shortwool' was used for the softest cloths.

The fleece might often have been washed while still on the animal's back. The sheep are driven into a pool filled with lye (an alkaline solution of wood ash) or lant (stale urine), which is worked well into the fleece to remove the accumulated dirt and rubbish from the wool. A few weeks later, enough of the natural grease or 'yolk' has returned to the wool for it to be easily worked and shorn. Wool could be shorn with a knife or shears, but was also 'rooed' or plucked from the sheep in June, or was pulled from the hides of slaughtered animals. Wool destined to be used in sea gear would have been treated with oils and fats to make it water repellent.

Wool can be spun straight from the staple, but wool combs can be used to disentangle and fluff up the raw wool for easier spinning. A new form of comb, with long handles at right angles to its teeth had appeared in Scandinavia during the Vendel period, and these could have been used to align the long staple wool fibres together in 'roves'. The new combs have been associated with the appearance of a new, hard, glossy cloth known as 'Birka type', made from a smooth yarn in which the fibres lie very even and parallel. A good deal of Viking-age woollen cloth uses yarn that falls between the two extremes of carefully combed smooth yarns and uncombed soft and bulky yarns. Fragmentary wool combs with 18 to 30 iron teeth, each 4-5in (10-13cm) long, have been found from Viking Norway and Anglo-Scandinavian York, while an almost intact example, complete with a 7in (17.5cm) lime-wood handle, was discovered at Fyrkat, Denmark. Wool combs are mentioned in *Grettis saga*, *Flateyjarbók*, in Carolingian capitularies and in the Old English *Gerefa* (Cambridge MS Corpus Christi 383). Wool cards were unknown in the Viking Age.

SPINNING

Before spinning, the fibre from the fleece or flax is often bound or dressed on a 'distaff', also called a 'rock' (ON *rokkr*). A surviving distaff from Viking York is made as a square-sectioned rod, about ½in (1.25cm) in cross section, tapering at both ends; it is incomplete but the surviving part is over 1ft (30cm) long, and the original length was probably not very much more than this; the top 8in (20cm) is roughly notched to keep the fibre in place. A complete example from Hedeby measures 14½in (37cm), while those from Oseberg are 13in (34cm) and 15in (38.5cm) long (*91*). The simplest form of distaff is a forked stick, and distaffs of this type may also have been used; the distaff used in *Rígsþula* st.16 seems to have been a switch of bendy wood.

Sat þar kona, sveigði rokk, breiddi faðm, bjó til váðar

A woman sat there, bent her distaff, stretched out her arms, ready to make woollen cloth

Spinning in the Viking Age was done with the spindle, a short, slender length of wood to which the yarn was attached; the turning of the spindle twists the fibres into a single yarn (*91*). Nearly complete spindles from Viking York were probably about 7in (18cm) long, and ⅜in (1cm) at their thickest point, but there are fragments of heavier spindles of over ½in (1.4cm) diameter; these were made of oak, ash or yew. Twenty-three complete spindles from Hedeby measured between 4-8½in (10-21.5cm) long and were mostly ¼-⅜in (about 0.5-1cm) thick. Where the wood could be identified, three quarters of the Hedeby spindles were made of yew. A particularly long yew-wood spindle from Ribe, Denmark measures 12in (30cm).

Spindles were weighted with a whorl, which acted as a plumb bob and flywheel, its weight helping to develop speed and allowing the spindle to spin for longer. Spindles from Hedeby showed the marks of the whorl about 1½in (4cm) from the tip. Spindle whorls were made of lead, glass, soapstone, potsherds, amber, bone and antler. At Birka, half were of stone, and a third were ceramic, but proportions vary from site to site according to local conditions. They could weigh anything up to 3½oz (100g), with most in the region of ⅜-1½oz (10-40g). Generally, the lighter the whorl, the finer the yarn and the shorter the fibres that can be spun, but a great deal depends upon the skill of the spinster and the technique she is using. In skilled hands, a heavy whorl might spin relatively fine yarn, but a light whorl cannot readily spin coarse yarn, so it is significant that some of the whorls from high-status centres such as Birka and Hedeby can weigh as little as ¼oz (5g), indicating the production of very fine fabrics at these sites.

In drop spinning, the spindle is set spinning by a brisk twist between the fingers of the right hand and then dropped; the right hand can then draw out more wool or flax from the distaff (which is held in the crook of the left arm or by the thumb of the left hand) occasionally giving the spindle another twist to keep it spinning. When the spindle reaches the ground, the spun yarn is wound up around the spindle shank, and the end nearest the unspun fibre is caught in the notch for the spinning to begin again.

This technique gives the yarn a clockwise twist, and this is referred to as Z-spun yarn, as opposed to S-spun yarn which has an anticlockwise twist (92). Linen from Northern Europe was always made with Z-spun yarn, but woollen twills sometimes used a combination of Z-spun warp with an S-spun weft. Penelope Walton Rogers has suggested that S-spun yarn might have been hip-spun, whereby the spindle is rolled along the right thigh and off the knee. The different spinning techniques used for warp and weft are associated with different grades of wool; Norse warp threads are hard-spun from combed fibres, and hip spinning might be better suited to making the softer bulkier yarns that were sometimes chosen for the weft. In modern traditions, drop spinners tend to use a spindle with the whorl at the bottom of the spindle, while hip spinners prefer the whorl at the top; spindles from Viking York are notched for yarn at both ends, allowing them to be used either way. But S-spun yarn can also be drop-spun by twisting the spindle with the left hand, or with the right hand by flicking the thumb backwards against the fingers.

Occasionally, two or more yarns were plied together, as in modern knitting yarn or string. Usually, the twist given to the ply is opposite to the twist of the individual spun yarn, so that two Z-spun yarns might be S-plied together (92).

The Oseberg find included two reels and a swift. Reels were used to wind the yarn into hanks or skeins for storage. The reels from Oseberg (93) are of the kind sometimes called a 'niddy noddy', with down-curved arms set on a 16in (40cm) bar. The wool is wound from corner to corner, and the bent arms allow it to be easily slipped off when the skein is fully wound. Simpler stick reels, consisting of a stick with a twig at each end might also have been used. Yarn can more simply be wound into balls of wool (and balls of yarn have been found in excavations at Århus Søndervold), but winding into hanks of a set length allows for the yarn to be washed and dyed and for ready calculations of both quality and quantity. When needed, a hank would be placed on the rotating swift, from which it could easily be unwound; it could then be rewound into a ball ready for use.

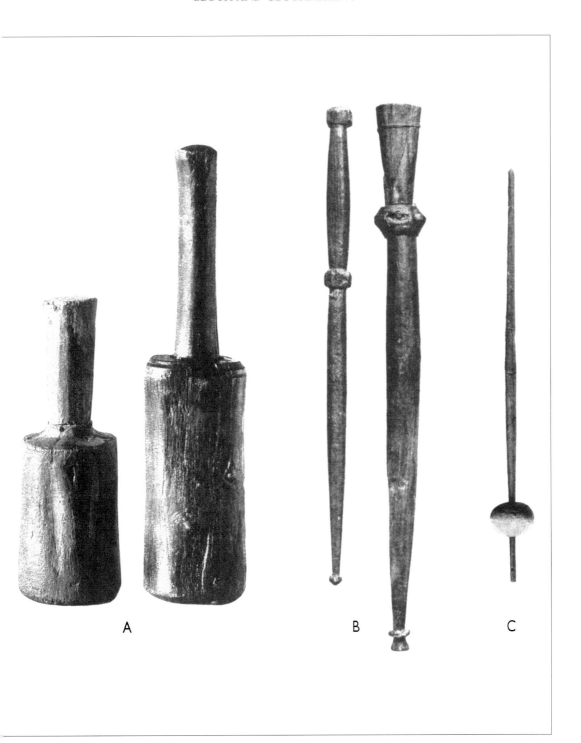

A   B   C

91 Beech wood tools for clothmaking from the Oseberg burial. A) Two beetles. Length 8½in (21.5cm), 12½in (32cm). B) Two distaffs. Length 13½in (34cm), 15in (38.5cm). C) Spindle. Length 11½in (29.5cm). *Shetelig 1920*

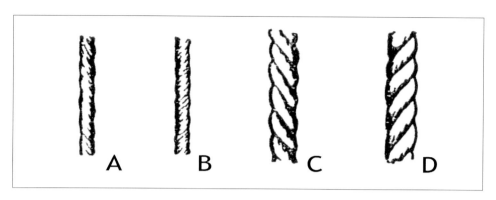

92 Yarns. A) S-spun. B) Z-spun. C) S-plied. D) Z-plied. *Geijer 1938*

93 Reel of beech wood from the Oseberg burial. 17 x 17in (43 x 43cm). *Shetelig 1920*

LOOMS AND WEAVING

The spun yarn could then be woven into cloth. The loom usually associated with Viking weaving is the warp-weighted loom. On this loom, the warp threads (those which run lengthways through the cloth) are hung from a moveable 'cloth beam', set across two uprights. At the bottom of the loom, the warp threads are tied to rows of weights to keep them taut. These loom weights, which were generally ring-shaped and made of pottery or stone, are the only part of the loom which generally survives as archaeological evidence. They are sometimes found still lying in rows, where a loom has been abandoned during weaving.

Loom weights from Birka are typically 4–5½in (11–14cm) in diameter, and 1–1¾in (2.5–4.5cm) thick. They weigh between 8oz and 4lb (200–1800g), with most in the range of 1–2lb (400–800g). Weights from the early Viking Age tend to be in the 8oz–1lb (200–500g) range, but in the later Viking period a number are found weighing about 1lb 12oz to 2lb (800–900g) and Andersson suggests that these heavier weights were used for linen.

The loom rests against a wall, so that the uprights are at a natural angle to the freely-hanging warp (94). Near the bottom of the loom is a fixed crossbar, called the 'shed rod'. It opens a 'shed' between the warp threads, with alternate warp threads either passing over the shed rod in line with the uprights, or hanging freely behind. Each set of threads is fastened to a different set of loom weights, and decorative markings on the weights might have been used to tell them apart. A moveable 'heddle rod' runs across the loom, resting on brackets fixed to the two uprights at chest height, and the freely-hanging warp threads are tied to this by long loops or 'heddles'. When the heddle rod is pulled out, the warp from the back of the loom is pulled to the front, while the warp on the shed rod stays put. This opens another shed between the warp threads.

Weaving on the warp-weighted loom typically takes two weavers, one standing at each side of the loom. One weaver passes the weft yarn through the open shed between the warp threads to the weaver on the other side, and then they move the heddle rod to open another shed before passing the weft back. As the weaving continues, the weft passes to and fro through alternate sheds as the heddle rod moves back and forth. Thus, the weft passes first behind one set of warp threads and in front of the other, then in front of the first and behind the other. More complicated weaves are made possible by using more heddle rods.

Every so often, the weft is beaten up against the edge of the woven cloth with a weaving sword about 30in (80cm) long, examples of which have been found from Viking sites in Norway and England. Pin beaters are also known from Viking archaeology; these unremarkable-looking little tools are 3–6in (8–16cm) long, and can be used for a variety of tasks, such as evening out warp spacing, picking out misplaced threads, and pushing the weft loosely into position before using the weaving sword, or 'playing the strings of the warp' as Moroccan weavers do today. Pin beaters associated with the warp-weighted loom are tapered at both ends or 'double-headed'.

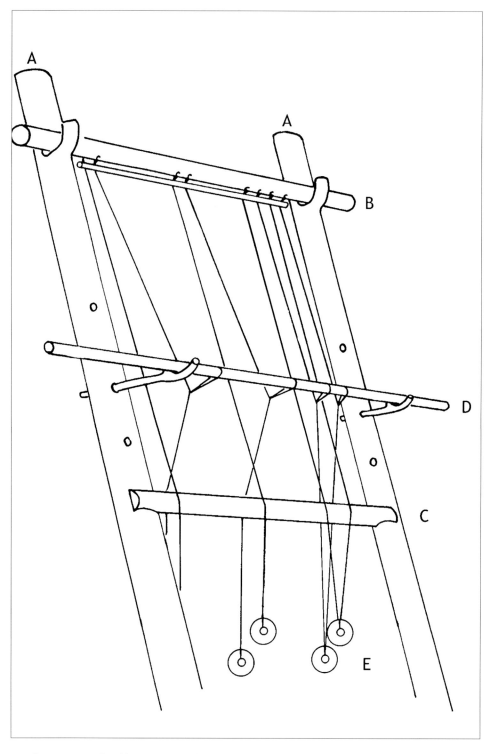

94 The warp-weighted loom: A uprights; B cloth beam; C shed rod; D heddle rod; E weights

As the weaving progresses, the finished part of the cloth can be wound up onto the cloth beam. Because the warp threads are attached to the weights only indirectly, the length of the warp can be greater than the distance from the cloth beam and the ground. Long lengths could be woven on these looms; the Icelandic lawspeaker received 240 ells of cloth, and a standard length of cloth in medieval Iceland was the *spytingr* of 60 ells, which was 90ft (27m) long. The weaving process as described here is given a Gothic twist in the poem *Darraðarljóð*, where valkyries work a warp-weighted loom with spears for heddle rods, guts for the warp, and human heads for the loom weights.

Also probably in use in Viking and Iron Age Scandinavia, was the freestanding two-beam loom. This loom is in many respects very similar to the warp-weighted loom, but the tension comes from a second beam at the bottom of the loom (95). The warp threads can go right round the loom, back and front, each being tied at both ends to a single rod or cord. The cloth is woven as a tube, but if the cord is withdrawn, the tube opens out into a rectangle, which can be used for other garments. Tubular-woven garments from Roman-era Denmark may well have been woven on this type of loom. After the fourth century, the Scandinavian tubular loom seems to have been neglected in favour of the warp-weighted loom. Though it might not have entirely fallen out of use, possibly surviving as a tapestry loom, evidence for the two-beam loom only reappears in the tenth century. Long lengths of cloth cannot be woven on the tubular two-beam loom, but in a more sophisticated variant, instead of weaving a tube around the loom, the lower beam acts as a turnable cloth beam, and longer lengths of woven cloth can be wound onto it.

Whereas cloth on the warp-weighted loom is woven from the top downwards, on the two-beam loom it is woven from the bottom upwards with the weaver sitting down. Different techniques mean that this loom is associated with a new weaving tool – the single-headed pin beater. These appear in urban archaeology of the tenth century, and at about the same time, loom weights begin to become less common in urban contexts. Weaving combs, used to beat down the weft, are also associated with the two-beam vertical loom, and have been found at Oseberg, Birka and elsewhere.

It is not known which type of two-beam loom may have been used in late Viking Scandinavia. A wooden structure from the ninth-century Oseberg burial has been identified as a small tubular two-beam loom, used to weave tapestries similar to those found in the same burial, but a row of holes along the lower part of the uprights suggests an alternative use as a braiding frame for making 'sprang' (see below); perhaps it was a multipurpose tool which could be used either for tapestries or sprang.

In the eleventh century or possibly earlier, weaving was becoming organised as an industry in urban centres across Europe, and the new craftsman weavers used a horizontal loom, probably a treadle loom. The horizontal treadle loom is very much faster than the vertical looms, but it is also very much more bulky and complicated. It relies on treadles which are linked via pulleys to heddle rods, opening and closing

95 Weaving on the two-beam loom and drop-spinning as practiced in the Viking Age, from an eleventh-century Italian manuscript. The weaver is apparently sitting on the floor behind her loom. The manuscript is the earliest illustrated copy of Hrabanus Maurus's *De Rerum Naturis*, dated (in a colophon) to 1023. *Montecassino MS 132*

sheds in the warp. Early archaeological evidence for this loom type comes from eleventh-century Hedeby, York, Opole and Gdansk. A contemporary description of the loom describes it in use by men working it with their feet; almost all evidence for the use of simpler loom types suggests that they were used by women in the domestic environment (although, curiously, there are instances of weaving swords recovered from men's graves in Norway). The new loom could weave very even and dense cloth with surprising speed. However, early horizontal looms were narrow, limited in width to the reach of the single weaver. The appearance of men at the loom might suggest that the faster horizontal looms had made large-scale cloth production truly commercially viable for the first time.

TYPES OF WEAVE, KINDS OF CLOTH

Textiles typical of Scandinavian dress in the Viking period are: fine tabby weaves with a high thread count in the warp; fine wool twills with Z-spun yarn; and heavy woollens with a woven pile. However, the proportions in which these cloth types are found varies from region to region, with tabbies, for instance, being rare on the island of Gotland (96). For a detailed country-by-country guide to the textiles of Viking Scandinavia, including a descriptive catalogue of several hundred textile fragments, see Lise Bender Jørgensen's *Forhistoriske Textiler i Skandinavien: Prehistoric Scandinavian Textiles* (1986).

Region	Tabby and repp 'including linen'	Plain twills (²/₁ and ²/₂)	Reversed twills	Sample size
Denmark	81%	14%	5%	229
Sweden*	66%	24%	10%	139
SE Norway**	56%	34%	10%	(73)
W Norway**	40%	30%	30%	(276)
Gotland	6%	79%	14%	34
Birka graves	62%	9%	29%	173
Hedeby graves	84%	12%	5%	86

96 Proportions of Viking-age cloth types found in graves from different parts of the Viking world. Figures based on Jørgensen 1986, except Birka (Geijer 1938) and Hedeby (Hägg 1991). Sample sizes (except Norway**) represent total numbers of twills and tabbies known in 1986; textile impressions from jewellery are disregarded. * Excluding Gotland and Birka ** Based on a notional sample size. In the absence of regional figures, the total count of textiles of each type for all Norway was divided in proportion to the number of graves per region containing that type of textile; percentages were calculated from these hypothetical figures

In describing cloth types, it is useful to note the density of the weave, which is conventionally measured by the number of threads to a centimetre; where warp and weft are different, the count for the warp is given first. Most Scandinavian cloth of the Viking Age has a thread count of 8-20 per cm, though considerably finer fabrics have also been found.

Tabbies

The simplest form of woven cloth is known as 'plain weave' or 'tabby'. The weft passes over one warp thread and under the next and so on, the returning weft passing under the warps which the first weft passed over, and over those it had passed under.

In the Viking Age, as today, plain tabby was the weave for almost all linens, using Z-spun yarn in both warp and weft (Z/Z; *colour plate 3*). Linen tabby is one of the most common cloth types of Viking-age Scandinavia, though it was less popular in western Norway. It can vary in quality from as few as 5 up to as many as 26 threads per cm or even finer; a linen tabby from the Viking grave at Balladoole, Isle of Man, had a thread count of 28 x 32 threads per cm, and a similarly fine piece comes from Viking York. However, linen used in shirts is mostly of 12-20 threads per cm. A particularly interesting find from York was the burnt remains of a linen patchwork, which shunned the more usual tabby weave in favour of pieces in a variety of twills, including a distinctive honeycomb-patterned twill with floating wefts.

Whilst the finest and fanciest weaves are of especial interest, illustrating both the skill of the weaver and the wealth of the wearer, it should not be forgotten that a great number of linens were simple hardwearing workaday cloths. Different qualities of linen cloth appear to have been indicated by the words *hörr*, *ripti* and *lín*, of which *hörr* is probably the poorest and *lín* the finest, but the exact distinction is now unknown.

Linen was less popular in Sweden and Norway, especially western Norway, than in Denmark, probably due to the harsher climates; on the island of Gotland it was virtually unknown. In the eleventh century, Adam of Bremen noted that the Norwegians, unlike the Swedes and the Danes, relied solely on their flocks for their clothing.

Woollen tabby ranges from 2 to 20 threads per cm. The coarsest woollen tabbies, sometimes woven with plied yarns, are likely to have been used as rough cloth for wrapping and covering objects rather than as clothing; very few such coarse tabbies have been excavated from graves, though they are not uncommon from settlement sites. The finest tabby for clothing commonly has 18-20 threads per cm in the warp against 12-14 per cm in the weft. But far coarser cloth was also used; for instance, Fragment 73 from Hedeby (clearly the shoulder of a shirt, *57*) has just 5-7 x 4-5 threads per cm.

Repp is a variant of tabby, where one system, warp or weft, is much more closely spaced than the other. Although uncommon in Denmark, in Sweden and Norway one in five of all tabbies is repp, which might account for a good deal of all woollen tabbies. Viking repp is typically a fine-quality cloth with a thread count of 20-33 x 10-19 per cm, up to 40 x 22. A piece of fine Z/Z repp from Gokstad, Norway, has a count of 26 x 5 per cm.

Fine woollen tabby and repp are among the distinctively Scandinavian textiles of the age. Eleven pieces of tabby and repp (mostly Z/Z) from Birka have counts ranging from 14 x 11 to 24 x 12 per cm. These strong, fine fabrics use combed shortwool yarn and are often dyed blue. They were sometimes used as linings and bindings, as at Birka, where one seems to have been lined a garment of diamond twill. This cloth type is also known from pre-Viking Ireland, where it might have originated.

Twills

If cloth is woven so that the weft passes over the warp threads two at a time, and the next line of weft returns across pairs of warp threads that are offset by only one thread, a noticeable diagonal pattern emerges. This kind of weave is called 'twill' (97). If the weft goes over two warp threads and under the next two, it is a 2/2 twill; if it goes over two and only under one it is a 2/1 twill. Both types of twill are found in Viking-age textiles, but 2/2 twill is very much more common, and in the early period 2/1 twills are unknown.

2/2 Z/S (with a Z-spun warp and an S-spun weft) twills are known all over Viking Scandinavia. The hard-spun warp is usually fairly fine, with a thread count of 8–18 per cm. The weft tends to be bulkier and the thread count is correspondingly lower at about 6-12 per cm. But the finest 2/2 twills can have as many as 24 threads by 16 per cm.

The appearance of 2/1 twills in the tenth century appears to coincide with the introduction of the two-beam loom. The thread count in 2/1 plain twill ranges from 10 x 6 per cm to 40 x 20 per cm, but this type of cloth remains relatively uncommon.

Veka twill and Gotland twill

Distinctive 2/2 plain twills from Gotland and Norway are woven with Z-spun yarn in both warp and weft. Gotland twill is well balanced, with equally hard-spun yarn for both warp and weft. It dominates the cloth of the island, and linen here is almost unknown. Gotland twill is mainly Z/Z, 12-15 x 10-14 per cm.

Norway's Z/Z plain 2/2 twill is quite different from the Gotland type, and is known as Veka type. This weaving tradition stretches back before the beginning of the Viking Age, and combines two types of fleece, the warp being of medium wool, with hairy medium in the weft; the warp is also harder spun than the weft. The warp is sometimes dyed blue with the weft left undyed, giving a striking blue diagonal effect.

Reversed twills

Both 2/2 and 2/1 twills were woven into patterns by regularly reversing the direction of the diagonal to make 'zigzag twill' (also called 'chevron twill' and 'herringbone twill') and 'diamond' (or 'lozenge') twill (97). These patterned twills can be grouped together as 'reversed twills', distinguished from plain or 'non-reversed' twills. In 2/2 reversed twills, the return diagonal is typically offset and the pattern can be called

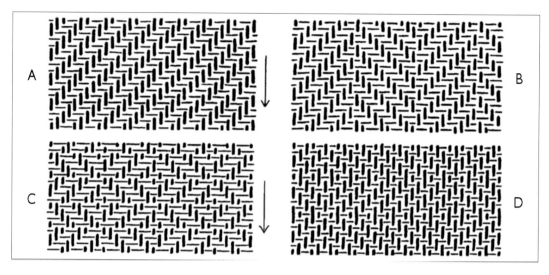

97 Diagram of major weaves used in Viking cloth. A) 2/2 twill. B) 2/2 zigzag twill. C) 2/2
diamond twill. D) 2/1 diamond twill. *After Geijer 1938*

'broken zigzag' or 'broken diamond twill'. Smooth-combed wool was generally
used for diamond twills, but zigzag twill could sometimes have a distinctly tweedy
look. 'Cross twill' or *Kreuzköper*, is technically a form of broken zigzag twill, but the
twill diagonal reverses so rapidly (after just two threads) that no clear pattern can
be seen.

2/2 zigzag twill can vary considerably from the thick and tweedy to the fine and
light, with a range of thread counts between 5 and 18 per cm. The better-quality
cloth is made from combed shortwool Z-spun yarn; a piece of zigzag twill from
Kaupang at the finer end of the scale had a count of 18-20 x 10 threads per cm. But
zigzag twill was considerably less popular than diamond twill.

Birka type

The finest woollen cloth in the Viking world was a variety of Z/Z diamond twill,
which appears in Scandinavia during the Vendel period. They were first noticed at
Birka, where there were some 40 surviving pieces, and are thus commonly called 'Birka
type'. These sophisticated wool twills are wonderfully light and fine, with a hard, glossy
finish. They were clearly luxury cloth, and commonly have 20-46 threads per cm in the
warp against 9-16 per cm in the weft; some specimens are considerably finer.

The Birka type is distinctively Scandinavian, being found almost only in the high-
status burials of the great Scandinavian trading centres and of western Norway. The
best are finer than the diamond twills of Western Europe, which are distinguished
by their S-spun weft. Outside Scandinavia, the Birka type is more-or-less limited
to occasional stray finds in areas of Viking dominance such as Dublin York and
Orkney.

Although it is generally the finest examples that have attracted the most attention (some of which have thread counts of up to 60 per cm), outside the major trading centres and the high-status Norwegian burials, the thread count is generally 18-36 x 10-20 per cm. A typical coarser example might have a warp of about 24 per cm and a weft at 12-16, but this is still a fine cloth.

A good deal of debate has focussed on where Birka-type cloth was woven. The old suggestion that Z/Z twills were the Frisian cloth known in Latin sources as *pallia fresonica* is no longer credible since they are in fact rare in Frisian areas, where the Z/S variety dominates; neither are they likely to have been traded through Russia from the Near East, since Staraya Ladoga, a major trading centre on this route, also favoured Z/S-woven fine twills. It now seems most likely that the Birka type was woven within Scandinavia. Some scholars have sought to define a single area within Scandinavia as the source of this cloth. Anne Stine Ingstad believed it might have been woven on the Baltic coast, but Lise Bender Jørgensen sees the Birka type as probably originating in western Norway alongside the coarser Veka type which is also Z-spun in both warp and weft.

Tenth-century Birka saw the advent of a yet finer woollen cloth in 2/1 diamond twill. This typically has 24-34 x 12-17 threads per cm, but the warp could be as close as 60 threads per cm. It is rare even at Birka, where it is known from nine examples, and is scarcely known elsewhere.

Piled cloth

Viking piled fabrics from Kildonan, Isle of Eigg (AD 850-900), from Jurby, Isle of Man (*c*.AD 900), from Lund, Sweden (eleventh century) from Heynes, Iceland (tenth century), and from Volynia, Ukraine (ninth century), all appear to have had a pile worked into the cloth during weaving. Those from Birka have proved too fragile for analysis. The basic weave is fairly coarse and open, allowing yarn to be tied in as a pile. The ground weave can be tabby or twill, and the pile either spun or unspun.

Viking York has yielded four piled fabrics, but they all use a different technique, whereby the yarn is darned into the already-woven cloth; perhaps these were local products imitating the Scandinavian fashion. Two fragments of a similar darned-pile fabric were found in the Viking burial at Cronk Moar, Isle of Man, where there was also a fragment of woven-pile fabric.

Piled fabrics could be used for coverlets and rugs, but were also used as cloaks. For Iceland, these shaggy cloaks were an important trade item, which are loosely regulated in early sections of *Grágás*, the earliest written Icelandic law code. Pile-woven cloth was often dyed; at least one example from York was dyed with madder, and one of the Birka examples is worked in a combination of red and blue dyed yarns. An example from Dublin has a natural dark-brown pile and weft, woven against a red warp. The reddish violet 'cloak' donated by Earl Godwin's daughter Gunnhild to the Cathedral of St Donaas in Bruges can still be seen (though it is now in the neighbouring Cathedral of St Salvator), but as it measures just 21 x 25in (54.5 x 64 cm), it is hardly a cloak.

According to *Grágás,* pile-woven cloaks could be undyed grey, white or black, or dyed red or blue; they could be plain or striped, and could be decorated with bands. It is possible that the dyed fleece from York was intended for use as the pile of such a cloak rather than for weaving.

Wadmal

Early literary sources repeatedly mention a cloth called *vaðmál* or 'wadmal'. For medieval Iceland, wadmal was a staple export, and a succession of laws regulate its production; the earliest surviving regulations are thought to date from the eleventh century and are preserved in the law code *Grágás.* Trade documents from medieval Britain testify to the import of this cloth from Iceland.

Based on these medieval descriptions, and on distribution of excavated cloth types, Penelope Walton Rogers and Else Østergaard have been able to identify a particular kind of cloth known to archaeology as a likely candidate for the historical label 'wadmal'. This is an undyed cloth, using a smooth natural brown warp against a pale soft and matted weft. The cloth has a soft matty texture as a result of fulling, a process whereby the cloth is 'waulked' or trodden underfoot in warm water or lant (stale urine); the cloth shrinks and thickens, becoming an impenetrable mat of felted fibres, which gives excellent protection against wind and rain.

Saga characters are sometimes described as dressed in wadmal clothing, and it is natural to envisage them dressed in cloth similar to that described here. However, though common in the later Middle Ages, this type of cloth is not at all common from Viking-era sites. The sagas were written long after close of the Viking Age, and whilst it is probable that the word *vaðmál* was in use during the Viking Age, it is not at all certain that it was originally applied to a specific type of cloth.

In the earliest legal reference, in *Grágás, vaðmál* is simply defined as a 2/2 twill woven to a width of 36in (90cm). Since 2/2 twill was the standard woollen cloth of the age, this regulation imposes no more than a standard width. The word *vaðmál* means simply 'cloth measure', and the regulations in *Grágás* are solely concerned with its measurement. Similarly vague are the rules on the production of piled fabrics; these are readily identifiable in the archaeological record, but analysis of surviving fragments suggests that there was no standard-isation beyond that specified in law. Although *Grágás* also sets a legal price for *varar-vaðmál* ('tradable measured cloth'), there might in reality have been some variation in the market price according to the merits of the cloth to be traded; a fixed legal value was necessary, since cloth could be used as an alternative to silver in compensation payments, and was used to pay the lawspeaker's salary of 240 ells.

So, in the earliest sources, the term *vaðmál* probably does not describe a type of cloth at all, but might simply refer to cloth woven to standard measure.

TABLET WEAVING

Groups of thin flat tablets of wood, bone or horn were used to make decorative braids. The square tablets were all pierced in each corner with a small hole, and the warp threads passed through the holes, with separate threads passing through each corner of every tablet (*98*). As the tablets are turned, a quarter turn at a time, so the warp threads in each tablet are twisted into parallel cords. The weft, which will be hidden in the finished braid, passes between the twisted warp threads, locking the twist in. By carefully varying how the tablets are threaded and turned, a skilled tablet weaver can make quite beautiful patterned braids.

Weaving tablets have been found in excavations at Lund, Birka, York and elsewhere, and range from about 1–2in square (2.5–5cm). The Oseberg queen was buried with a partly completed tablet weaving, containing 52 tablets; she had clearly been working on this before she died. More than any other single find, the half-finished braid in particular reveals a real interest in textile arts that may have been typical among women of her class; managing 52 tablets takes a good deal of skill and experience.

Braids and tapestries were probably the textile arts particularly favoured by the rich; it is doubtful that the Oseberg queen would have put her hand to ordinary weaving (she was buried without the tools for it), and it may be that ordinary women would have been equally unfamiliar with tapestry and braiding. I am not aware of evidence for the use of tablet weaving outside high-status contexts in Viking-age Scandinavia, and surviving bands often include threads of silk and precious metal.

Tablet weaving in gold and silk found in the graves of Birka was probably imported from the Byzantine world, but similar and even finer pieces, such as those from Dublin or Mammen, may also have been made in Scandinavian or Western European contexts. But the notion of gold braids as an exotic luxury is perhaps preserved in *Guðrúnarkviða II* st.26, where they are woven by Hunnish maidens.

Tablet-woven bands were used to decorate shirts, hats and caftans, and one could also apparently be worn as a simple fillet round the head. In earlier periods, they seem to have been mainly used to decorate the edges of garments, and their position in the grave can be used to determine the end of a sleeve or the hem of a shirt, but in the Viking period, tablet weaving can be used to decorate the body of a garment, as in the illustration of the English King Æthelstan in Cambridge MS Corpus Christi 183 (*colour plate 14*) or the illustration of Thorkell Hávi in the Eadui Psalter (*colour plate 13*); this is perhaps most clearly demonstrated in an archaeological context in Birka grave BJ.958, where a tablet-woven band crosses the chest as it does in these manuscript illustrations. These braids probably cover a horizontal seam, which secures the lining of the garment below the neck opening in the same way that it is secured by diagonal seams on the shirt from Viborg (*50, 51*).

A tablet-woven braid could be used as a 'starting border' on the warp-weighted loom, the weft of the braid becoming the warp of the loom, but no examples from Viking Scandinavia have come to light.

98 Braiding tablets from the Oseberg
burial. 1¾ x 1¾in (4.3 x 4.3cm).
Shetelig 1920

SPRANG

In the tomb of the Oseberg queen was a frame which might have been used for making sprang (99). This frame is made of beech, and is just under 4ft (47in, 119cm) high, a little more than 2ft (26in, 66cm) wide at the top and a little less than 3ft (34in, 86cm) at the bottom. A row of holes runs down the lower length of the uprights, so the lower beam can be moved up during braiding, as the warp gets tighter. The Oseberg frame has also been interpreted as a two-beam tapestry loom, and it is possible that it was actually designed as a multipurpose tool.

In making sprang, a warp is laid by winding a single thread repeatedly around the top and bottom beams. The threads are first plaited together two-by-two with the fingers, and the plait is locked by weaving two sticks between the threads. The sticks and plaits are pushed to top and bottom, leaving unplaited warp between them. The process is repeated until two areas of netlike fabric are gradually built up at the top and bottom of the frame. Because the threads are fixed top and bottom, a symmetrical pattern is produced. By working according to set patterns, more elaborate designs can be worked into the mesh.

Most Viking sprang was probably made in linen which rarely survives in the archaeological record. In the sixteenth century, Olaus Magnus noted that the Scandinavian women devoted their efforts to 'the whitest netting which they call "*spraangning*"' (*candidissimo … retiario quod spraangning vocant*, Bk13 ch48), which they used for decorative hangings and fine women's clothing. A 5in-wide (13cm-wide) sprang in S-spun silk from Dublin may well have been woven in a Norse context from imported yarn, though sprang is also known from the early medieval Mediterranean.

It is not certain what sprang was used for in the Viking world, but it forms an elastic net which has been used at various times for stockings and snoods.

TAPESTRY

Tapestry was not, so far as is known, woven for clothing in the Viking world, but deserves mention here as it was the other decorative textile art apparently pursued by the Oseberg queen. Several pieces of tapestry were found buried with her in the mound (17, 54), and it is likely that they were woven by her, perhaps with the assistance of the woman buried alongside her. In the medieval Icelandic poem *Guðrúnarkviða II*, in which the legendary princess Guðrún is imagined in the company of another princess, the royal women weave tapestries together, including scenes from Guðrún's own life; the cycle of legends of which Guðrún is a part was a subject for real tapestries in the Viking Age. Tapestries have been found in royal graves from the Vendel period at Valsgärde, Sweden, and on the island of Karmøy, Norway. The cemetery at Birka included two fragmentary pieces of tapestry, while examples from Skog and Överhogdal, Sweden, probably represent the art as it was practised at the close of the Viking Age.

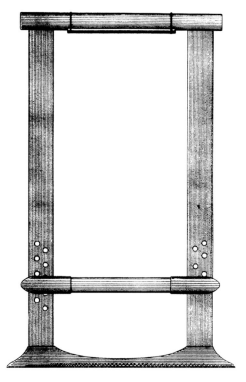

99 Wooden frames for textile work
from the Oseberg burial.
A) *above:* a frame for tablet weaving.
B) *left:* this frame could have been
used for making either sprang or
tapestries. *Shetelig 1920*

The tapestries from Skog and Överhogdal were woven as linen strips just under 14in (35cm) wide. To make the pattern, coloured yarns of wool are wrapped around the warp threads during weaving; this technique is called 'soumak'. The Oseberg tapestries are narrower at 6-9in (16-23cm) wide and use soumak only to outline the figures, which are filled in with coloured brocade; the examples from Skog and Överhogdal are pure soumak, but all these tapestries use a bold outline, with a contrasting colour for infill.

The Oseberg tapestries were possibly woven on the small upright frame found in the burial (99); this is discussed above as a braiding frame for sprang, but the find of a weaving comb at Oseberg (a tool distinctive of the two-beam loom) suggests that it would also have been used as a small two-beam loom suitable for tapestry work. From the size of this frame, it has been estimated that the Oseberg tapestries originally measured between 5ft and 6ft 6in (1.5-2m) long. By comparison, a complete surviving section from Överhogdal is just under 6ft (182cm) long. If this interpretation of the Oseberg frame is correct, two large fragments from Överhogdal previously thought to come from a single length measuring about 13ft (4m) should probably be seen as separate pieces.

In the sagas, tapestries are used to adorn important houses when a feast is prepared.

NEEDLE BINDING

'Needle binding' is the translation of a common Scandinavian term (Danish *nålebinding*, Norwegian *nålebinde*, Swedish *nålbindung*), which is used for a textile technique not unlike crochet. Using a single needle, a series of interlocking loops of yarn can be bound together to make socks, hats or mittens. A circle of small loops is stitched through an initial single loop; another row of loops is then bound to this circle, and so on until the item is finished. Finds from the Viking period are relatively few but a needle-bound sock was found at Coppergate, and two examples of mittens in needle binding are known from Iceland, as well as fragments from Finland and Dublin. The normal yarn is plied wool, but a panel of needle binding in gold forms part of a silk from Mammen.

The technique was apparently unknown in England before the Viking settlement, suggesting that the needle-bound sock from York, which was found in an Anglo-Scandinavian context, might have been a Scandinavian product, or, as it is bound in a very simple version of the technique, perhaps an English copy (*colour plate 9*).

SILKS

Silk was one of the most important commodities underpinning the Viking mercantile expansion. From documentary evidence, we know that small quantities of silk were making their way to Britain and the far west of Europe before the ninth century, but it is not until the beginning of the Viking Age that silks begin to appear more frequently in the archaeological record. This change is especially dramatic in sites in Scandinavia and in areas of Viking influence such as York and Dublin.

Viking trade routes led down the Don to Byzantium and the Black Sea, and down the Volga to the Caspian, bringing them into direct contact with the silk road fetching goods from the Indo-China and the Far East. These trade routes brought silks not only to the Scandinavian homelands, but made them available for the first time to ordinary citizens in Britain, Ireland and mainland Europe. The supply came largely from the Near East (Byzantium and the eastern Mediterranean), but among the Birka silks is a single self-patterned Chinese fabric, which probably came north to Scandinavia along the Volga. Coin hoards in Russia and Scandinavia suggest two peaks in this trade, between *c.*AD 800-820 and *c.*AD 890-950, and there is some evidence that the majority of Viking silks were deposited around these two periods.

Irish sources associate silk with the Norsemen, and an Irish poem celebrating the capture of Dublin in AD 1000 boasts 'We took silk from the stronghold!' (*Tugsam siccir as a dún, Cogadh Gaedhel* ch.68). More than a hundred silks have been found in modern excavations of Viking Dublin.

Most silks are in tabby weave. There are narrow gauzy silks, generally either 6in (15cm) or 9in (23cm) broad between the selvedges, woven in Z-spun yarn and sometimes dyed purple; there are broader pieces with an unspun weft on a Z-spun warp and dyed red or blue, and there are narrow red ribbons sometimes dyed with Mediterranean kermes. These ribbons range from ½-1½in (1.3-3.8cm), generally towards the middle of this range, and unlike the other tabbies they often use S-spun yarn; otherwise the silk is unspun.

Fifty graves from Birka contained silk weft-faced compound twill or 'samite', which would originally have had patterns picked out in red and natural-coloured threads; these were generally cut into thin strips. Similar thin strips of samite come from Mammen Oseberg and Dublin. These were clearly mainly used as facings, trimmings and bindings, and the very narrow hems reveal how expensive they must have been; in one case from Dublin, a piece just ⅜in (1cm) wide has been stitched to another to make up a useable width.

Samite is almost certainly the cloth known as *goðvefr* or *guðvefr* ('god-weave, weaving of the gods'), a term which occurs more in poetry than prose, presumably because poets deal more readily with fabulous wealth than do sagamen. Thus in *Atlakviða*, the Hunnish nobility are dressed in *goðvefr* (st.38), and in *Hamðismál*, the Niflungar dress in *goðvefr* before they undertake their fatal mission (st.16); in *Laxdæla saga* ch.12, the flamboyant Gilli, nicknamed 'the Russian', is dressed 'in samite clothes' (*í guðvefjar-klæðum*). References to Old Norse *goðvefr* and Old English *godweb* 'of two colours' (ON *tvílitaðan guðvef*, OE *twegea bleó godwebb*) and to *godweb* 'patterned with gold' (*godweb mid golde gefagod*) confirm its identification as samite. The value placed on *goðvefr* in literature is matched by the evident value of samite in the Viking world as revealed by archaeology; the suggestion that *goðvefr* denotes shot silk taffeta is, I think, less convincing, and cotton is out of the question.

FURS AND SKINS

Against the silks and the silver which they brought north, the Vikings traded furs. The fur trade is a prominent feature of Arab accounts of the Rus, and is mentioned in the earliest, Ibn Khurradadhbih's early ninth-century *Treatise on the Highways and the Kingdoms*, which says that they traded as far away as China and Baghdad. In the early tenth century, fox and beaver furs were noted by Ibn al-Faqih, and Ibn Rusta wrote that 'their sole occupation is trading in martens, ermines and other furs,' which they sold for silver (adapted from Montgomery's translation). Al-Muqaddasi (d. *c*.990) supplies a longer list, which has been rendered as 'sable, Siberian squirrel, ermine, marten, weasel, beaver, coloured hare' (quoted in Davidson 1976). This eastern trade was pursued by the Icelandic settler Björn mentioned in *Landnámabók* and in *Þórðar saga hreðu* ch.2, who gained the nickname *Skinna*-Björn, 'Skins'-Björn.

Ohthere, a Norwegian merchant who visited the court of King Alfred, told him that he took tribute from the Saami in the north of Norway, which was partly paid in pelts. Alfred's account notes that 'the greatest must pay fifteen marten skins and five reindeer skins and one bear skin, and ten ambers of feathers, and a kirtle of bearskin or otterskin, and two ships' ropes' (*se byrdesta sceall gyldan fiftyne mearðes fell and fif hranes and an beran fel, and tyn ambra feðra, and berenne kyrtel oððe yterenne, and twegen sciprapas*). These would presumably have been the goods which Ohthere brought to England. Scandinavian traders continued to bring furs to England throughout the period, and the Domesday Book records marten skins imported to Chester in the late eleventh century. Indeed, Norwegian merchants dealt so much with furs that they referred to them by the familiar terms 'white wares' (*ljós varar* i.e. ermine and probably arctic fox) and 'grey wares' (*grá varar*). The tribute from the Saami also forms the subject of some of the early chapters of *Egils saga* (ch.7, ch.14-17).

These furs were luxury items and were used as trimmings and as warm linings for silks and other fine cloths. Red fox, pine marten, red squirrel, brown bear, otter, lynx and beaver were among the fur-bearing species recorded in the Birka graves, while remains from the Black Earth included evidence of ermine.

Humbler skins were also worn, as perhaps by the 'goat-kirtled' bride in *Rígsþula* (*geita-kyrtla*, st.23). Thorbjörg, the seeress of *Eiríks saga Rauða*, wore a black lambskin hood, lined inside with white catskin, and catskin gloves (ch.3); these skins might have held magical significance for her, but the appearance of catskin and lambskin alongside various kinds of cloth in lists of trade goods in the Icelandic law code *Grágás*, suggests that these skins were also in regular use among ordinary people. Goatskins and horsehides are mentioned by Arab observers. Sealskin garments are mentioned in the sagas, and are apparently described as a feature of Germanic costume by the Roman Tacitus (*Germania*, ch.17). The piled fabrics described above are clearly imitative of shaggy sheepskin or goatskin, and probably largely replaced it for anyone who could either buy them or make them.

DYEING AND BLEACHING

Day-to-day dress in the sagas is apparently undyed, and coloured cloth is worthy of comment in itself. Although dyes are regularly detected in woollen cloth from the Viking era, a large number of woollens used for clothing were left undyed. Wool for dyeing comes from white fleeces. Naturally pigmented wools are rarely dyed, but contrasting natural colours are sometimes woven together in warp and weft. By the same token, white wools are rarely left undyed, so the choice of dyed or undyed clothing begins with the farmer's choice of stock, a choice that might be dictated by generations of farming tradition.

Until the 1980s, ideas of the range of available colours and dyestuffs, and of the prevalence of dyed clothing were based mainly on literary evidence and on the colours that archaeologists reported as visible in excavated textile fragments. It is now possible to chemically analyse cloth fragments from the Viking Age for traces of dyestuffs. This analysis is not foolproof, but it is infinitely superior to judging by eye; not only does the eye not detect the fainter or more heavily decayed dyes on earth-stained cloth, but fragments which may look dyed sometimes prove to have been coloured simply by the soil they were buried in, or by metal salts from a nearby object. Since many textile fragments owe their preservation to the presence of such metal salts, this has led to a number of mistaken claims for dyed textiles.

Through the work of Penelope Walton Rogers in York, analysis of Viking-period textiles from Scandinavia has revealed four main dyes: woad for blue; lichen purple; red from madder or sometimes bedstraw; and an as yet unidentified plant dye for yellow, referred to as 'yellow-X'. Among textiles from Scandinavia, there is an overwhelming preponderance of fabrics dyed with woad (*100*).

Fruits seeds and fruit-stalk fragments of woad (*Isatis tinctoria*) were found in a box among the grave goods of the Oseberg queen, and woad was already being grown in Denmark by the Roman Iron Age. To make the dye, the young leaves are crushed and fermented, and the resulting colourless dye is dissolved in a vat of hot alkali such as lant or lye. The moist cloths, yarns or wools are stirred in this vat, then wrung out and hung up to dry. It is only during drying that the cloth takes on a blue colour. Birka-type fabrics are usually dyed a deep blue, as are the fine shortwool tabbies which are also found in high-status graves. Blue is also by far the commonest colour for clothing in the sagas.

Lichen gives a purple or reddish colour that was used in Classical times to eke out the more expensive shellfish purples. Roman cloth was dyed with the Mediterranean lichens *Roccella tinctoria* and *R. fuciformis*, but other species of lichen found in Scandinavia Ireland and Britain produce a similar dye, which may have been used for the Viking textiles. Varieties of *Lecanora*, *Ochrolechia* and *Parmelia* have been used for dyeing, as well as *Roccella*. A particularly likely candidate for Viking purple is *Lichen tartareus*, known as *korkji* in Færoese, a word which is probably derived from Old Irish *corcur* meaning 'purple'. This lichen (along with *Parmelia saxatalis*) is also traditionally known

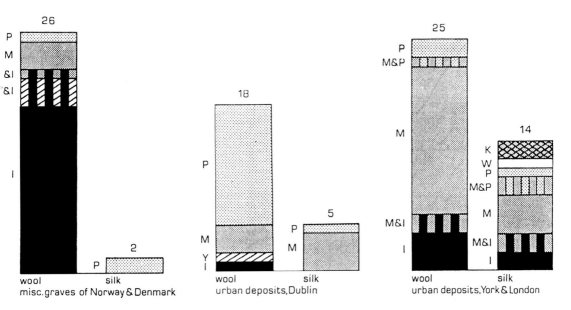

100 Proportions of dyestuffs found in samples of cloth from Scandinavia, England and Ireland. I = indigotin (woad or indigo); K = kermes; M = madder; P= lichen purple; W = Weld; Y = yellow-x. *Walton 1989, courtesy of the Anglo-Saxon Laboratory, York*

in Iceland by the name *litunarmosi*, 'dyeing lichen'. As with woad, lichen is fermented in lant to produce a dyestuff, and, also like woad, it is a 'vat dye', but the dye bath can be either acid for a reddish dye or alkaline for a bluer purple. Woollen textiles from Viking Dublin showed a great fondness for lichen purple, as did those from Narsaq, one of the earliest sites for the Eastern Settlement in Greenland.

Walnut shells (from the Common Walnut, *Juglans regia*) for dyeing were found at Hedeby and in the Oseberg burial. At Hedeby, the bulk of the dyed cloth had been dyed with walnut, and it was probably also used in the Oseberg tapestries. An American species of walnut (*Juglans cinerea*) was found at the Viking settlement at L'Anse aux Meadows, Newfoundland, where it must have been imported, perhaps from New Brunswick. Used without a mordant, walnut can give a lightfast rich reddish brown. Walnuts are best used green, and are soaked in water and boiled to release their tannins.

Madder (*Rubia tinctorum*) was grown in Carolingian France and probably in England. However there is no evidence that madder was grown in Scandinavia, where madder-dyed textiles are rare; when they have been recorded, as at Skringstrup and Vinjum, they are often of a type thought to originate in Europe. Madder was traded in the markets of ninth-century Quentovic and Paris, and could have been brought to Scandinavia for use in dyeing, but whether it arrived as ready-dyed cloth or was locally dyed with an imported dyestuff, madder-red cloth in Scandinavian burials is always associated with wealth and imported goods. It is found for instance, in the textiles from Oseberg, where one woman, presumably the queen, was dressed entirely in red, while her retainer was dressed in blue. In the tenth-century poem *Hrafnsmál*, Thorbjörn Hornklofi lists the red cloaks of the court poets alongside their gold rings as a symbol of the king's favour, while in *Atlakviða*, red clothes are listed among other promised riches. Similarly, in the Icelandic sagas red cloth is invariably a sign of wealth and foreign trade. Thus, in *Eiríks saga Rauða* ch.11, when the Skrælingjar trade furs for red cloth, they are trading for merchandise which the Norsemen themselves value highly.

Instead of using imported madder, Scandinavian dyers sometimes continued the Migration-era tradition of using native plants such as the bedstraw *Galium boreale*, as in the embroidery for the Mammen cushion cover. However, bedstraw-dyed textiles are also uncommon.

Both madder and bedstraw need a mordant. The mordant introduces metal salts to the cloth, which allows the dye to 'bite'. The resulting colour is stronger and is both light-fast and water-fast, so will not fade or wash out as easily. Scandinavian dyers have traditionally used the native clubmoss (*Diphasiastrum complanatum*) as a mordant; unlike most plants, clubmoss contains high levels of aluminium. Outside Scandinavia, dyers have generally preferred alum, which can occasionally occur naturally in the earth. Alum is probably the better mordant, but clubmoss appears to have been preferred because of its local availability. Iron oxide can also be used as a mordant, giving a rusty red compared to the brighter colours of aluminium mordants.

Significant quantities of clubmoss were discovered in the Anglo-Scandinavian levels at York, which are thought to have been imported from Scandinavia. Weaving traditions at York appear to have been typical of the rest of England and Europe at large, and the prominence of red-dyed cloth is also un-Scandinavian. But to achieve a good madder red, either clubmoss or alum was needed. Alum, a natural deposit found in areas of volcanic activity, could have been imported from the Mediterranean, and was traded in eleventh-century London (*Legis Regis Edwardi Confessoris: Libertas Civitatum* 8). Clubmoss however, was readily available in Scandinavia. The clubmoss from York is thus probably only indicative of York's major trading links, and is not evidence of a distinctively Scandinavian dyeing tradition in Anglo-Scandinavian York.

The adjective *val-rauðr* occurs in a list of excessively splendid gifts offered by Attila the Hun in the ninth-century poem *Atlakviða* (st.4), where it describes *serkir* or 'tunics', probably denoting the Mediterranean-style *tunica* as distinct from the Scandinavian *skyrta* or *kyrtill*. This word is commonly translated as 'blood-red' but more probably means 'foreign-red' (specifically 'Celtic-' or 'Roman-red'), which appears to confirm that red-dyed cloth was not a Scandinavian product. It might refer specifically to the Mediterranean use of alum, to the widespread use of madder in Britain, or to kermes-dyed crimsons and vermilions (which in the Viking period have been found only in silk cloth); a kermes-red tunic from a Migration-era grave at Evebø, Norway, might be such a *serkr val-rauðr*. The phrase might be an echo of the red *tunica* awarded to high-ranking barbarians in the Roman army.

The kermes dye which colours some Viking silks comes from the kermes beetle (*Kermes vermilio*) which lives on the Mediterranean kermes oak (*Quercus coccifera*). In medieval times, kermes dye was traded across Europe, but where it is found as a dye for silk, the cloth was probably dyed at source. Blue silks might have been dyed with indigo (*Indigofera tinctoria*) rather than woad, but the pigment (indigotin) is the same in both plants. Silks might also have been left undyed in their natural golden colour, and *Heimskringla* speaks of hair 'yellow like silk' (*gult hár sem silki*, *Ólafs saga Kyrra* ch.1), and similarly an English medical text refers to a jaundiced patient as 'yellow as good silk' (*ageolwað swa god seoluc*), but this yellow might also have been artificially enhanced.

The enigmatic yellow-X dye is strangely absent from English sites. This might suggest that it is derived from a plant which does not grow in Britain, but it might simply reflect the different dyeing traditions of Britain and Scandinavia. English dyers favoured dyestuffs which need a mordant, and used weld and greenweed for yellow. Scandinavian dyers preferred vat dyes like woad and lichen, and yellow-X probably falls into this category too.

Woollen cloth is described as dyed 'in the wool', 'in the yarn' or 'in the cloth', depending on at what stage in its production it has been dyed. The find of madder-dyed unspun wool from Anglo-Scandinavian York may be evidence for spinning and weaving with dyed wool, but this wool may equally have been meant for use as an unspun pile rather than for spinning and weaving. The Veka-type cloth of Norway has a blue-dyed warp with an undyed weft, and must therefore have been dyed either in the wool or in the yarn. Other individual finds have striped and checked patterns which cannot be achieved by dyeing in the cloth. It has been suggested that the Oseberg queen's red clothes were dyed in the cloth, though this cloth was probably made outside Scandinavia.

Dyes have not yet been confirmed on linen cloth from the Viking Age. Linen is usually only preserved through the action of metal salts, which can give it a blue cast, but on analysis none of these blue linens have yet shown evidence of dyeing. Cheap linen will have been left in its natural greyish or brownish hue, whilst high-quality linens would usually have been bleached rather than dyed. The linen is first steeped or boiled in lye, a solution of wood ash and lant, then spread out to bleach in the sun. A similar process might have been used in bleaching hair and in *Snorra Edda*, Svanhildr is bleaching her hair on the riverbank when Jørmunrekkr's horses ride her down, as are Guðrún and Brynhildr when they quarrel. Bleached cloth would have varied in quality, and could have been one of several shades approaching whiteness; the whiter the cloth the more expensive it will have been. Thus, in *Orkneyinga saga* ch.55, a fine linen garment coveted by Earl Haraldr is described as 'white as snow' (*hvítt sem fönn*) and is presumably whiter than the shirt and linen breeches he is already wearing, while according to the Byzantine Leo the Deacon, the shirt worn by the tenth-century Rus prince Svyatoslav was noticeably whiter than those of his retinue.

Nonetheless, although linen does not accept dyes as readily as wool, dyed linen may well have been available, even if relatively rare. Pliny knew of blue, red and purple-dyed linens in Roman times, and according to *De Carolo Magno*, red linen breeches were worn by the Franks. Some of the Birka linens, which have not yet been tested in the lab, were very possibly dyed. The medieval Icelandic poem *Sigurðarkviða inn skamma* refers to 'foreign linen well coloured' (*valaript vel fáð*, st.66), and the blue *serkr* worn by the noblewoman, Moðir, in *Rígsþula*, would probably have been made of dyed linen.

Some idea of the extra expense of dyed cloth comes from Diocletian's edict on maximum prices mentioned above (Introduction). The best wool sold for 100-175*d.* per pound, washed but undyed, whilst ordinary wool 'of the best middle quality' sold for 50*d.* The same wool, dyed with lichen purple, sold for between 300*d.* and 600*d.* per pound, the price depending solely on the quality of the dye. At the same date, a manual labourer such as a farm hand or water carrier could expect to earn no more than 25*d.* a day above board and lodging.

SEAMS AND SEWING

Needles were made of bone or metal. Bone needles from Birka and Hedeby range from 1½-7½in (4-19cm) in length, but are generally in the range of 3½-4in (9-10cm), with an eye of in (3mm). Metal needles are of copper alloy or more often iron, and measure between 1½-4in (4-10cm); the eye is either punched as a round hole, or formed into a 'long eye' by welding together the tips of a forked shank.

Thread used for sewing is usually a plied yarn matching the fibre of the cloth; thus woollen yarn sews wool and linen sews linen. Woollen yarn is mostly made from combed wool, and so is smooth and strong; it is sometimes dyed, but does not necessarily match the colour of the cloth. Silk is normally sewn with unplied silken thread, but sometimes linen is used.

The seams used on woollen cloth are generally unremarkable; yarn from York is between 30-60thou (0.8-1.5mm) in diameter and there are from two to eight stitches per inch (1-3 per cm). A variety of hem types is found, all with the aim of preventing the cloth from fraying at the edge. Various simple stitches are used to fix one piece of cloth to another, sometimes overlaid with decorative stitching in a contrasting coloured yarn. Sometimes a woollen cord or braid was attached to a seam or selvedge for strength; these were sometimes hidden within the garment.

Silk hems use as little material as is possible, and so are most often rolled. The yarn is fine, between 10-30thou (0.3-0.8mm) and the stitching fairly tight at 10 to 15 stitches per inch (4-6 per cm).

The most interesting seams are in linen, and good examples are found at York and at Viborg. The thread is mainly fine, between 15-40thou (0.4-1.0mm), and more closely stitched even than silk at 8 to 13 stitches per inch (3-5 per cm). Linen seams from York are mostly of the 'run and fell' kind. In a typical example, the two fabrics are first laid face-to-face, and sewn with a simple running stitch or backstitch. One of the edges is trimmed shorter than the other, before the cloth is opened up and the edges pressed to one side. The untrimmed edge is then tucked under the other, and stitched in place. The shirt from Viborg uses a variety of elaborate seams, many of them oversewn with parallel decorative felling.

The use of such seams and the closeness of the stitching strongly suggest the use of a smoother of some sort, to flatten the cloth during dressmaking. Linen creases easily, and if it is not kept smooth it is difficult to work accurately. The run and fell seam exploits the nature of the cloth by deliberately creasing the linen into place along the seam before stitching it down. This would have been done with a smooth heavy 'slick'.

Slicks, or linen smoothers, are known from Viking-era archaeology in Scandinavia and elsewhere. Twenty-eight have been recovered from Anglo-Scandinavian York, twenty-five of glass and three of stone. Stone slicks are known from before the Viking Age, with the earliest glass examples appearing in ninth-century Norway and Sweden. Over a hundred glass slicks were found at Hedeby, measuring 3-4in (7-10cm) in diameter and 1-2in in height (2.5-5cm). The glass is usually green, but so dark as to seem black; occasionally it is a pale transparent green. Analysis has shown the glass to have a high lead content, which adds to its weight. The list of cloth-working tools in the Old English *Gerefa* includes *slic*, and these objects were still in use in eighteenth-century Norway for smoothing garments, especially seams, after laundering.

A slick would have been essential in constructing the elaborate seams of the Viborg shirt, which are perfectly flat and painstakingly sewn. Sometimes seams run close together in perfect parallel for decorative effect.

There is documentary evidence that slicks were not only used in dressmaking. The ninth-century Annals of St Bertin describe a slick in use in the entry for 862, where a slave woman in Thérouanne is smoothing her master's linen shirt for him to wear to Mass; somewhat disconcertingly, the shirt exudes blood and is presented to the bishop who declares it a miracle. The slave woman uses a 'smoother' (*leviga*) which she drags across the cloth, pressing down as she goes. Glass slicks similar to Scandinavian examples appear at about this date in France.

EMBROIDERY AND OTHER DECORATIVE WORK

There is remarkably little surviving Scandinavian embroidery from the period, though simple embroidery at Oseberg and Birka seems to have been typically placed alongside seams and appliqués. They are typically executed in stemstitch and backstitch, with two threads of two-plied wool, the first thread being a core which the other thread loops around. A series of five rings executed in this style marked the edge of a silk fragment at Oseberg. The seam of the Mammen cushion cover was overlaid with decorative herringbone whipstitching.

The Mammen burial is peculiarly rich in embroidered cloth, and, indeed, empty needle holes reveal that a good deal of embroidery in linen has been lost. The Mammen embroideries employ various decorative motifs from contemporary Scandinavian and Western art, including animals, human heads and acanthus leaves. Representational embroidery also comes from the Norwegian Oseberg burial, where, as at Mammen, it decorates a madder-red garment; like the red fabric it decorates, embroidery was undoubtedly a sign of great status. At Oseberg, the representational embroideries have been seen as representing an import from the British Isles, and despite the use of some Scandinavian-style motifs, the same interpretation seems appropriate at Mammen.

There are very few fragments of conventional embroidery from Birka, confirming the impression that this was an unusual textile art in Scandinavia, associated with men and women of the highest status, and possibly also associated with foreign influence or exotic luxury.

A technique known from Birka is similar to embroidery using gold and silver wire. This was dubbed *Ösenstich* by Agnes Geijer, and has been described as 'reverse chain stitch'. It is usually used as ornament on silk, but sometimes it joins two silks together, and at other times it appears without any woven ground. It is found in 10 examples from Birka, five from Gotland and a single piece from Ingleby, Derbyshire, where it accompanied a warrior of the ninth-century 'Great Army' to his grave.

Most distinctive, and Geijer believed unique, was *Slingenstich* or 'twined wire', in which the pattern is made with two ends of a single wire. One end, the 'sleeper', lays out the pattern, while the other 'live' end stitches around it to keep it in place. Twined wire can be used to make settings for pieces of mica, foliated glass, sheets of gold or gilded leather. Among the best work in this technique is the beautiful Golden Stag, which was wrought in solid gold wire on silk and was inlaid with mica above a silver passement.

Geijer believed that the Birka costume ornaments made of gold and silver wire, which she saw as work of a 'remarkably high standard', must represent imports from 'somewhere in the Orient', suggesting that 'isolated and far cruder imitations may have been produced in Scandinavia'. There are 92 such pieces from Birka, but similar finds come from Mammen, Denmark, and Valsgärde, Sweden. But just as there is no inherent reason why fine cloth could not be woven in Scandinavia, so there is no reason why fine ornaments could not have been made there too. A device for drawing wire has been found at Birka, so the wire for making such pieces was locally available. Perhaps the less accomplished examples were amateur pieces, either worn by the maker or given as a keepsake.

Another decorative technique used at Birka was passementerie. A gold or silver wire (either solid, or wound around a core) is coiled in knotwork patterns and appliquéed to the garment, which is invariably silk, or plaited into long laces; some passementerie appears to have decorated headgear.

CLOTHES, CLOTH AND VIKING SOCIETY

The story of cloth and clothing never strays far from other aspects of social history. What people wore is only ever half the question; it is at least as important to understand such issues as why they wore it, what messages other people might read from the clothes they had chosen, and who made the clothes and the cloth they were made from. Some aspects of these questions have already been tackled in other chapters of the book. This section will look briefly at just a few aspects of the function and meaning of clothing in Viking-age Scandinavian society.

PIT HOUSES AND TEXTILE PRODUCTION

House pits are a feature of Germanic archaeology well before the Viking Age, and they frequently contain evidence of textile production. They generally take the form of a roughly rectangular pit, usually with one or more large postholes at either end. A typical pit might be about 10 x 14ft (3 x 4m), and 2½ft (75cm) deep. In Scandinavia, round house pits are also known, but these too are typically provided with two large postholes at opposite sides of the pit.

There has been a good deal of debate over the form and function of the type of building associated with these features with regard to Anglo-Saxon England, but here we are concerned only with the pit house proper, in which the floor of the pit is also the floor of the house; it may sometimes have had wooden floorboards, but in many cases, the floor seems to have been left as bare earth, with internal fittings leaving stakeholes in the floor of the pit itself.

Pit houses are commonly found alongside other kinds of house, so it is likely that they had a distinct purpose. They often contain loom weights and other evidence of textile production, and have long been interpreted as weaving huts. Some scholars have felt that this is too narrowly defined a purpose, and have expanded their reconstructed function to the status of general workshops and stores, a suggestion that is sometimes confirmed by the presence of corn or agricultural tools in place of textiles. Nonetheless, it is textile production in particular with which pit houses are most consistently linked by archaeology.

W. Haio Zimmermann argues that, as textile workshops, these sunken buildings could have provided the damp atmosphere best suited for working linen and vegetable fibres. This means that, rather than simply being a type of building which happens to have been used for textile production, the pit house can be seen as a building which is specifically designed for that purpose, and which is uniquely fit for the task. It also explains the significance of the pit, which becomes not just a means of building a house without walls, but an important element in the construction of what is in effect an underground chamber.

To maximise the damp-retaining properties of the pit, the spoil could have been used to make earthen walls and roof. In reconstructions with timber or wattle walls and thatched or shingled roofs, this spoil is an unwanted by-product to be disposed of, but if roof and walls are made of earth, it becomes an essential part of the structure instead. Turf roofs are made in Scandinavia to this day; squares of sod are laid over twigs and gravel on a surface of overlapping strips of birch bark; the whole is built on a base of wooden boards. The boarding used to support the earth roof might provide an alternative explanation for the burnt boards lying on top of the loom weights in West Stow SFB15, which have previously been read as evidence for a ground-level floor built over the pit.

In a typical thatched or shingled roof with a pitch of a half right angle (45°) or more, the two sides can simply lean against each other in the middle, supporting each other's weight as in the traditional A-frame. But the pitch of a turf roof has to be fairly shallow, no more than about a quarter of a right angle (27½°). This means that a large proportion of the weight is directed downwards in the middle, so the ridge beam has to be supported. The same principle is at work when you build a house of cards; if the angle is too shallow, the cards fall down. So, the regular occurrence of postholes at either end of the pit house might in itself imply a turf roof.

Building in turf is consistent with Scandinavian tradition, where it has been used for other types of building too, and it is not remarkable that pit houses should have turf walls in this context. Evidence that the turf wall is an inherent part of the pit house even outside Scandinavia comes from Milk Street in London, where the spoil from the pit had been piled against the outside wall to a thickness of about 3ft (1m) and grassed over. This wall may have been continuous with the outer surface of the roof.

Something akin to these turf-roofed pits is described by Tacitus in his *Germania* ch.16, where he suggests uses to which such a pit house might have been put:

Solent et subterraneos specus aperire eosque multo insuper fimo onerant, suffugium hiemis et receptaculum frugibus, quia rigorem frigorum eius modi loci molliunt, et si quando hostis advenit, aperta populatur, abdita autem et defossa aut ignorantur aut eo ipso fallunt, quod quaerenda sunt.

They are also wont to dig out an underground cave and to pile loads of dung on top, as a winter shelter and a harvest store, since such enclosed spaces soften the severity of the cold, and if at some time an enemy should come, he ravages in the open, but he either does not know the hidden dugouts, or he ignores them because they are hard to find.

Tacitus had not actually seen the shelters he is describing, but based his description on earlier accounts, probably often from military sources, and he is most interested in their use as hideouts. Thus, his shelters are well hidden, and possibly almost flat-roofed, but they must have been based on a similar pit and prop construction to the pit house as reconstructed above. The low-pitched green turf roof proposed for an ordinary pit house might often have looked more like a grassy knoll than a house, if the end walls were similarly hidden by turf. Underground hideouts are also mentioned in *Heimskringla, Óláfs saga Tryggvasonar* ch.49 (where, as in Tacitus, it is hidden under dung), and in the opening chapter of *Hrólfs saga Kraka* among other places. It is probably in such a shelter that we should envisage the woman of the Old English poem known as 'The Wife's Lament', which she describes as 'a cave of earth' (*eorðs cæfe*).

Tacitus does not refer to the use of such structures in textile production, but Pliny, writing about linen making in his *Historia Naturalis* (Book 19 Part 1 ch.2), tells us that 'in Germania they go about this work dug down underground' (*in Germania autem defossae atque sub terra id opus agunt*). It is hard to imagine a more convincing explanation of the phrase 'dug down underground' than the reconstruction of the pit house suggested here. Pliny's comment confirms that linen making is at least part of the explanation of the Germanic pit house, while Tacitus suggests other reasons why they might have been built.

From pit house CME at Århus Søndervold, Denmark, the charred remains of two balls of yarn and the cut-off ends of warp threads have been identified as flax, showing that linen was woven in this building and remains of linen textiles have also been found in other pit houses. Pit house CME also yielded fragments of wool, and wool and linen might well have been woven in the same building, but the distinctive pit construction is due to the linen production. At Næs in Denmark, a site with evidence of large-scale linen production, a total of 79 pit houses was found, most of them with evidence of textile production, including loom weights, spindle whorls, bone needles and glass slicks. In Norway, where linen cloth is rarer, and where linen production was probably minimal, pit houses are correspondingly rare.

The loom weights in Viking pit houses are usually found in long rows, suggesting the position of the loom when in use, or stowed neatly in a corner. Eva Andersson has observed that nearly half the loom weights are found in the north-east of the building, while the entrance normally faced south-west, to take best advantage of available daylight during the warmer part of the year, when the door could be left open. With the loom placed on the pit floor, below the height of the door in the north-east of the building, the light from the open doorway would have fallen straight onto the weaving in progress. Some pit houses have long, shallow internal pits, often containing loom weights, which are similar to pits found in the weaving houses of Pfalz Tilleda, Germany. Zimmermann suggested these were to enhance humidity, but it may be that they were intended to get the loom at the best possible angle to the light.

Although the earliest evidence for linen in Denmark comes from the early Roman Iron Age, the first Danish pit houses do not appear until late Roman times. Linen must first have come to Scandinavia as an import, and the culture of linen making followed rather later. Since, as well as new expertise, linen making involved new departures in architecture and agriculture, such a delay is not surprising. Linen production, when it came, must have required major reorganisation.

Pit houses are a consistent feature of Germanic archaeology, which are likely to have had one or more specific uses; they have frequently been found in association with textile-working artefacts, and can sometimes be associated specifically with linen making. A turf roof would complete the effect, implicit in the pit itself, of a chamber enclosed by earth, and similar chambers are described in Anglo-Saxon, Norse and Classical sources. The turf roof would need the support of an extra beam, which could explain the central postholes commonly found at either end of the pit. Such an earth-bound chamber would provide ideal conditions for linen making, and appears to match Pliny's description of a Germanic linen workshop. In view of these factors, the conclusion seems inescapable that pit houses were roofed in turf, and that one among their functions, probably their primary function, was the production of linen.

TEXTILE WORKSHOPS AND BIRKA–TYPE CLOTH

The even quality and production techniques of some of the more sophisticated textiles of the Viking world, in particular cloths of the Birka type, suggest the existence of established production centres, where cloth could be manufactured to a consistent standard. The extremely fine quality of the Birka-type fabric also demonstrates that it was produced in a secure and wealthy setting, where a great deal of time and care could be lavished on its production.

In Charles the Great's Frankia, female textile workers were organised under the watch of a higher-ranking female overseer into a *gynaecium*. The Old English *Gerefa* (Cambridge MS Corpus Christi 383) describes an English estate set up for textile production, which may have been based on a similar system; the estate would have supplied its own raw materials for the workshop. This might also have been the pattern in Scandinavian societies, and would give a social setting for the weaving of the fine Z-spun twills. If so, we would expect these high-quality cloths to have been the products of major estates, probably royal estates. The close association of the Oseberg queen with textile production might point to royal patronage for such weaving and spinning workshops in the Viking world.

Such workshops would probably have been made up at least in part of slave women, and perhaps the retainer burial at Oseberg was one such woman. The early eleventh-century Norman poet Warner of Rouen satirizes the Irish poet Moriuht, who traced his wife to a textile workshop in Normandy, after they had both been taken by Vikings and sold into slavery (*Moriuht*, ll.276-8); the Normans at this date still maintained a close relationship with the Viking world. Tenth-century Anglo-Saxon wills reveal that textile workers in Anglo-Saxon England, such as weavers, fullers and seamstresses, could be slaves forming part of an estate. The mother of Sveinn Tjuguskegg, who was known as 'Seam'-Æsa (*Saum-Æsa*), was probably such a slave.

Frances Pritchard suggests that the use of foreign slaves in textile production will have helped to spread ideas amongst the textile cultures of the Viking Age. Similar cultural exchange will have been associated with the exchange of brides between the élites of Germanic societies. A term for such a foreign bride in Anglo-Saxon poetry is a 'peace weaver' (*freoðu-webbe*, *Beowulf* l.1942 *et al.*), and the word may allude to her literal occupation as well as to her metaphorical role.

There is ample evidence for involvement in textile production at the highest levels of society, amongst which the Oseberg queen stands out as a prime example; she was buried with all the equipment she could have needed to turn raw wool and linen into the finest textiles. Evidence for textile production was apparently found at the palatial hall identified as Skíringssalr, which was excavated in 2001 at Huseby near Kaupang, Norway, but this has yet to be fully analysed.

The early twelfth-century Annals of St Neots record a story, which probably originates in Norse tradition, that the sisters of Ingvar and Ubbi (sons of Ragnarr Loðbrók) wove their banner, 'Raven'. In Norse literature, Brynhildr (*Helreið Brynhildar* st.4) and Hervör (*Hervarar saga* ch.4), both noblewomen, are criticised for failing to pursue textile arts. In Europe, Charles the Great had his daughters taught to work wool using the distaff and spindle (*filias vero lanificio adsuescere coloque ac fuso*, *Vita Karoli* 19). Judith wove a *peplum* for her royal husband, while Irmentrude was described as expert in what Sedulius calls 'the art of Pallas'. Charles would praise the skill of princesses and abbesses in making textiles for princes or bishops. Even today, folktale still associates the finest textile workers with the royal court.

If textiles were indeed made by royal households and other great estates, we must envisage their products as the finest of cloths. Perhaps, it was not always the queens and princesses themselves who were foremost in this work (the textile equipment in the grave of the Oseberg queen did not include an ordinary loom), but such work would surely have been carried out by their retinues. And the products of these royal workshops would have clothed the royal house and provided material for the gifts of clothing that the king and queen bestowed. Kings' gifts of clothing occur regularly in the sagas; if such gifts had been woven and sewn under the direction of the queen, the *kudos* of the recipient would have been considerably enhanced; the alternative scenario, where such clothes were purchased by the crown for use as gifts, seems much less satisfactory. Silks of course, had to be imported, but royal silks, like royal gold, might often have been won as tax, tribute or booty, or received as gifts from foreign kings. However, *Hauks þáttr* in *Flateyjarbók* describes how a king's garments could also be gained through trade.

It is not, then, necessary to assume that all cloth of the Birka type was woven in the same workshop or even in the same country. Indeed, the small-scale production of high-quality cloth may have been a regular appurtenance of the court, and queens' weavers might have been as universal as kings' warriors. The products of such distinguished weavers would have been distributed as gifts according to royal favour. The preponderance of petty rulers in ninth-century western Norway and the later dynastic struggles may help to explain the concentration of Birka-type cloth in that area.

Not all such workshops would have been royal establishments; the great number of excavated examples of Birka-type cloth suggests a widespread production base, and Eva Andersson draws attention to light spindle whorls from Birka and Hedeby, which, she points out, must have been used in the production of exceptionally fine cloth.

Textile workshops would probably have been found on most major estates, but the notion of small-scale production aimed at supplying the needs of the owners and furnishing gifts to social equals and high-ranking social inferiors could help explain why this luxury cloth type is so rare overseas. If it was produced solely as a medium of gift exchange, it might never have been traded; and if it was not traded within Scandinavia, neither would it have been traded abroad.

COLOURED CLOTHES

Anyone reading the Icelandic sagas with even a casual interest in clothes will be struck by occasional references to coloured clothing. Usually, the colour is specified, but it seems that colour is remarked on simply for its own sake. Coloured clothes are worn by people of rank when they dress their best for the Althing or for a wedding; the other time when people in the sagas are likely to wear coloured clothes, is when they about to do anything which touches their honour, such as killing an enemy. Clearly, most people wore undyed cloth most of the time. This picture of everyday clothes made of undyed wool is in keeping with the finds from later-medieval Greenland where almost all the cloth was undyed, but made use of two shades of natural brown wool; undyed cloth may have been the norm for rural communities throughout the period.

Rather more cloth from Viking-age archaeological sites has turned out to be dyed than the evidence of the sagas might suggest. This could be because the majority of textile finds come either from burials or from urban settlements, both contexts where one might reasonably expect a greater emphasis on smart clothing. Fabrics recovered from burials are likely to be best clothes or perhaps specially made burial clothes, and so are more likely to be dyed than everyday wear. In finds from the harbour at Hedeby, only half the garment textiles were undyed, suggesting that urban communities might also have placed more emphasis on sartorial show. Whilst, the bulk of the rural population probably wore plain, undyed clothes most of the time, more colourful clothes may have been popular in towns, where clothes really could 'make the man', and where dyestuffs may have been more readily available. However, the situation described in the Icelandic sagas and borne out by finds from medieval Greenland might also partly reflect the growing isolation of these Atlantic communities in the later Middle Ages, when dyed clothes might have been less common than they had been during the Viking Age.

Blue is the commonest colour in the sagas (cloaks in particular are very often blue), while blue and green clothes are also most common in the Scandinavian archaeological record (*100*). Though the word *blár*, 'blue', covers all shades of blue including the very darkest, it is by no means synonymous with *svartr*, 'black'; in terms of clothing, *blár* denotes dyed blue cloth, while *svartr* denotes naturally-pigmented black cloth. Dyed clothes are worn with pride by their owners at public gatherings and other significant occasions. Víga-Glúmr wears his blue cloak when he upholds the family honour through killing; his brother, seeing him in the cloak, knows at once that something has happened. Valla-Ljótr, in *Valla-Ljóts saga* ch.1 and *Bolla þáttr* ch.9 (*Laxdæla saga* ch.87) has two outfits:

> *Þat var búningr hans hversdagliga at hann hafði svartan kyrtil ok refði í hendi, en ef hann bjóst til víga þá hafði hann bláan kyrtil ok öxi snaghyrnda.*

> It was his everyday dress that he had a black kirtle and a staff in his hand, but if he got ready to kill, then he had a blue kirtle and a horned axe. (*Bolla þáttr* ch.9)

Wearing one's best clothes for a killing, signals the deliberate nature of the act and its importance. Few people would metaphorically soil their best clothes with a shameful act, even if they will risk literally soiling them with their opponent's blood; by wearing their best clothes the killers make a clear declaration that they can be proud of what they are about. It amounts to a public statement of commitment to the killing, which recalls the legal distinction between 'killing' (*víg*) conducted in public as a matter of honour, and 'murder' (*morðr*) done in secret or under cover of darkness. When in *Hamðismál* st.16, the brothers Hamðir and Sörli dress in their finery before undertaking their suicidal mission, they are not only showing their commitment to vengeance against Jörmunrekk, they are also preparing themselves for death, and the same may also be true in the saga episodes mentioned above, for no one can ever foretell the outcome of violence with certainty.

Inevitably, since woad blue is the commonest dye in both literature and archaeology, it is usually blue clothes that are donned before a saga killing. Marina Mundt has linked the wearing of blue before a killing with a statement in *Þiðreks saga* ch.174 that 'the colour blue shows a cold breast and grim heart' (*Ok merkir blár litr kallt brjóst ok grimt hjarta*). But this saga has been shown to be a collection of translations from German heroic legend; the customs and traditions it represents are German rather than Scandinavian. It is not possible to believe that, in a society where most people who wore dyed clothing wore blue, that colour could be associated with negative characteristics.

It has also been suggested that the colour blue was particularly associated with death, and that this is why blue clothes are worn by killers in the sagas and by the dead in their graves. In support of this, we might note that Ibn Fadlan describes the clothes worn by the dead Rus chieftain as being newly made for the funeral. But clothes retrieved from burials sometimes show signs of wear and repair, as for instance at Adwick-le-Street, England. The preponderance of blues and greens in Scandinavian archaeology corresponds to a contrasting preponderance of reds in Britain and purples in Ireland. In a lengthy passage noted by Penelope Walton Rogers describing the cloths of various nations, the eleventh-century Latin poem *Conflictus Ovis et Lini* confirms that different nations favoured different colours for their clothing (l.161–212), noting, for example, the popularity of madder red in Britain (l.175–6). The Scandinavian taste for blue and green dyes is probably reflected in the adjective 'blue-green' (*gormglas*) used of the Vikings in the Irish *Cogadh Gaedhel* ch.91.

Red clothes in the sagas seem to indicate particular splendour; they are sometimes the gifts of kings, and are often worn with other coloured clothes or costly jewellery. In the romance *Örvar-Odds saga* ch.27, when Oddr drops his disguise of birch-bark clothes, he is wearing a red tunic and a gold arm ring; the contrast could not be greater. In the poem *Atlakviða* st.4, 'foreign-red' (*val-rauðr*) tunics are numbered among a list of extravagant gifts, while in *Haraldskvæði* st.19 the red cloaks of King Haraldr's poets are symbolic of their ample rewards; both these poems probably date from the ninth century. This picture of red clothes as a mark of rank or luxury is confirmed by archaeology, where madder-dyed clothes are found only in graves of the highest status.

White clothes on the other hand, either of bleached linen or undyed white wool, when they are mentioned in the sagas, are invariably the mark of the Christian. But this is more literary convention than historical fact, based on the whiteness of the Christening robe. It is not credible that non-Christians should have deliberately avoided white linen, since linen formed an important part of both men's and women's clothing in the Viking Age. Wherever white clothes appear in the sagas without religious overtones, they are simply termed 'linen clothes'. However, runestone references to dying in white clothes probably represent deathbed Conversions or baptisms deferred until death.

WEDDING CLOTHES

Her wedding day was probably the one time above all others that a woman wanted to look her best, and a bride's wedding clothes may have been quite distinctive. In the poem *Guðrúnarhvot* st.16, Guðrún describes how she decked her daughter in gold and silks before giving her away in marriage, and it may have been traditional for the girl's mother to dress her for her wedding, though only the wealthiest could have afforded such luxurious trappings as these.

Both *Rígsþula* and *Þrymskviða* describe the bride's clothing, and both emphasise the wearing of linen and hanging keys. Keys have been found in women's burials and are thought to have been symbolic of the housewife's status as mistress of the house; the laws of Cnut specifically charge the woman with responsibility for her keys and for all goods she has locked away (Laws II Cnut, 76.1-76.1a). In poetry, hanging keys are associated specifically with brides, and this may be because the bride has newly achieved the right to wear the keys, which are therefore displayed prominently on her costume. Whether they were necessarily worn by married women at other times is less certain; they may have been a ceremonial feature of women's costume, worn only on specific formal occasions such as wedding and burial when their symbolic value was paramount. Ibn Fadlan's famous description of the Rus notes that the women wore a hanging knife but does not mention hanging keys.

At Birka, keys are four to five times more likely to be found in women's graves than in men's, but they are not always found in graves containing oval brooches which, as I have argued above, were the mark of the wedded wife. Keys are also found in graves of women buried without oval brooches, including Bj.756, 758, 777, 831, 893, 970 and 971. These women apparently had power over their own resources that was recognised in their burial rites, yet were buried without the oval brooches which seem to have symbolised marriage.

In *Þrymskviða*, the god Thórr is disguised as a bride and is 'bound in bride's linen' (*bundu þeir Þór þá brúðar líni*, st.19) and the words 'bride's linen' are repeated several times in this poem. It is probably the custom of veiling the bride that is the origin of the phrase 'to go under linen' (*gá und líni*) meaning to wed; this phrase occurs twice in *Rígsþula* (once in the alternative form *gá und ripti*). In *Laxdæla saga* ch.69, not only the bride, but all the women wear linen headdresses for the wedding feast. The word for the veil in *Þrymskviða* is *lína*, meaning 'line, thread or rope', but when the giant Thrymr wants to kiss the bride, he has to stoop 'under the veil' (*und línu*, st.27); *lína* is used in kennings for 'woman' by Kormákr (*Kormáks saga* st.20 ch.6, st.52 ch.17).

A type of headdress called *motr* features significantly in *Laxdæla saga*, and may have been specifically linked with marriage. In ch.43 it is intended to be given as a wedding gift by the groom, while in ch.44 Kjartan makes an implicit link between it and marriage, when he says 'I think the *motr* suits you well, and I believe it would be best for me to own both together, the *motr* and the maiden' (*Vel þykir mér þér sama motrinn ... ætla ek ok at þat sé best fallið at ek eigi allt saman, motr ok mey*). The word appears to be a loanword in Norse; it is related to Old Frisian *mother* and Old Low German *moder* 'a woman's neckcloth', among others; the Lithuanian *muturis* appears closest to the apparent meaning of the Norse word, designating a white linen cloth worn on the head of the newly married bride. Like other women's headgear, the *motr* is wound around the head (ch.43).

CLOTHES AS GIFTS

Very often it seems, one's best clothes would be received as gifts. Generally, a rich man could afford to dress better than a poor man, but clothing given as gifts would reflect the giver's wealth at least as much as the receiver's.

Hávamál st.41 advises that friends exchange gifts of clothes and weapons, and the sagas are full of examples of such gifts, which are generally given at Yule or as parting gifts when a guest is about to leave; sometimes they are also given to a poet in exchange for a poem. Usually, the gift is given by a social superior, but gifts are also given among equals and from a follower to his lord.

These gifts are always of the best clothing, but are not always new. Indeed the fact that the clothes have been worn by the giver sometimes seems to add to their value; this is particularly the case if they are the gift of a king. Thus, in *Egils saga* ch.55, King Æthelstan gives Egill 'a costly cloak, which the king himself had worn before' (*skikkja dýr, er konungr sjálfr áðr borit*). In *Víga-Glúms saga*, a blue cloak (*skautfeldr blár*) given to Glúmr by his grandfather is important to the family 'luck' (*gæfa*), and we should probably imagine that such gifts always brought with them an element of the giver's luck. Thus, it is more than simply the implication that it was fit for a king that makes Egill's cloak special, the gift of the king's own cloak brings with it something of the king's special mystique and luck. When Egill gets clothes from his friend Arinbjörn (*Egils saga*, ch.67), they are newly made from English cloth, but this is apparently due to Egill's great size.

Scandinavian society in the Viking Age was a gift-based society as much as a monetary society, but it is wrong to think of gift exchange as a primitive form of trade. Trade could be carried out according to more-or-less agreed equivalent values measured in cattle, in silver, or even in ells of cloth. Gifts are harder to value, not least because a part of their worth is derived from the act of giving, and could never be realised through trade. The value of clothing, particularly luxury clothing, is hard to assess in monetary terms.

Once given, a gift might be passed on again. Perhaps, its value increased when a garment was given again, because as a gift, it had already been a uniquely precious object to the new giver. And unlike the first giver, the new giver can probably not afford to replace what they are giving away. In *Flóamanna saga* ch.15, Thorgils gives a kirtle to Thorstein that is called 'Auðun's Gift' (*Auðunarnaut*), and the previous history of the gift is preserved in its name. And the cloak which Gunnlaugr gives his beloved Helga had been a gift to him from King Æthelræd; after he dies, this cloak *Gunnlaugsnaut* takes a special place in Helga's life, and she asks for it to be brought out when she is dying herself.

Unlike gifts of clothing, gifts of rings are akin to monetary reward. The ring has an intrinsic value as bullion as well as the value of its craftsmanship, and this is recognised in the habit of breaking jewellery up, reducing it to hacksilver. Ibn Fadlan saw the neckrings of Rus women as symbolising their husbands' wealth, and they probably conformed to a standard weight. Archaeologists have observed that standard weights appear to have been used for gold and silver rings. In *Egils saga* ch.55, along with the gift of his cloak, King Æthelstan gives Egill two gold arm rings in return for his poetry, each of them weighing a mark. In *Njáls saga* ch.138, when Hallbjörn gives Eyjólfr a gold ring, its value is immediately calculated by the saga writer at 1200 yards of best wadmal. Similarly, in *Heimskringla*, Eyvindr Skáldaspillir's cloak pin, for which every Icelander contributed a penny, had a fixed monetary value, which Eyvindr instantly redeemed and converted into livestock.

It was said 'a gift demands a return' (*ey sér til gildis gjöf*, *Hávamál* st.145). Thus in *Landnámabók*, Hildigunn gives her son Einarr a newly made kirtle when she asks a favour. And in *Ljósvetninga saga* ch.13, Guðmundr gets a very fine cloak from a Norwegian merchant in return for his hospitality through the winter; Guðmundr later gives the cloak to his brother Einarr to ensure his support; Einarr tries to return the cloak when he realises what is demanded of him, but Guðmundr will not take it back. However, when Ingibjörg gives Kjartan her *motr*, it represents a renunciation of her interest in him, since she will not now be wearing it for him herself (*Laxdæla saga* ch.43).

Clothes were also routinely provided for travellers (cf. *Hávamál* st.3), but this is best understood as an act of hospitality rather than specifically as gift giving.

THE GIFT OF A SHIRT

A uniquely significant gift was the gift of a shirt from a woman to a man. Unlike other gifts of clothes, a given shirt was newly made. This is a lover's gift, and can only respectably be given between betrothed or married couples, or as a gift from a mother or sister. Thus, in *Gísla saga* ch.9, Ásgerðr's reluctance to cut a shirt for her husband and her willingness to cut one for his friend takes on real significance, the more so when her husband overhears her. In *Kormáks saga* ch.17, Kormákr visits his old flame Steingerðr who is now married and 'asks her to make him a shirt' (*biðr hana gera sér skyrtu*); it is not that he needs a shirt, but he wants to know how she will react to his loaded request. In *Örvar-Odds saga* ch.12, Oddr gets a magic shirt from Ölvor before marrying her. And later when he carries back Hjálmarr's body to his lover Ingibjörg, 'she was sewing Hjálmarr a shirt' (*hún saumaði Hjálmari skyrtu*, ch.15); she dies on that instant (in the grittier *Hervarar saga*, she takes her own life;

ch.4) and they are buried in each other's arms, Hjálmarr's dying gift of a ring to her completing this deathly wedding. In *Laxdæla saga* ch.34, Guðrún inverts the usual custom; the shirt she sews will lead to divorce instead of marriage.

The needlecases and scissors which accompanied so many Viking women of all ranks to their graves, would have been used to make these shirts, as well as other clothes for the family, and the elaborate seams on the shirt from Viborg show that the making of such a shirt could be truly a labour of love.

A collection of Anglo-Saxon maxims recorded in the Exeter Book probably also refers to such a gift ('Maxims' I, II, l.94–8):

> … *leof wilcuma Frysan wife, þonne flota stondeð … wæsceð his warig hrægl ond him syleþ wæde niwe …*

> … her beloved is welcome to the Frisian woman, when his boat is at rest … she washes his dishevelled robe and gives him a new garment …

The 'new garment' she gives him to greet his return must be a shirt, which she will have made in his absence; the bonds of love are renewed. *Hávamál* st.3 also emphasises the importance of providing fresh clothes for a traveller, and we might imagine that similar scenes greeted homecoming Vikings, when they returned from the voyages of war and trade through which they dominated the age.

BIBLIOGRAPHY

This bibliography cannot claim to be comprehensive. I have tried to include, amongst others, every book or article which I have found especially useful, or which I believe to have contributed significantly to our understanding of the subject, but even given this limited aim, I expect there are some omissions.

It is unnecessary here to list separate editions of each and every saga which is cited; suffice it to say that excellent editions are available in the *Íslenzk Fornrít* and the *Editiones Arnamagnæanæ* series. Readily available translations are no substitute for research purposes, since words denoting separate garments are often translated by the same term, whilst other words are sometimes translated with different meanings; however, Viðar Hreinsson's edition of saga translations (which regrettably translate *blár* consistently as 'black' rather than 'blue') and Caroline Larrington's poetic translations are useful for general reference. Unless otherwise indicated below, quotations in Latin are taken from the Loeb editions.

Ågren, Torbjörn 1995 'Fur in Birka: an Examination of Hair Residue on Penannular Brooches' *Laborativ Arkeologi* 8

Amedroz, A.H.F. & Margoliouth D.S. 1921 *The Eclipse of the 'Abbasid Caliphate*

Andersson, Eva 1998 'Textile Production in Late Iron Age Scania – a Methodological Approach' in Jørgensen & Rinaldo 1998

Andersson, Eva 1999 *The Common Thread: textile production during the late Iron age – Viking age*

Andersson, Eva 2003 *Tools for Textile Production from Birka and Hedeby*

Arbman, Erik Holger 1944 *Die Gräber* (*Birka I*: 2 volumes)

Arneborg, Jette & Gulløv, H.C. *Man, Culture and Environment in Ancient Greenland, Danish Polar Centre Publication* 4

Arneborg, Jette & Østergård, Else 1994 'Notes on Archaeological finds of textiles and textile equipment from the Norse western settlement in Greenland' in Jaaks & Tidow 1994

Arwidsson, Greta (ed.) 1986 *Systematische Analysen der Graberfunde (Birka: Untersuchungen und Studien II:2)*

Avdusin, D.A. & Puskina, T.A. 1988 'Three chamber graves at Gniozdovo' *Fornvännen* 83

Backe, Margareta *et al.* (ed.) 1985 *In Honorem Evert Baudou*

Bau, Flemming 1981 'Seler og slæb i vikingetid: Birka's kvindedragt i nyt lys' *KUML*

Bersu, Gerhard & Wilson, David M. 1966 *Three Viking Graves in the Isle of Man*

Blindheim, Charlotte 1945 'Vernesfunnen og kvinnedrakten i norden i vikingtiden' *Viking* XI

Blindheim, Charlotte 1947 'Drakt og smykker. Studier I jernalderens drakthistorie i norden' *Viking* XI

Blindheim, Charlotte, Heyerdahl-Larsen, B., Ingstad, A.S. & Seeberg, E.S. 1999 *Kaupang-Funnene: Bind II*

Bosworth, Joseph and Toller, T. Northcotc 1898 *An Anglo-Saxon Dictionary*

Boucher, François 1965, 1996 *A history of costume in the West*

Brögger A.W., Falk H., Grieg S. and Shetelig H. 1917-1928 *Osebergfunnet* (4 volumes)

Brøndsted J. 1936 'Danish Inhumation Graves of the Viking Age' *Acta Archaeologica* 7

Bugge, Dr Alexander 1911 'Costumes, Jewels and Furniture in Viking Times' *Saga Book* VII

Campbell, James 1980 *Viking Artefacts: a select catalogue*

Carus-Wilson, E.M. (ed. N.B. Harte and K.G. Ponting) 1983 *Cloth and clothing in medieval Europe: essays in memory of Professor E.M. Carus-Wilson*

Christensen, Arne Emil, Ingstad, Anne Stine and Myhre, Bjørn 1992 *Oseberg Dronningens Grav*

Cleasby, Richard, Guðbrandur Vigfússon and Craigie, Sir William A. 1874, 1957 *An Icelandic-English Dictionary*

Coatsworth, Elizabeth 2005 'Stitches in Time: Establishing a History of Anglo-Saxon Embroidery' in Netherton and Owen-Crocker 2005

Cramp, Rosemary 1984 *County Durham and Northumberland (Corpus of Anglo-Saxon Stone Sculpture* v.1, 2)

Crowfoot, Grace M. 1948 'Textiles from a Viking Grave at Kaldonan on the Isle of Eigg' *Proceedings of the Society of Antiquaries of Scotland*

Crowfoot, Grace M. 1966, untitled sections on textiles (pp. 43-44 and 80-83) in Bersu & Wilson 1966

De Vries, Jan 1962 *Altnordisches Etymologisches Wörterbuch*

Dronke, Ursula (ed., trans.) 1969-1997 *The Poetic Edda* (2 volumes)

Dumville, David and Lapidge, Michael (ed.) 1985 *Annals of St Neots with Vita Prima Sancti Neoti*

Dunlop, D.M. 1957 'The British Isles according to medieval Arabic Authors' *The Islamic Quarterly* April-July 1957

Ellis Davidson, Hilda Roderick 1976 *The Viking Road to Byzantium*

Ewing, Thor 2006 *"í litklæðum'* – Coloured Clothes in Medieval Scandinavian Literature and Archaeology' in McKinnell and Kick 2006

Falk, Hjalmar 1919 *Altwestnordische Kleiderkunde*

Fanning, Thomas 1994 *Viking Age Ringed Pins from Dublin*

Farke, Heidemarie 1998 'Der Männerkittel aus Bernuthsfeld – Beobachtungen während einer Restaurierung' in Jørgensen & Rinaldo 1998

Fentz, Mytte 1992 'An 11th century Linen Shirt from Viborg Søndersø, Denmark' in Jørgensen & Munksgaard 1992

Fentz, Mytte 1994 'Viking Age Replicas in Research and Communication' in Jaacks and Tidow 1994

Fjellström, Phebe 1985 'The Hlað. A Viking Hair Ornament' *in* Backe *et al.* 1985

Foote, Peter (ed.), Fisher, Peter and Higgens, Humphrey (trans.) 1998 *Olaus Magnus: description of the northern peoples, Rome 1555*

Foote, Peter, Hermann Pálsson, and Slay, Desmond (ed.) 1973 *Proceedings of the First International Saga Conference, 1971*

Freke, David 2002 *Excavations on St. Patrick's Isle, Peel, Isle of Man, 1982-88: Prehistoric, Viking, Medieval and later*

G. Waitz (ed.) 1883 *Annales Bertiniani*

Geijer, Agnes 1938 *Die Textilfunde aus den Gräbern (Birka III)*

Geijer, Agnes 1979 'The Textile Finds from Birka' *Acta Archaeologica* 50 (also in Carus-Wilson *et al.* 1983*)*

Geijer, Agnes 1979 *A History of Textile Art*

Gervers, Veronika 1983 'Medieval Garments in the Mediterranean World' in Carus-Wilson *et al.* 1983

Ginters, Valdemars 1981 *Tracht und Schmuck in Birka und im ostbaltischen Raum: eine vergleichende Studie*

Godman, P. and Collins R. (eds) 1990 *Charlemagne's Heir: New Perspectives on the Reign of Louis the Pious (814-840)*

Gordon, Stewart (ed.) 2001 *Robes and Honor: The medieval world of investiture*

Granger-Taylor, Hero & Pritchard, Frances 2001 'A Fine Quality Insular Embroidery from Llan-gors Crannóg, near Brecon' in Redknapp *et al.* 2001

Gräslund, Anne Sofie 1980 *Birka IV: The burial customs, a study of the graves on Björkö* Olaus Magnus

Groenman-van Waateringe, Willy 1984 *Die Lederfunde von Haithabu (Haithabu Bericht 21)*

Guðjónsson, Elsa E. 1962 'Forn röggvarvefnaður' *Árbók hins Íslenzka Fornleifafélags*

Haefele, Hans F. 1959 *Notker der Stammler, Taten Kaiser Karls des Grossen (MGH SS rer. Germ. N. S. 12)*

Hagen, Karin Gjøl 1992 *Solplissé: en reminisens av middelalderens draktutvikling? En komparativ studie i plisserte stoffer fra Birka, Vangsnes, middelalderens Trondheim, Uvdal og Setesdal*

Hägg, Inga 1968 'Some Notes on the Origin of the Peplos-Type Dress in Scandinavia' *Tor*

Hägg, Inga 1974 *Kvinnodräkten i Birka*

Hägg, Inga 1982 'Einige Beobachtungen über die Birkatracht' in Jørgensen & Tidow 1982

Hägg, Inga 1983 'Viking Women's Dress at Birka: a Reconstruction by Archaeological Methods' in Carus-Wilson *et al.* 1983

Hägg, Inga 1984 'Textilfunde aus dem Hafen von Haithabu – Aspekte und Interpretation' *Offa* 41

Hägg, Inga 1985 *Die Textilfunde aus dem Hafen von Haithabu* (*Haithabu Bericht 20*)

Hägg, Inga 1986 'Dic Tracht' *in* Arwidsson 1986

Hägg, Inga 1991 *Die Textilfunde aus der Siedlung und aus den Gräbern von Haithabu* (*Haithabu Bericht 29*)

Hald, Margrethe 1972 *Primitive Shoes: an archaeological-ethnological study*

Hald, Margrethe 1980 *Ancient Danish Textiles from Bogs and Burials: a comparative study of costume and Iron Age textiles* (previously published in Danish as *Olddanske Tekstiler,* 1950)

Hase, C.B. (ed.) 1828 *Corpus Scriptorum Historiae Byzantinae*

Haupt, Moriz 1859 'Hermanni Contracti Conflictus Ovis et Lini' *Zeitschrift für deutsches Alterthum* 11

Heckett, Elizabeth Wincott 1987 'Some Hiberno-Norse Headcoverings from Fishamble Street and St. John's Lane, Dublin' *Textile History* 18, no.2

Heckett, Elizabeth Wincott 1990 'Some silk and wool head-coverings from Viking Dublin: uses and origins – an enquiry' in Walton & Wild 1990

Heckett, Elizabeth Wincott 2002 'Irish Viking Age silks and their place in Hiberno-Norse society'

Heckett, Elizabeth Wincott 2002 *Viking Age Headcoverings from Dublin*

Henry, Phillippa A. 1998 'Textiles as Indices of Late Saxon Social Dynamics' in Jørgensen & Rinaldo 1998

Hoffman, Marta 1974 *The Warp-weighted Loom*

Holder-Egger, Oswald 1911 *Einhardi Vita Karoli Magni* (*MGH SS rer. Germ. 25*)

Holm-Olsen, Inger Marie 1974 'Noen Gravfunn fra Vestlandet som kaster lys over Vikingtidens Kvinnedrakt' *Viking*

Hougen, B. 1940 'Osebergfunnets billedvev' *Viking* 4

Hyer, Maren Clegg 2005 'Textiles and Textile Imagery in the *Exeter Book*' in Netherton and Owen-Crocker 2005

Ierusalimskaja, Anna A. 1996 *Die Gräber der Moscevaja Balka: Frühmittelalterliche Funde an der Nordkaukasischen Seidenstrasse*

Ingstad, Anne Stine 1979 'To kvinnegraver med tekstiler fra Kaupang' *Univ. Olds. 150 Jubileumsårbok*

Ingstad, Anne Stine 1982 'The Functional Textiles from the Oseberg Ship' in Jørgensen & Tidow 1982

Ingstad, Anne Stine 1988 'Textiles from Oseberg, Gokstad and Kaupang' in Jørgensen, Magnus & Munksgaard 1988

Ingstad, Anne Stine 1992 'Hva var textilerne vært brugt til?' in Christensen, Ingstad and Myhre 1992

Ingstad, Anne Stine 1999 'Tekstilene' in Blindheim *et al.* 1999

Iversen, M. 1991 *Mammen. Grav, kunst og samfund i vikingetiden*

Jaaks, Gisela & Tidow, Klaus (ed.) 1994 *Archäologische Texilfunde--Archaeological Textiles: Textilsymposium Neumünster 4.-7.5. 1993* [NESAT V]

Jansson, Ingmar 1985 *Ovala Spännbucklor: En Studie av Vikingatida Standardsmycken med Utgångspunkt från Björkö-fynden*

Jenkins, D. (ed.) 2003 *The Cambridge History of Western Textiles* (2 vols)

Jones, Gwyn and Jones, Thomas (trans.) 1974, 2000 *The Mabinogion*

Jørgensen, Lise Bender 1986 *Forhistoriske Textiler i Skandinavien: Prehistoric Scandinavian Textiles*

Jørgensen, Lise Bender 1990 'Hørvævninger og oldtidsvæve' *KUML*

Jørgensen, Lise Bender 1992 *North European Textiles before 1000 A.D*

Jørgensen, Lise Bender 1994 'Ancient Costumes Reconstructed' in Jaaks & Tidow 1994

Jørgensen, Lise Bender 2003 'Scandinavia, AD 400–1000' in Jenkins 2003

Jørgensen, Lise Bender 2003 'The Balts, the Slavs and the Avars' in Jenkins 2003

Jørgensen, Lise Bender 2003 'The continental Germans' in Jenkins 2003

Jørgensen, Lise Bender, Magnus, Bente & Munksgaard, Elisabeth (ed.) 1988 *Archaeological Textiles: Report from the 2nd NESAT Symposium 1.-4.V.1984* [NESAT II]

Jørgensen, Lise Bender & Munksgaard, Elizabeth (ed.) 1992 *Tidens Tand 5: Archaeological Textiles in Northern Europe: Report from the 4th NESAT Symposium 1.-5. May 1990 in Copenhagen* [NESAT IV]

Jørgensen, Lise Bender & Rinaldo, Christina (ed.) 1998 *GOTARC* Series A, Vol. 1: *Textiles in Northern European Archaeology: Report from the 6th NESAT Symposium, 7-11th May 1996 in Borås* [NESAT VI]

Jørgensen, Lise Bender & Tidow, Karl (ed.) 1982 *Archäologische Textilfunde 6.5-8.5.1981. Textilsymposium Neumünster* [NESAT I]

Kenward, H.K. & Hall, A.R. 1995 *Biological Evidence from 16-22 Coppergate (The Archaeology of York: The Environment 14/7)*

Krag, Anne Hedeager 1994 'Reconstruction of a Viking Magnate Dress' in Jaaks & Tidow 1994

Krag, Anne Hedeager 1998 'Dress and Power in Prehistoric Scandinavia, c550-1050 AD in Jørgensen & Rinaldo 1998

Lang, James 1991 *York and eastern Yorkshire* (*Corpus of Anglo-Saxon Stone Sculpture* v.3)

Lang, James 2001 *Northern Yorkshire* (*Corpus of Anglo-Saxon Stone Sculpture* v.6)

Larrington, Caroline (trans.) 1996 *The Poetic Edda*

Leahy, Kevin 2003 *Anglo-Saxon Crafts*

Lehtosalo-Hilander, Pirkko-Liisa 1984 *Ancient Finnish Costumes*

Lindqvist S. 1941-1942 *Gotlands Bildsteine* (2 volumes)

Lønborg, Bjarne 1999 'Vikingetidens kvindedragter' *KUML*

Madsen, Anne Hedeager 1990 'Women's dress in the Viking period in Denmark, based on the tortoise brooches and textile remains' in Walton & Wild 1990

Magoun, Francis Peabody (ed. Jess B. Bessinger Jr. and Robert P. Creed) 1965 *Franciplegius: Medieval and Linguistic Studies in Honor of Francis Peabody Magoun, Jr.*

McDonough, Christopher J. (ed., trans.) 1995 *Moriuht: a Norman Latin poem from the early eleventh century*

McGregor, A, Mainman, A.J. & Rogers, N.S.H. 1999 *Bone, Antler, Ivory and Horn from Anglo-Scandinavian and Medieval York* (*The Archaeology of York: Craft, Industry and Everyday Life* 17/12)

McKinnell, John S. and Kick, Donata 2006 *The Fantastic in Old Norse-Icelandic Literature/Sagas and the British Isles. Preprint Papers for the Thirteenth International Saga Conference*

Minorsky, V. (trans.), Bosworth C.E. (ed.) 1982 *Hudud al-'Alam*

Møller-Hansen, Keld & Høier, Henrik 2000 'Næs – en vikingetidsbebyggelse med hørproduktion' *KUML*

Montgomery, James E. 2000 'Ibn Fadlan and the Rusiyyah' *Journal of Arabic and Islamic Studies* 3

Montgomery, James E. 2001 'Ibn Rusta's Lack of Eloquence, the Rus and Samanid Cosmography' *Edebiyât* 12

Montgomery, James E. forthcoming 'Arabic Sources on the Vikings' in *The Viking World*, ed. N. Price and S. Brink

Moore, Michael 2001 'The King's New Clothes: Royal and Episcopal regalia in the Frankish Empire' in Gordon 2001

Mortensen, Mona 1998 'When they speed the shuttle: the role of textile production in Viking Age society as reflected in a pit house from Western Norway' in Jørgensen & Rinaldo 1998

Mould, Quita, Carlisle, Ian and Cameron, Esther 2003 *Craft, industry and everyday life: leather and leatherworking in Anglo-Scandinavian and medieval York*

Mundt, Marina 1973 'Observations on the Influence of Þiðreks saga on Icelandic writing' in Foote *et al.* 1973

Munksgaard, Elisabeth 1974 *Oldtidsdragter*

Munksgaard, Elizabeth 1990 'The costumes depicted on gold-sheet figures (*guldgubbar*)' in Walton and Wild 1990

Munksgaard, Elizabeth 1991 'Kopien af dragten fra Mammengraven' in Iversen 1991

Munro, John H. 2003 'Medieval Woollens: Textiles, textile technology and industrial organisation, *c*.800-1500' in Jenkins 2003

Netherton, Robin and Owen-Crocker, Gale R. (ed.) 2005 *Medieval Clothing and Textiles* 1

Nockert, Margareta 1991 *The Högom find and other Migration period textiles and costumes in Scandinavia*

Nockert, Margareta 1997 *Bockstenmannen och hans dräkt*

Nörlund, Poul 1924 'Buried Norsemen at Herjolfsnes' *Meddelelser om Grønland* 67

Noss, Aagot 1974 'Draktfunn og drakttradisjon i det vestnordiske området: frå vikingtid til høgmellomalderen' *Viking*

Østergård, Else 1991 'Textilfragmenterne fra Mammengraven' in Iversen 1991

Østergård, Else 2004 *Woven into the Earth: textile finds in Norse Greenland*

Owen, Aneurin 1841 *Ancient laws and institutes of Wales*

Owen-Crocker, Gale R. 1986, 2004 *Dress in Anglo-Saxon England*

Owen-Crocker, Gale R. 2005 'Pomp, Piety, and Keeping the Woman in Her Place: The Dress of Cnut and Ælfgifu-Emma' in Netherton and Owen-Crocker 2005

Petersen, Jan 1928 *Vikingetidens Smykker*

Poole, R.G. 1989 'The Textile Inventory in the Old English *Gerefa*' *The Review of English Studies* 40

Pritchard, Frances 1988 'Silk Braids and Textiles of the Viking Age from Dublin' in Jørgensen Magnus & Munksgaard 1988

Pritchard, Frances 1992 'Aspects of the Wool Textiles from Viking Age Dublin' in Jørgensen & Munksgaard 1992

Rasmussen, Liisa & Lönborg, Bjarne 1993 'Dragtrester i grav ACQ, Köstrup' *Fynske Minder*

Redknapp, Mark *et al.* 2001 *Pattern and Purpose in Insular Art*

Reichert, Hermann 1992 *Heldensage und Rekonstruktion – Untersuchungen zur Thidrekssaga (Philologica Germanica* 14)

Roesdahl, Else & Wilson, David M. 1992 *From Viking to Crusader*

Roscoe, Jane Christine 1992 *The Literary Significance of Clothing in the Icelandic Family Sagas* MA Thesis, University of Durham

Ryder, Michael L. 1982 'European Wool Types from the Iron Age to the Middle Ages' in Jørgensen & Tidow 1982

Ryder, Michael L. 1985 *Sheep and Man*

Schlabow, Karl 1976 *Textilfunde der Eisenzeit in Norddeutschland (Göttinger Schriften zur Vor- und Frühgeschichte*, Bd.15)

Sears, E., 'Louis the Pious as *Miles Christi*: the Dedicatory Image in Hrabanus Maurus's *De laudibus sanctae Crucis* [In praise of the Holy Cross]', in Godman and Collins 1990

Shetelig, Håkon 1920 *Osebergfunnet 3*

Skre, Dagfinn and Styylegar, Frans-Arne 2004 *Kaupang: the Viking town*

Smyser, H.M. 'Ibn Fadlan's Account of the Rus with Some Commentary and Some Allusions to Beowulf' in Magoun 1965

Speed, Greg & Walton Rogers, Penelope 2004 'The Burial of a Viking Woman at Adwick-le-Street' *Medieval Archaeology*

Straubhaar, Sandra Ballif 2005 'Wrapped in a Blue Mantle: Fashions for Icelandic Slayers?' in Netherton and Owen-Crocker 2005

Svabo, J.C. 1966 *Dictionarium Færoense*

Sveinbjörn Egilsson 1860 *Lexicon Poëticum Antiquae Linguae Septentrionalis*

Thorpe, Benjamin 1840 *Ancient laws and institutes of England*

Tilke, Max 1990 *Costume Patterns and Designs*

Todd, James Henthorn (ed., trans.) 1867 *Cogadh Gaedhel re Gallaibh*

Tronzo, William 2001 'The Mantle of Roger II of Sicily' in Gordon 2001

Tschan, Francis J. (trans.) Adam of Bremen 1959, 2002 *History of the Archbishops of Hamburg Bremen*

Valtýr Guðmundsson 1893 'Litklæði' *Arkiv för Nordisk Filologi 9*

Vaughan, R. (ed.) 1958 'The Chronicle attributed to John of Wallingford' *Camden Miscellany* XXI, Camden 3rd ser. 90

Vebæk, C.L. 1993 *Narsaq – a Norse landnáma farm (Meddelelser om Grønland, Man & Society 18)*

Viðar Hreinsson (ed.) *et al.* 1997 *The Complete Sagas of Icelanders, including 49 tales*

Waitz, G (ed.) 1878 *Pauli Historia Langobardum (MGH, Script. Rer. Germ. 48)*

Walton Rogers, Penelope 1993 'Dyes and wools in Norse textiles from ø17A' in Vebæk 1993

Walton Rogers, Penelope 1997 *Textile Production at 16-22 Coppergate (The Archaeology of York: The Small Finds 17/11)*

Walton Rogers, Penelope 1998 'The raw materials of the textiles from GUS' in Arneborg & Gulløv 1998

Walton Rogers, Penelope 1999 'Textile Making Equipment' in MacGregor Mainman & Rogers 1999

Walton Rogers, Penelope 2003 'The Anglo-Saxons and Vikings in Britain, AD 450-1050' in Jenkins 2003

Walton, Penelope 1989 'Dyes of the Viking Age: a summary of recent work' *Dyes in History and Archaeology 7*

Walton, Penelope 1989 *Textiles, Cordage and Raw Fibre from 16-22 Coppergate* (*The Archaeology of York: The Small Finds* 17/5)

Walton, Penelope 1990 'Dyes and wools in Iron Age textiles from Norway and Denmark' *Journal of Danish Archaeology* 7

Walton, Penelope 1990 'Textile Production at Coppergate, York: Anglo-Saxon or Viking?' in Walton & Wild 1990

Walton, Penelope 1991 'Dyes and wools in textiles from Bjerringhøj (Mammen), Denmark' in Iversen 1991

Walton, Penelope, and Wild, John P. (ed.) 1990 *Textiles in Northern Archaeology: NESAT III Textile Symposium in York 6-9 May 1987* [NESAT III]

Welander, R., Batey, C. & Cowie, T.G. 1978 'A Viking Burial from Kneep, Uig, Isle of Lewis. *Proceedings of the Society of Antiquities in Scotland* 117

Whitelock Dorothy 1955 *500-1042* AD (*English Historical Documents* Vol.1)

Wild, John Peter 1988 *Textiles in Archaeology*

Wild, John Peter and Jørgensen, Lise Bender 1988 'Clothes from the Roman Empire: Barbarians and Romans' in Jørgensen, Magnus & Munksgaard 1988

Wilson, David M. (ed.) 1976 *The Archaeology of Anglo-Saxon England*

Zeki Velidi Togan, Ahmed 1939 'Ibn Fadlans Reisebericht' *Abhandlungen für die Kunde des Morgenlandes* Bd.24 Nr.3

Zimmermann, W. Haio 1982 'Archäologische Befunde frümittelalterlicher Webhäuser. Ein Betrag zum gewichtwebstuhl' in Jørgensen & Tidow 1982

INDEX

If you are interested in purchasing other books published by The History Press,
or in case you have difficulty finding any of our books in your local bookshop,
you can also place orders directly through our website

www.thehistorypress.co.uk